# THE KINGDOM *of the* ANTICHRIST

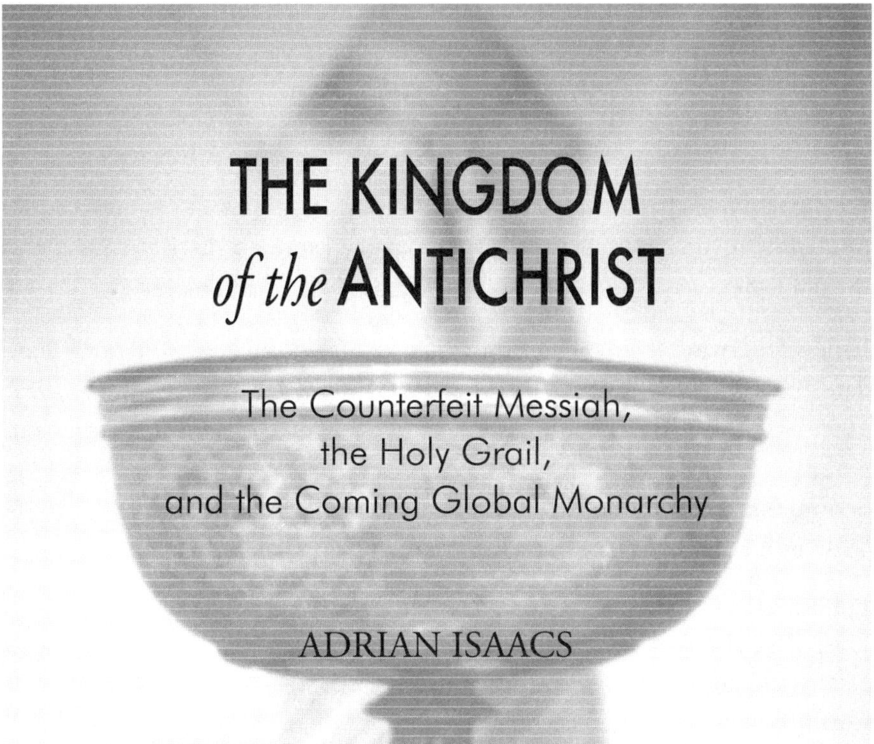

# THE KINGDOM *of the* ANTICHRIST

## The Counterfeit Messiah, the Holy Grail, and the Coming Global Monarchy

ADRIAN ISAACS

Deep River Books

SISTERS, OREGON

THE KINGDOM OF THE ANTICHRIST
The Counterfeit Messiah, the Holy Grail,
and the Coming Global Monarchy


Published by
Deep River Books
Sisters, Oregon
http://www.deepriverbooks.com

ISBN 10: 1-935265-28-8
ISBN 13: 978-1-935265-28-3

Library of Congress Control Number: 2010936868

Printed in the USA

Cover design by Joe Bailen

# Table of Contents

To Him who loves us and released us from our sins by His blood—and He has made us to be a kingdom, priests to His God and Father—to Him be the glory and the dominion forever and ever. Amen. Behold, He is coming with the clouds, and every eye will see Him, even those who pierced Him; and all the tribes of the earth will mourn over Him. So it is to be.

*Amen.* (Rev. 1:5–7 NASB)

This book is dedicated to the Lord Jesus Christ,
who has loved me and brought me to Himself
through awakening me to the glory of His soon return.
May He take the words on these pages, powerless apart from His grace,
and use them for the furtherance of His kingdom.

# Preface and Acknowledgements

*The Kingdom of the Antichrist* is the end result of many years of research and work. Its purpose is to counteract the overwhelming and growing influence of esoteric/pagan spirituality in Western society. Often presented as a series of "new revelations" or "new discoveries," modern esoteric and pagan spirituality calls into question many of the traditional and foundational beliefs of the faith that many in the West still treasure deeply: *Christianity!*

Astounded at the striking similarity between elements of esoteric spirituality and "history," and what the Bible says will transpire during the days of the Antichrist, I set out to write a book that would expose these "new revelations" for what they are: unbiblical theories that are actually helping to prepare the world to receive the Antichrist. I was amazed to hear arguments suggesting that Jesus had been married to Mary Magdalene, leaving a trail of royal European descendants who could one day arise to sit on His messianic throne. I was also amazed to hear arguments suggesting that the destiny of humanity was to unite under one world government and one world religion through the agency of a new messiah/Christ figure. Such rhetoric clearly points to the Antichrist—either by detracting from the true Christ or by promoting a false Christ.

The purpose of this book is not to paint a definitive picture of how the Antichrist's kingdom *will* come together. Aside from the obvious perils of trying to predict the future, no student of God's Word should ever venture out to definitively state how a prophetic passage will be fulfilled if the biblical text does not *clearly* provide for such assurance of interpretation. Many things we simply cannot know with certainty until they happen. Certain concepts addressed in this book—the so-called "bloodline of Christ," the "new world order," Maitreya, Rex Deus, etc.—are not meant to be definitive claims as to how biblical prophecy will be fulfilled, but are meant rather to illustrate the anti-Christ nature of esoteric spirituality, and their *possible* link to the coming Antichrist. Nevertheless, we can be certain of this one thing: there is a counterfeit spiritual system rooted in the ancient past running through the centuries that will culminate in the kingdom of the Antichrist. This counterfeit system is the main subject of this book. Examples such as the ones mentioned above are manifestations of this system.

Many people have contributed toward the completion of this work, either through inspiration, encouragement, technical assistance, or graciously allowing me to use their material. I must first of all thank my supportive wife, Tammy, for encouraging me to finish this project, for her patience with me as I dedicated countless hours to completing it, and for accompanying me on research trips. I must also thank my parents, Albert and Judy Isaacs, for their constant support and encouragement, along with my loving sister Nadine, and my brother-in-law Ricardo.

I would also like to thank all of the additional people who have in anyway contributed to the production of this book. All of you know who you are, and I am extremely grateful for your assistance.

Most of all, I must thank the Lord Jesus Christ, who saved me and made all of this possible by giving me breath each day, and leading me to the truths of His Word.

*Adrian Isaacs*
*Toronto, Ontario*
*April 2010*

# 1

## The Esoteric Revelations

Is humanity progressing toward a global utopia of peace, prosperity, and perfection, or racing toward the Antichrist, Armageddon, and the Apocalypse? For approximately 1,700 years, Western society has adopted a largely Judeo-Christian worldview. As such, many Westerners have in some form or another identified with the Christian faith—either being fervently active in their belief or simply sympathetic toward it due to their upbringing. This, however, may be changing. Despite a strong Christian heritage, many today find themselves questioning the traditional account of Jesus Christ and the faith He inspired.

While many may not utterly reject Christianity as a religion, they may feel, perhaps somewhat intuitively, that the Christian message is in need of revision in light of new trends in global spirituality and recent "discoveries" concerning Jesus Christ and His early followers. Today, numerous *esoteric* theories and "revelations" are coming forward that offer an un-orthodox account of who Jesus was. The term "esoteric" refers to that which is hidden from most, but known by a select few. Esoteric philosophy is a form of thought maintaining that certain knowledge and truth lie hidden from the casual observer and can only be understood by those initiated into an organization that promotes such philosophy.[1] The great Christian commentator H. A. Ironside stated many years ago:

> Esoteric religion, I may say, is the religion *par excellence* of the Antichrist.[2] I do not think we will be far wrong if we identify this coming delusion [a deception associated with the Antichrist] with the occult systems of Gnostic origin, so largely prevailing and so rapidly spreading at the present time.[3]

Currently taking place in Western society is a clash between the traditional Christian account and the new esoteric accounts concerning Jesus Christ, the history of the church, and the future of mankind. New "revelations" and theories are being disclosed that offer a radically different view of history as it pertains to Christianity and the future as it pertains to all humanity.

## The Bloodline of Christ and the "Revelation" of Sion

One of these theories suggests that Jesus and one of His closest female followers in the Bible, Mary Magdalene, were married. This was alluded to in the runaway 2003 best-selling novel *The Da Vinci Code*, by Dan Brown. It is also the major theme of the 1982 best-seller *Holy Blood, Holy Grail*. According to this book, Jesus and Mary may not only have been married, but may have also been the ancestors of powerful noble families in Europe protected by an esoteric organization called the *Prieure de Sion*. A stated ambition of this organization is the restoration of a long-deposed French royal bloodline to the thrones of France and a united Europe. It is hypothesized that this bloodline may be linked to the "descendants" of Jesus and Mary.

If this bloodline-of-Christ theory were proved true, then two thousand years of church history and teaching would be called into question, and Christianity would be faced with an unimaginable crisis. Despite the historical problems of such a theory, many continue to be enamoured and charmed by the possibility that Jesus had been married, and are reevaluating the faith that perhaps was a significant part of their upbringing. Many who adhere to this bloodline-of-Christ/Priory-of-Sion theory believe that the Christian message of a crucified and risen God was all a hoax designed to give the Catholic Church ecclesiastical hegemony over the European populace. But what really is the truth?

## The Grail Revelation

What exactly is the Holy Grail? According to some, the term "Holy Grail" is derived from the French phrase *Sang Real*, which means "Blood Royal" or royal blood. In his best-selling book, Bloodline of the *Holy Grail: The Hidden Lineage of Jesus Revealed,* Laurence Gardner claims that the *Sangreal* is in fact a messianic bloodline incorporating the Judaic royal house of David, Jesus, and Jesus' "heirs."[4] In this context, the Holy Grail is not a cup but an ancient and dynastic bloodline. This bloodline, we are told, descends from both Jesus Christ and his brother James to individuals living today. Gardner states that strains of the bloodline can be traced through the noble registers of Britain and Europe.[5]

Concerning the history of the West, Grail adherents such as Gardner believe that the Christian church is nothing more than an institution built upon lies devised to maintain influence and authority over society. The church-endorsed kingdoms and governments of European history that possessed no "Grail strain" were apparently usurpers of the thrones of the "true" nobility—the "heirs of Jesus." We are told that this dynastic bloodline was heavily persecuted and silenced by the medieval church, which explains why Christianity became the "faith of the West."

Gardner's definition of the Grail is just one of many. As we shall soon discover, the Grail is in fact so much more, and serves as the perfect symbol for that which esoteric philosophy seeks.

## The Tomb of Christ Revelation

In 2007, documentary filmmaker Simcha Jacobovici presented the possibility that the "lost tomb" of Jesus had been found. His controversial book *The Jesus Family Tomb: The Discovery, the Investigation, and the Evidence That Could Change History* presented the theory that Jesus' physical resurrection is a myth, and that His bones were placed in a Jerusalem tomb, along with those of Mary (His mother), Mary Magdalene, and other supposed family members.

Legends, myths, and theories concerning bodily remains of Jesus Christ are not limited to the Jacobovici story. Some, including Richard Andrews and Paul Schellenberger, best-selling authors of *The Tomb of God,* have presented the possibility that Jesus' bones are secretly being kept hidden in a remote area in the south of France, carried there from Jerusalem centuries ago by the famed Knights Templar. The Templars, supposedly possessing esoteric knowledge that contradicted orthodox teaching, are believed to have retrieved the bones from the Holy Land and smuggled them off to France where they await excavation. The impact on the Christian West, and in fact Islam, should Jesus' "bones" be presented to the world, would be monstrous! Many today already suspect that a "decaying" Jesus is far more plausible than a resurrected and returning Jesus.

## The Messianic Revelation

One theory to be promoted in recent years that also casts Jesus in a new light concerns two bloodlines stemming from Israel's King David and High Priest Aaron, as well as a "legacy" supposedly left by King Solomon, David's son. It has been suggested that the lineages of David and Aaron can be traced down through history to a clan of European families that were intimately associated with the Knights Templar. The families, we are told, may be preserving two Judaic "messianic" lines—one political (Davidic) and one priestly (Aaronic)—for the eventual establishment of the kingdom of heaven on earth through the advent of two new messiahs.[6]

Christopher Knight and Alan Butler's *Solomon's Power Brokers: The Secrets of Freemasonry, the Church, and the Illuminati* presents a radical yet somewhat disturbing theory concerning the "legacy" of Solomon. Here, the priestly families are termed "Star Families." The authors document their hypothesis that a dynastic priesthood linked to King Solomon and his temple has exerted tremendous influence over the development of Western civilization. The authors *do not* suggest that the Star Family goal is a Jewish goal, but rather an esoteric and ecumenical goal where all gods are honored with no one religious group claiming a monopoly on spiritual truth. They believe the essence of Star Family theology to be that there is one supreme deity above all "national" gods. The gods of various nations and cultures may be legitimate, but are ultimately inferior to some supreme universal cosmic energy.[7] Thus, the gods of every nation were to be equally honored with the end result being a unified world.

The following quote from *Solomon's Power Brokers* concerns what the authors believe may be the final outcome of the Star Family plan:

> We believe it probable that once the Israeli state has achieved a relatively stable relationship with its neighbours, someone in high office will discreetly propose that Jerusalem

should become the new headquarters of the United Nations, a politically neutral ground belonging to no single country. That person is likely to be the secretary-general of the United Nations. He or she may speak the words but it will not be their idea. It will come from deep within the Star Families.

From there, with the convergence of nations and currencies, it will be a natural step to convert Jerusalem into the global capital of a United Earth.

King Solomon's vision will have been achieved, but in a way far beyond what he envisaged. The most enigmatic, and at times the saddest, city that has always been the navel of the planet will have attained its ultimate goal: The harmonious union of humankind.[8]

**The Masonic/Illuminati/Rosicrucian Revelation**

Who are the Freemasons, and what is their real agenda? Depending on whom one listens to, the Masons are either plotting world domination or simply looking to enhance the quality of life for multitudes around the globe. Mysteries abound concerning this strange and enigmatic fraternity. Often linked to the Freemasons is another esoteric group—the Illuminati. Together, these two groups are believed by some to be striving for the creation of a global state run by an elite class of politicians, businessmen, and spiritual leaders.

Some researchers have also documented a close link between Freemasonry and yet another esoteric group—the Rosicrucians. It has been argued that the true goal of the Masonic/Rosicrucian cabal is the creation of a "New Atlantis" or a "New Jerusalem." Atlantis is said to be symbolic of the ideal society where peace, universal democracy,[9] ancient philosophy, and scientific achievement characterize a "Golden Age" of mankind. The Atlantis of legend is said to have consisted of ten kings who were then ultimately under the authority of an eleventh. This arrangement has been said to represent the natural and proper form of human government.[10] Interestingly, ten kings, also under the authority of an eleventh, will preside over the kingdom of the Antichrist. The New Jerusalem, which is referred to in the Book of Revelation as descending from heaven to earth, is taken by some esoteric adherents to symbolize the advent of heaven on earth, the creation of a perfect global society based on esoteric philosophy and ancient occult wisdom.

Freemasonry has been brought to the forefront of popular culture, partly due to the incredible success of the *National Treasure* movie series. The series portrays the heavy Masonic influence upon the founding fathers of the United States of America. Interestingly, America's currency bears a phrase that many feel is a reference to the Masonic/Illuminati/Rosicrucian plan—the *Novus Ordo Seclorum*, which translates as *New Order of the Ages.* The phrase is found on the one-dollar bill underneath the pyramid and the emblazoned eye of Horus. The "New Order of the Ages" is believed to lie at the very heart of all that the Masonic Order strives for. Could this "New Order" be one and the same with the kingdom of heaven promised in the Bible, or might it be a counterfeit?

## The New Age Revelation

Today, many throughout Western civilization prefer a more personal, subjective spirituality over organized religions such as Christianity. Part of the reason for this is the unfortunate disillusionment many claim to have experienced with the church, perceiving it as an institution lacking evidence and relevance in a scientific and modern world. Historian Martin Lunn declares:

> The Church has depended upon the faith of its followers for 2000 years and conveniently for them faith is belief without evidence. Christianity has been unable to provide any convincing proof of much that it wants its followers to believe and for more than the last century has had to defend itself in the face of a variety of scientific discoveries that it wishes would just go away. . . . Some of us think that there has been a "softening up" process over the last couple of decades to lead mankind toward some kind of spiritual revelation.[11]

While Lunn is not quite accurate in stating that faith is "belief without evidence," he does seem to be on to something when he suggests that mankind may be heading toward some type of "spiritual revelation." A new spirituality seems to be unfolding in the twenty-first century—one based on the idea that God can be reached through multiple paths. It stresses knowledge over faith, enlightenment over repentance, and world unity over world evangelism. It is a type of spirituality where men and women throw off the "limitations" of old religion in favor of a "new religion" where every person may worship God (or the gods) as they see fit. The problem with this logic is that it presents a god who is limited to and subject to our own imagination. Such a god is no god at all but a creation of our own mind. If God can be whatever one perceives Him to be, then God can potentially be evil, unloving, racist, unjust, and partial. For God to truly be God, He must exist independently of who we are or who we *think* He is. We don't create Him—He has created us.

The new spirituality that is currently unfolding is often identified as "New Age" spirituality. The phrase *New Age* is a way of labeling a unique astrological time period that some believe is currently dawning—one that will consist of a spirituality based, not on Christian truth, but on esoteric and pagan philosophy. It is believed that for the past two thousand years mankind has been operating in what is called the "Piscean Age," an age characterized by intolerance and failure.[12] The astrological sign for Pisces is a fish, a symbol often associated with Christ and Christianity. Thus, to New Age and occult followers, the last two thousand years have been characterized by the "failure" and "intolerance" of Christianity. They see a "new age" dawning, the shifting from the age of Pisces to the age of Aquarius, where peace, tolerance, and unity among nations are to characterize human civilization. In their book *Rosslyn: Guardians of the Secrets of the Holy Grail*, Tim Wallace-Murphy and Marilyn Hopkins write:

> It is widely recognized that we live in a transitional period between two astrological eras. We are leaving the Age of Pisces, a 2000-year period characterized by failure, brutal intolerance, changeability and despondency. For the last forty years we have been in transition, moving into the age of Aquarius. According to astrologers, under the influence of this sign there will be a strong emphasis on science used not for its own sake, but in the service of humanity. It is believed to be a time of growing international cooperation and possible world government when mankind can apply warm-hearted generosity to practical ends. It is also predicted that there will be a reconciliation between science and the ageless stream of truths that run through man's unconscious.[13]

Sadly, even some so-called Christian leaders have joined the esoteric and New Age adherents in their call for a new spirituality and a new Christianity. In his 2004 national best seller *The Pagan Christ*, Tom Harpur, a former professor of New Testament at the University of Toronto, argues for a more "cosmic Christianity" that is free from the literal interpretation of Scripture. He also denies the "personal Jesus," opting for a more spiritual Christ over the historical one. In his book, he clearly identifies, perhaps unwittingly, with the ultimate esoteric goal—the brotherhood of man:

> Whatever the defenders of orthodoxy have to say, and I am well aware it will be plenty, they cannot deny that the literalist, exclusivist Christianism held by the majority of Churches—"Our Church and our View of Jesus remains the only way"—is extremely divisive and will never lead to the solidarity of humanity.[14]

Another prominent "Christian" leader, whose teachings are more akin to esoteric/New Age spirituality than traditional Christianity, is Bishop John Shelby Spong. Spong calls for the reformation of Christianity away from the literal interpretation of Scripture. He denies the virgin birth, the atonement of Christ on the cross, and the bodily resurrection of Jesus Christ. Many of Spong's key beliefs are outlined in his book *A New Christianity for a New World: Why Traditional Faith is Dying and How a New Faith is Being Born.*

## The Revelation of Maitreya

Occult adherents and esoteric philosophers often scoff at such "literalist Christianism" concerning a literal Antichrist. But this is to be expected. As they declare their hope to see a utopian new age, one way to deal with the Bible's warning of a coming Antichrist is to treat such warnings as figurative or symbolic. Rather than rest in the revealed Word of God and rely on God Himself to create heaven on earth, esoteric adherents seek to build paradise on earth by their own methods and devices. Thus, any warning of a coming Antichrist is ludicrous to them. They truly believe they are building a better world. As such, they must find ways to explain away the biblical warnings—one method being to "over-symbolize" them. The Antichrist then becomes a system of evil. Armageddon becomes strictly symbolic of the conflict between good and evil.

In the new age to come—and in fact leading up to it—esoteric spiritual mysteries are to be gradually revealed in a more public manner to the general population leading to a sort of spiritual "great awakening" among the nations. This spiritual revolution seeks to bring about a change in human consciousness, as well as to establish a true global society upon the earth:

> A new spiritual climate is emerging wherein the old gnosis is being used like a warrior's sword against the aggression of destructive technologies. This change in consciousness is as startling as all those that preceded it. We live in an era characterized by a high moral idealism and a deep spiritual thirst. The great task that now confronts us is to seek a new ecology of the spirit.[15]

> The new Aquarian age is prophesied to be one in which science will be harnessed to the service of humanity—an age of increasing international harmony within which mankind can apply warmhearted generosity to practical and humanitarian ends. . . . We must utilize this spiritual awareness as the motor for action in the temporal world. Action is indeed the magic word![16]

According to New Age and esoteric sources, the shift into the age of Aquarius and the accompanying transformation of spiritual consciousness is to be overseen by one called the World Teacher. This individual, also regarded as the Christ, goes by the unique name of Lord Maitreya, and is hailed as the one sought for by all religions. To the Jew, he is to be the messiah. To the Christian, he is to be the returned Christ. To the Muslim, he is the Imam Mahdi, and to the Buddhist, he is to be the final Buddha.[17] Maitreya is apparently a chief agent in a sort of New Age "Hierarchy of Masters":

> Maitreya has attained a high seating in the Hierarchy of Masters, answering only to Sanat Kumura, or Lucifer, the star who was cast from Venus to earth. Proponents teach that at the dawn of each new age, Sanat Kumura sends forth a Christ to impart knowledge that will bring about the spiritual

> transformation of loyal adherents. Many leaders, organizations, cultists, and pseudo-religions await the appearance of Lord Maitreya as the messiah of the Aquarian Age.[18]

As Jesus was the "messiah of the Piscean Age" (from a New Age standpoint), so Maitreya is to be the messiah of the Aquarian age.

British painter and author Benjamin Creme has done more to promote the appearance of Maitreya than any other individual. Creme currently tours Europe, Asia, and North America, holding conferences to educate people about the World Teacher. In the early 1980s, Creme was interviewed by *The New York Times*, and made known to the world the imminence of Maitreya's appearance. According to Creme, Maitreya will make his appearance during what has been called the Day of Declaration, where all of humanity will be invited to receive Maitreya as the World Teacher:

> Before long, an international press conference will be held at which Maitreya will present his credentials. This will lead to the Day of Declaration, when he will appear on the radio and television networks of the world linked by satellite. On that day Maitreya will mentally overshadow the whole of humanity simultaneously. All will hear his words inwardly in their own language. This telepathic communication will reach everyone, not only those watching or listening, and hundreds of thousands of miraculous healings will take place throughout the world. On that day, there will be no doubt that Maitreya is the Christ and World Teacher. His open world-wide mission will have begun.[19]

Creme claims that Maitreya has been living discreetly in London, England, since 1977, where he awaits the Day of Declaration. Creme also claims to have received several telepathic messages and prophecies from Maitreya that speak of humanity becoming a divine race, the creation of a global society, and the unifying of people's minds with the knowledge of certain ancient mysteries.[20] Of course, Creme has been unable to deliver on his promises and predictions. Decades have transpired since he first began to promote publicly the advent of Maitreya, and no World Teacher has come forth. Creme attributes this delay in Maitreya's coming to a lack of readiness on the part of humanity. Nevertheless, Creme states definitively that Maitreya is already here, and is simply awaiting the right moment to make his public appearance.

The New Age description of Maitreya calls to mind characteristics of both the biblical Antichrist and the False Prophet. Is Maitreya a bona fide candidate for one of these two offices?

## Pulling It All Together

Is Christianity still relevant in today's world? What is the truth behind many of the above "revelations," and do they warrant a revisiting and a reinterpretation of the biblical witness concerning Jesus? What is their relevance with respect to the coming Antichrist? Before we can adequately answer these questions, we must first become familiar with what the Bible says concerning both the *true* Messiah, Jesus Christ, and the one commonly referred to as the Antichrist.

# 2

## Who is the True Messiah?

On September 11, 1990, former U.S. President George H. W. Bush announced the creation of a new world order—a world where the nations of the north, south, east, and west can all live in harmony.[1] A comparable scenario was voiced by President Mahmoud Ahmadinejad of Iran, who, at the annual session of the United Nations General Assembly in September 2006, made known his desire to see one whom he called "the real savior" arrive and establish peace, justice, and unity on the planet.[2] It is a natural human inclination to desire a better existence and an ideal world. The esoteric and occult vision of a new age of peace, unity, and justice through the advent of a new messiah is partly born out of this desire to see mankind elevated to a greater level of existence. However, true global peace, justice, unity, and human elevation can only come through the true Messiah, not through human effort.

### The Davidic Messiah

The Bible reveals that God will indeed establish a glorious kingdom on earth to be ruled by one man—the Messiah. The word Messiah is derived from the Hebrew word *masiah* or *maschiach*, meaning "anointed."[3] The Greek translation of the word is *Christos*, the word which the word *Christ* is derived. According to Jewish usage of the term between 300 BC and AD 300, *Messiah* specifically meant one who would descend from King David and fulfill the messianic promises given to the royal house of David[4] (Isa. 9:6–7). The term is used much more broadly today, often in association with anyone who would appear as a sort of savior or superhuman figure. In this context, the Antichrist can be regarded as a counterfeit messiah.

According to Jewish tradition, there are at least five key things associated with the Messiah:[5]

1. He will descend from King David.
2. He will gain authority over the land of Israel.
3. He will gather the Jews from around the world to Israel.
4. He will restore the Jews to complete observance of Torah Law.
5. He will usher in global peace.

The first four pertain specifically to the Jews. The final one pertains to all mankind. The global peace that mankind has desperately sought to achieve resulting repeatedly in disappointment and disillusionment shall finally be brought about by the Messiah. God's promise is that He will in time usher in a true golden age upon the earth, led by the Messiah, to be enjoyed by God's people (Zechariah 14:9; Isaiah 9:6–7).

## The Prophet, the Priest, and the Temple

We are told in the Bible that the Messiah will be preceded by a forerunner who prepares the way for the Davidic king:

> "Behold, I am going to send you Elijah the prophet before the coming of the great and terrible day of the Lord. He will restore the hearts of the fathers to their children and the hearts of the children to their fathers." (Malachi 4:5–6)

There are two key vessels used by God in preparation for the kingdom of heaven—a prince and a prophet. In the book of Exodus, when God was delivering the children of Israel from bondage in the land of Egypt, He used two vessels—Moses, who was the deliverer, and Aaron, who was the "mouthpiece" of Moses.[6] Aaron, along with his sons, was the one whom God granted the priesthood of Israel to as a "lasting ordinance."[7]

Central to the Jewish priesthood was the temple, which stood in the city of Jerusalem. Constructed first by King Solomon (David's son) in the tenth century BC, the temple was a house for God, an earthly dwelling place for the Holy One of Israel. There is today no temple in Jerusalem, the last one having been destroyed by the Romans in AD 70. However, a future temple will play a significant role during the reign of the Davidic Messiah.[8]

## The Identity of the Messiah

The gospel of Luke introduces us to a curious individual by the name of Simeon, of whom the Bible says was "righteous and devout, looking for the consolation of Israel" (Luke 2:25). This is a reference to the comfort that would be given to Israel by the Messiah's coming. The text states that it had been revealed to Simeon by God that he would not die until he had seen the Messiah. We know from the second chapter of Luke that this account involving Simeon occurred shortly after the birth of Jesus.

Concerning the Messiah's coming, Daniel 9:25 states: "So you are to know and discern that from the issuing of a decree to restore and rebuild Jerusalem until Messiah the Prince there will be seven weeks and sixty-two weeks." Found within this one verse is a key that unlocks the mystery to the Messiah's identity, as well as reveals when He would appear to Israel. He was to appear seven weeks and sixty-two weeks (sixty-nine weeks) after the decree to restore and rebuild Jerusalem, which had been desecrated by the Babylonians.

It is imperative to understand that the Hebrew word translated as "week"—*shabua*—does not refer here to a period of seven days but seven *prophetic years*, with each year consisting of 360 days. Thus, when the prophet writes that the Messiah will appear sixty-nine weeks after the decree to rebuild Jerusalem, he is stating that 483 prophetic years (sixty-nine weeks, with each week consisting of seven 360-day years) will transpire from the time the decree was given until the Messiah's arrival. What does history have to say concerning this?

As recorded in Nehemiah 2:1–8, the decree was given to rebuild Jerusalem by King Artaxerxes in 444 BC. Several reputable biblical scholars and commentators have noted that when we add 483 prophetic years (sixty-nine weeks) to 444 BC, we are brought forward to one of the most significant periods in Israel's history, and to a most remarkable day. Sir Robert Anderson, Arno Gaebelien, Clarence Larkin, and Harold Hoehner are some of the people who have researched this prophecy of the seventy weeks. While each author may not necessarily agree on every fine point, they all come to the same startling conclusion: that the expiration point of the 483 years occurred in and around AD 30–33. If Simeon was indeed familiar with this prophecy, and well versed in the chronology, he would have known that the time of the Messiah's appearance in Israel was at hand.

The question then needs to be asked: Was there anybody in Israel between AD 30 and 33 that fit the description of Israel's Messiah? Indeed there was! One of the most remarkable messianic prophecies, found in the book of Zechariah, sheds light on this:

> Rejoice greatly, O daughter of Zion! Shout in triumph, O daughter of Jerusalem! Behold, your king is coming to you; He is just and endowed with salvation, Humble, and mounted on a donkey, Even on a colt, the foal of a donkey. (Zechariah 9:9)

This prophecy concerning the arrival of Jerusalem's king (the Messiah) was foretold by Zechariah in the sixth century BC. Regarding the prophecy of the seventy weeks of Daniel, many authors and scholars such as Harold Hoehner provide the precise date in history when the sixty-nine weeks expired. Hoehner states that this date is the tenth day of the Hebrew month of Nisan in AD 33. This translates to March 30, AD 33, a date familiar to many Christians. On this day, Zechariah 9:9 was fulfilled as Jesus for the first time publicly and openly presented Himself as Israel's Messiah. This event known as the triumphal entry, and recorded in all four Gospels, involved Jesus riding into Jerusalem as the long-awaited Messiah of Israel, just as Zechariah had foretold, and precisely at the expiration point of the sixty-nine weeks of Daniel!

Was Jesus of the house of David? Indeed, both the gospels of Matthew (1:1–17) and Luke (3:23–38) provide detailed genealogies proving Jesus' Davidic descent. Additionally, there are numerous other Messianic prophecies fulfilled in Jesus, proving beyond all reasonable doubt that He is indeed the Messiah. It is worth listing just a few here:

| Messianic Criteria | Old Testament Prediction | New Testament Fullfilment in Jesus |
|---|---|---|
| Messiah born of a virgin and called "Immanuel" | Isaiah 7:14 | Matthew 1:18, 23–25; Luke 1:26–35 |
| Messiah to be the Son of God | Psalms 2:7 | Matthew 3:17 |
| Messiah to be born in Bethlehem | Micah 5:2 | Matthew 2:1 |
| Messiah to be a "light to the Gentiles" | Isaiah 60:3 | Acts 13:47–48 |

| Messianic Criteria | Old Testament Prediction | New Testament Fullfilment in Jesus |
|---|---|---|
| Messiah to be raised from the dead | Psalms 16:10 | Acts 2:31; Mark 16:6 |
| Messiah's hands and feet to be pierced | Psalms 22:16; Zechariah12:10 | Luke 23:33; John 20:25 |
| Messiah to be rejected by His own people | Isaiah 53:3 | John 7:5, 48 |
| Messiah to be hated without cause | Psalms 69:4 | John 15:25 |
| Messiah to be king | Psalms 2:6; Zechariah 9:9 | Luke 1:30-33 |

These are just nine of the almost three hundred prophecies concerning the Messiah that were fulfilled precisely in Jesus Christ. It is important to understand that these prophecies were written by different individuals over a span of centuries.[10] Furthermore, these prophecies were uttered centuries before their fulfillment. Daniel, who received the great seventy-week prophecy already discussed, lived approximately six centuries before Christ, yet recorded the precise time of Jesus the Messiah's arrival. Imagine if someone living six centuries before the day President Barak Obama was sworn in had been able to predict the identity of the forty-fourth president, and the day he would be sworn in! Unthinkable! Yet, this is the case with the prophecy of the seventy weeks and the Messiah. These facts prove conclusively the divine inspiration of the Bible, as well as Jesus' identity as the long-awaited Messiah of Israel, and the hope of all nations.

## The Messiah Rejected

One might understandably ask: "If Jesus is the Messiah, where is the kingdom of heaven?" The Gospel accounts make it clear that the political and religious leadership of Israel, along with the Romans, did not embrace Jesus and His message. He was in fact viewed as a threat to their establishment. Consequently, He was rejected by the Jews and crucified on a Roman cross. But even this was predicted (Isaiah 53:3; Psalms 22:16). That Jesus was the individual referred to in the prophecy of the seventy weeks is further confirmed by Daniel 9:26, which states that "Messiah will be cut off and have nothing." The word *cut* used here means "to destroy" or "to consume."[11] Isaiah 53:8 also uses the phrase *cut off* to denote the Messiah's removal from the "land of the living"—certainly a strong reference to death.

Through Israel's failure to see Jesus as the Messiah, the plan of God was accomplished,[12] as the rejection of the Messiah meant the death of the

Messiah, which was needed for forgiveness of sins to be possible.[13] God did not *cause* Israel to reject Christ, but rather, in His foreknowledge, He knew that they would. This rejection then became part of the means by which God would provide redemption for the world.

The Scriptures reveal that before establishing His glorious world kingdom, the Messiah would first die on behalf of His people. His death was to serve as the payment for all human sin, making it possible for a holy God to forgive sinful people. In dying, the Messiah suffered the predicament that every sinner deserves to suffer—death and separation from God. Thus, the love of God is displayed to the world. Mankind deserves to suffer the wrath of God because of sin, "for all have sinned and fall short of the glory of God" (Romans 3:23).

However, rather than pour His wrath out upon you and me, God decided to become a man in the person of Jesus Christ and allow Himself to be killed in order to suffer the penalty for all sin, which is death (Romans 6:23). Now sinners can be righteously forgiven. Why? The death of Jesus pays the penalty for their sin! Jesus took upon Himself the guilt of sin incurred by the world and suffered for it. God has chosen to demonstrate His love for His creation by giving of Himself completely on our behalf. He became a man, and as a man, gave up His life so that you and I could be forgiven and live eternally. His subsequent resurrection from the dead is a proclamation of victory over sin and death, and reveals that the work of Jesus Christ has fully made amends between humanity and God. This is the basis of our relationship with God—love! The *essence* of the Christian life is to know God intimately through the life, death, and resurrection of Jesus Christ.

Israel's rejection of her Messiah ultimately meant that the kingdom of heaven would not be established at Christ's first coming. Thus, the very kingdom they longed for was postponed. However, as the apostle Paul makes clear in the eleventh chapter of Romans, God will restore Israel and fulfill His promises to her, which include the establishment of a glorious kingdom on earth to be ruled by the Davidic Messiah, Jesus.

## Pulling It All Together

Esoteric and New Age sympathizers are eagerly awaiting a new utopia, a "kingdom of heaven" upon the earth. They believe that the Christian declaration of a coming Antichrist and a coming Apocalypse is incorrect, or perhaps incomplete. They even make reference to the Bible in defence of their position:

> Many fundamentalist Christians, as well as a large proportion of the general public, believe that apocalyptic prophecies herald the end of the world. The visions conveyed by biblical sources, esoteric tradition and teachings from all the great religions tell a very different story. There is a startling similarity between the Essene, Christian and Hindu beliefs concerning the cataclysmic events usually associated with the apocalypse. These traumatic times are believed to herald not the end of civilization as we know it, but the dawn of a new era where life will be transformed into "heaven on earth."[14]

The utopian kingdom of heaven sought after by proponents of esoteric and New Age philosophy is in fact an imitation and counterfeit to the true kingdom of heaven promised by God in the Bible. With this counterfeit kingdom will come a counterfeit messiah, who will be the Antichrist!

There is a subtle warning given by Jesus to the people of Israel in His day concerning their rejection of Him as the Messiah: "I have come in My Father's name, and you do not receive Me; if another comes in his own name, you will receive him" (John 5:43).

Jesus' words reveal a dangerous tendency of the human heart. When the truth is rejected, a lie is often embraced. This world has rejected its true King, Savior, and Messiah. In so doing, the door has been opened for a counterfeit king, savior, and messiah to be embraced who will offer the world what it wants, without demanding what God demands. Many would deny that they reject Jesus Christ. They would perhaps say, "I believe Jesus was a good man" or "I believe Jesus was a great prophet." Some deny His deity but accept his historicity. Others claim He was married. Some may even believe He was a legitimate candidate for Messiah. However, unless we believe the *full* account that *Scripture* makes concerning Him, and *only* that account, we have not believed in the true Jesus (1 John 5:5–13).

Authors Michael Baigent, Richard Leigh, and Henry Lincoln note that they would prefer to see a solely human messiah presiding over a unified Europe than a supernatural messiah at Armageddon. This is the attitude of many who reject the biblical witness concerning Jesus. The Antichrist could not ask for a clearer invitation!

# 3

# The Kingdom of the Antichrist

## The Antichrist

The term "antichrist" is actually only found in two books of the Bible—the first two epistles of the apostle John. In the context of John's writings (1 John and 2 John), antichrists were specifically those who denied that Jesus was the Christ (1 John 2:22) and that He had come in the flesh (1 John 4:1–3; 2 John 7). John was warning against an unbiblical view of Christ that was rooted in the heretical form of thought known as Gnosticism. The Gnostics believed that the physical world was evil in contrast to the spiritual world, which they perceived as pure. Flesh was evil while spirit was good. Thus, in their minds, the Christ could not possibly have "come in the flesh." The concept of an incarnate God was a contradiction of Gnostic thought. How could the perfectly pure spirit being take up residence in evil human flesh? John defines the one who would deny the physical, human manifestation of the Christ as an antichrist (2 John 7).

In defining the term "antichrist" as such, John is not emphasizing a coming political world ruler, but rather is calling attention to false teaching concerning Jesus Christ that was already present in his day.[1] John also refers to something called "the spirit of the antichrist" (1 John 4:1–3), which was, in his day, already in the world. This spirit, John reveals, is behind the motivation to deny Jesus—specifically that He came "in the flesh."

In 1 John 2, the apostle does make a statement that seems to suggest the preeminence of one antichrist above all others:

> Children, it is the last hour; and just as you heard that antichrist is coming, even now many antichrists have appeared; from this we know that it is the last hour (1 John 2:18).

It is this passage more than any other that has led Christians throughout the centuries to label the great enemy of Christ as the Antichrist. Here, John warns of a coming antichrist that was to be associated with a period of time he refers to as "the last hour." He later defines antichrists as those who deny Jesus Christ—specifically those who deny that He is the Christ, and that He came in the flesh. Thus, *the* antichrist John refers to here is one who is against Christ—one who "denies that Jesus is *the* Christ." Even though John's primary concern is false teaching, the term "antichrist" has been intricately linked by the church to that one great political enemy of Christ who is to come.

**The Beast of the Apocalypse**

The book of Revelation, which identifies this great enemy as "the beast," reveals much concerning this individual. We are told that the beast will exercise authority over the entire planet (Revelation 13:7), and will indeed be worshipped by all who dwell on the earth who are not following the true God of heaven. We are also told that it is Satan who energizes him and gives him his throne (Revelation 13:2).

The authority and influence of this beast will be tremendous. He is entrusted with the kingdoms of this world—to rule over them as a grand monarch. He is to be a political world ruler who ascends to power shortly before Jesus returns to this earth. The fact that he will be willingly followed by the majority of the earth's inhabitants indicates that his rule—at least initially—will be one that is applauded by the people of the world. He will not come on the scene as a tyrant, but rather as a man of peace. Revelation 6:1–4 hints that this is indeed the case, as the Antichrist is pictured here arriving on the scene on a white horse (the first of four horsemen of the Apocalypse) holding a bow, but having no arrow. The arrowless bow indicates that the rider of this white horse is not anticipating any conflict as he goes out "conquering and to conquer." Furthermore, the second horseman is said to have been granted the power to "take peace from the earth." Obviously, this second rider can take peace from the earth only if peace was the condition on earth before his arrival.

### The Antichrist and the Times of the Gentiles

In Luke 21:24, Jesus alludes to a period of time called the "times of the Gentiles"—a period of time featuring the rule of Gentile (non-Jewish) nations in the earth prior to the advent of the true messianic kingdom of heaven. We are given a detailed look at this Gentile time frame in the Book of Daniel, as the Hebrew prophet Daniel himself was able, through God's provision, to decipher a dream by the king of Babylon that outlined the times of the Gentiles from Babylon to the return of Jesus Christ. As recounted in Daniel 2:31–35, King Nebuchadnezzar witnessed in his dream a magnificent metallic statue divided into five sections: a head of gold, breasts and arms of silver, a bronze belly and bronze thighs, iron legs, and feet and toes of iron and clay. The statue was then destroyed by a stone "cut out without hands" that struck the statue on its iron and clay feet.

Daniel 2:36–45 reveals that each section of the statue—along with the stone cut without hands that falls on the statue and destroys it—represents a world kingdom. Nebuchadnezzar himself, we are told, is the head of gold (Daniel 2:36–38). After Babylon, another kingdom would arise represented by the silver. After this would arise a third empire, and then a fourth—represented respectively by the bronze and iron. The fifth division—the iron/clay feet—represents a different phase of the fourth empire. Finally, we are told that the stone cut without hands is none other than the kingdom of heaven established on the earth at some point in the future, supplanting all former Gentile rule (Daniel 2:44–45).

The Bible, as well as secular history, enables us to identify the kingdoms outlined in Daniel's prophecy. We already know that King Nebuchadnezzar's Babylon is the head of gold, which ruled the known world from 606 to 538 BC. The silver, then, represents the empire that succeeded Babylon—Medo-Persia (Daniel 5:30–31). Medo-Persia ruled the known world from 538 to 330 BC, after which came the rule of the empire symbolized by bronze—Greece (Daniel 8:20–21). While the fourth and final Gentile kingdom is not mentioned by name in the book of Daniel, European history does make it abundantly clear that the empire symbolized by the legs of iron is Rome! It was the Romans who defeated the Greeks and followed in the succession of Gentile world powers and had a significant influence over the land of Israel. Note, however, that during the final phase of the fourth empire of Nebuchadnezzar's statue, a nonmetallic element is introduced—specifically, the clay. Some commentators have suggested that the iron—a metal common to all four empires—represents autocratic rule, whereas the clay—unique to the final phase of Rome—represents democratic rule.

The interpretation given to Daniel clearly reveals that the fourth kingdom is illustrated by both the legs of iron *and* the feet and toes of iron and clay. There is no fifth Gentile empire. Consider as well that it is upon the feet of iron and clay that the stone kingdom, the kingdom of God, falls. Simply stated, it is the Roman Empire that the kingdom of heaven is to displace. At first, this appears to present a problem. The Roman Empire has long collapsed, yet the kingdom of heaven has clearly not been established as a visible, physical kingdom upon the earth. How do we reconcile this? To answer this question, we shall now take a look at Daniel's own vision of Gentile dominion, as recorded in Daniel 7.

In Daniel 7:1–27, the prophet sees a vision of four beasts that, we are told, represent four kings (or kingdoms). The first beast, which resembled a lion, was followed by one that resembled a bear, which in turn was followed by one resembling a leopard. The fourth beast, which greatly intrigued Daniel, resembled nothing that he could conceive of. It is simply described as a "dreadful and terrifying" beast (Daniel 7:7).

Scholars disagree as to the precise interpretation of the first three beasts in this vision, but generally agree on the identity of the fourth beast. Some hold that the first three beasts in Daniel's vision correspond with the first three divisions of Nebuchadnezzar's statue: the gold, silver, and bronze. Others maintain that the words, "will arise from the earth," found in Daniel 7:18, indicate that all four beasts, from Daniel's perspective, were future, and therefore could not correspond precisely with Nebuchadnezzar's statue, which already featured one of the four kingdoms in power. While this is a valid argument, it is nonconsequential when trying to identify the final Gentile kingdom, as scholars from both views are in agreement as to the identity of the fourth and final beast.

There are four crucial points that need to be understood concerning this final beast. First, this beast is a fourth kingdom on the earth. Second, it possesses ten horns (Daniel 7:19–23). Third, an eleventh horn comes up from among the ten horns and subdues three one of them (Daniel 7:8). And finally, dominion is taken away from the eleventh horn by the "Ancient of Days" (Daniel 7:21–22).

For the sake of clarity, let us consider the first and fourth point concerning this beast together. The Ancient of Days, a title referring to God, is said to remove the fourth kingdom and replace it with "an everlasting kingdom." Clearly, this everlasting kingdom corresponds to the "stone" kingdom of Nebuchadnezzar's vision that is said to endure forever. Remember that it is upon the statue's feet of iron and clay that the stone falls. Thus, the empire replaced by the kingdom of heaven in Daniel 2 is the same empire replaced by the kingdom of heaven in Daniel 7. Notice as well that at the base of the statue are ten toes that Daniel declares are kings (Daniel 2:44). Interestingly, the fourth kingdom described in Daniel 7 also has ten horns, out of which Daniel is told are ten kings that spring up out of the fourth world empire (Daniel 7:24). Therefore, the fourth kingdom of Daniel 7 is identical to the fourth kingdom of Daniel 2, and that kingdom is Rome. This fourth beast represents the final Gentile world kingdom to rule before God takes global authority from the Gentiles and fulfills His covenant promises to Israel by establishing the kingdom of heaven on earth. Since God has not yet established the visible kingdom upon the earth, it can be concluded that the great prophetic timeline established by Nebuchadnezzar's statue has yet to reach its conclusion. But how then does one account for the demise of the Roman Empire without the establishment of the kingdom of heaven?

## The Once and Future Empire

One of the certainties of biblical prophecy is the eventual revival and restoration of the Roman Empire. It is important to understand that according to Nebuchadnezzar's statue depicting the times of the Gentiles, each kingdom is to be overthrown by the one that follows it. The Medes and Persians conquered Babylon. Greece conquered the Medes and the Persians, and the Romans replaced Greece. However, Rome was never actually defeated or supplanted by a succeeding world power. It simply crumbled and dissolved into numerous individual nations. Pieces of the ancient Roman Empire have since existed as separate kingdoms, as it was mainly just the unity and imperial power of Rome that was lost.[2]

The Bible makes it clear that the imperial aspect of the Roman Empire will be revived, leading to Rome's reestablishment as a dominant, unified world power. As Daniel states, it is in the days of the final kings of the Roman Empire (Daniel 2:45) that "the God of heaven will set up a kingdom which will never be destroyed." Rome, the final Gentile world kingdom, still has a role to play. Arno Gaebelein writes:

> The ten horns on the fourth beast correspond to the ten toes of Nebuchadnezzar's dream image; they are ten kings. The Roman Empire has never existed in this form. . . . The Roman Empire must therefore be revived politically. It will be one great world power, an undivided empire, yet in it there will be ten kingdoms.[3]

The ten toes and the ten horns of the two visions depict a revived Roman Empire under the leadership of ten kings. At some point in the future, the Roman Empire will take on the form of a ten-kingdom confederacy, united yet divided. All ten kings are the heads of kingdoms, with each of the kingdoms arising from the fourth world empire, which is Rome.[4]

What is the significance of the eleventh horn that comes up after the first ten? Daniel's prophecy reveals that this "little horn" "speaks out against the Most High"—a title for God. This little horn has no regard for God's authority or supremacy. He serves as a God-defying emperor over a new Roman Empire, and is the one God takes the kingdom from when He sets up the kingdom of heaven on earth. Being the ruler of the final Gentile kingdom, this little horn is none other than the Antichrist—the beast of the Apocalypse. The kingdom of the Antichrist, then, will assume the form of a revived Roman Empire in the days ahead.

## The False Prophet and the Tribulation Period

The Antichrist will not work alone in the quest to establish a global dictatorship but will be aided by a second beast, the False Prophet (Revelation 13:11–18; 19:20), who actually causes the people of the earth to worship the

Antichrist (Revelation 13:12). The False Prophet is somewhat of a counterfeit of two individuals mentioned in Scripture. He is presented as a herald to the first beast, compelling the world to follow and worship the Antichrist. In this way, the False Prophet serves as an "anti–John the Baptist." It was John who prepared the way for the Messiah and urged the people to prepare their hearts to receive Jesus. Through the two beasts of Revelation 13, Satan presents to the world (and Israel in particular) a counterfeit king and priest. The False Prophet mimics John the Baptist, heralding the Antichrist as the one to be worshipped. This is no minor detail. In fact, it reveals how meticulous Satan is in his imitation of things divine.

The False Prophet also appears to be an imitation of the prophet Elijah. Again, this is an astonishing glimpse into the careful plotting of Satan as he attempts to stage a counterfeit messiah. Concerning the true Messiah's advent in Israel, God, speaking through the prophet Malachi, states:

> "Behold, I am going to send you Elijah the prophet before the coming of the great and terrible day of the Lord. He will restore the hearts of the fathers to their children and the hearts of the children to their fathers, so that I will not come and smite the land with a curse." (Malachi 4:5–6)

God's Word states that before the day of the Lord, which includes the coming of the true Messiah to Israel, a forerunner will be sent to prepare the way so that God would not have to "smite the land with a curse." This forerunner is said to be "Elijah," with whom John the Baptist is closely linked. Elijah is the one who called fire down from heaven on Mount Carmel in a "fire test" with the prophets of the god Baal. The purpose of the test was to identify who was the true God—Baal or the Lord. The account is found in 1 Kings 18:20–46. Here, both Elijah and the prophets of Baal prepare a sacrifice for their God to consume by fire. Whoever answered by fire would be regarded as the true God. When the prophets of Baal cried out to their god, there was no response. The sacrifice on the altar remained intact. However, when Elijah called upon his God, fire totally consumed the altar. It was the fire from heaven that confirmed to the people who the true God was.

To this very day, the vast majority of Jews do not recognize Jesus Christ as the Messiah. Consequently, they are still looking for the Messiah to make his appearance. Those Jews who are familiar with the Scriptures will understand the importance of Elijah's role in heralding the Messiah. They would also certainly be familiar with Elijah's famous fire test to prove who the one true God is. It cannot be without significance, then, that the False Prophet will call fire down from heaven, as indicated in Revelation 13:13. When the False Prophet arrives on the scene and points to the Antichrist as the one to be worshipped, he will be fulfilling the role of an "Elijah" by mimicking the role that Elijah is to play in heralding the true Messiah. When he then proceeds to mesmerize the world by calling fire down from above, Israel and all the nations may very well believe that this deceiver is serving the true God, since Elijah also called fire down from heaven to prove that his God was the true God. The outcome of this is frightful to consider. The Antichrist, under this scenario, may very well be received as the long-awaited messiah.

The Antichrist and the False Prophet will arise during a seven-year period of divine judgement upon the earth often referred to as the tribulation period. The final three and a half years of this seven-year period have been called the great tribulation due to the intensity of divine judgement that occurs during these years. The entire tribulation period is a time when God's wrath is poured out on a world that has rejected Jesus. Some may object to this, asking how a loving God could allow the world to go through such harsh judgements. In reality, God has given mankind thousands of years to learn His ways. Certainly, in light of the millennia of human history that has transpired, seven years of judgment is an incredibly short period of time. Indeed, God's mercy is deeper, wider, and higher than we can ever imagine. Furthermore, a careful study of the book of Revelation reveals that God will show mercy to many who are faithful to Him during that horrendous period of time.

Pure justice demands that judgement of wrongdoing must eventually come. It is not a matter of God being mean or unfair but, rather, just! He has provided His Son Jesus Christ as a sacrifice for sin, that all may be forgiven and saved from the wrath to come by placing their faith in Christ. Those who reject this provision are subject to divine vengeance.

**Pulling It All Together**

Scripture is clear that one man will at some point in the future arise to seize control of the entire globe, bringing all nations and peoples under his authority. His empire will be the kingdom of the Antichrist. It is widely believed that he will be received by Israel as her long-awaited messiah, possibly claiming Davidic ancestry. He will appear on the scene as the answer and cure to the ills that plague humanity. However, in the end, he will prove to be an emissary of hell. He will in fact be Satan's representative on earth, fully energized by the Devil himself.

As we close this chapter, it should be noted that the message of biblical prophecy, despite its warnings of a coming tyrannical world leader, is not a message of gloom and annihilation. It is not another "2012" disaster prediction. Though the Antichrist will rule, his reign will be extremely short. At the end of the seven-year tribulation, Jesus Christ Himself will return to defeat the Antichrist and set up the messianic kingdom, ushering in a thousand years of peace, justice, and righteousness upon the earth.

# 4

## The Revelation of Babylon

The seventeenth chapter of the book of Revelation introduces us to one of the most intriguing entities in all of Scripture. In this chapter, we are introduced to a woman known as Babylon the Great, a seductive harlot seated upon the Beast that is the Antichrist and his kingdom:

> Then one of the seven angels who had the seven bowls came and spoke with me, saying, "Come here, I will show you the judgment of the great harlot who sits on many waters, with whom the kings of the earth committed acts of immorality, and those who dwell on the earth were made drunk with the wine of her immorality." And he carried me away in the Spirit into a wilderness; and I saw a woman sitting on a scarlet beast, full of blasphemous names, having seven heads and ten horns. (Revelation 17:1–3)

The seven heads identify this beast with the beast of Revelation 13, while the ten horns correspond to the ten toes of Daniel 2, the ten horns of Daniel 7, and the ten horns of Revelation 13. Without a doubt, this beast represents the revived Roman Empire under the rule of the Antichrist. But what is the identity of the woman who sits upon the Beast?

## Queen of the Apocalypse

The passage continues:

> The woman was clothed in purple and scarlet, and adorned with gold and precious stones and pearls, having in her hand a gold cup full of abominations and of the unclean things of her immorality, and on her forehead a name was written, a mystery, "Babylon the Great, the mother of harlots and of the abominations of the earth." And I saw the woman drunk with the blood of the saints, and with the blood of the witnesses of Jesus. When I saw her, I wondered greatly. And the angel said to me, "Why do you wonder? I will tell you the mystery of the woman and of the beast that carries her, which has the seven heads and the ten horns. The beast that you saw was, and is not, and is about to come up out of the abyss and go to destruction. . . . Here is the mind which has wisdom. The seven heads are seven mountains on which the woman sits, and they are seven kings; five have fallen, one is, the other has not yet come."
>
> "The ten horns which you saw are ten kings who have not yet received a kingdom, but they receive authority as kings with the beast for one hour. These have one purpose, and they give their power and authority to the beast." . . . And he said to me, "The waters which you saw where the harlot sits, are peoples and multitudes and nations and tongues. And the ten horns which you saw, and the beast, these will hate the harlot and will make her desolate and naked, and will eat her flesh and will burn her up with fire. For God has put it in their hearts to execute His purpose by having a common purpose, and by giving their kingdom to the beast, until the words of God will be fulfilled. The woman whom you saw is the great city, which reigns over the kings of the earth" (Revelation 17:4–8, 9–10, 12–13, 15–18).

The best way to uncover the identity of this woman is to highlight her various characteristics, starting with the plain declaration of the last verse of chapter 17. Notice that verse eighteen identifies this woman as a city—one that "reigns over the kings of the earth." When John recorded these words, of all the cities he could have envisioned, Rome seems to be the most likely! John was a Roman prisoner exiled to the Isle of Patmos when he received the revelation. It was the Roman Empire that ruled the known world in his day. Furthermore, the beast that the woman rides is the Roman Empire. The text also states that the seven heads of the beast represent seven mountains upon which the woman sits. Geographically, Rome is built upon seven hills.[1] Jerusalem is also said to be situated upon seven hills/mountains, and has been identified by some as the "great city" of Revelation 17. However, many of the other details found in this passage seem better suited to a Roman entity than to Jerusalem. It is fascinating, however, that both Jerusalem and Rome are said to be seated on seven hills/mountains. Jerusalem is where Jesus will reign from in His kingdom, while Rome was the capitol of the empire that reigned when Jesus was crucified.

Notice also that the woman sits on "many waters," and that these waters represent "peoples and multitudes and nations and tongues." Clearly, this woman's influence is not confined to one city, but extends globally. Those upon the earth drink from the gold chalice she holds and become "drunk with the wine of her immorality."

Verse two states that the kings of the earth "committed acts of immorality" with her. Remember that the woman is a harlot. The imagery here depicts the leaders of the world developing intimate relationships with this global Roman entity. She sits upon the beast, depicting her control over the political sphere of the empire. She reigns *over* the kings of the earth, indicating that for a time, the political leaders of the earth actually bow before her. She crowns kings and emperors, commanding the allegiance of the empire.

The woman is adorned in colors of purple and scarlet, wearing gold, pearls, and precious stones. She is abundantly wealthy. Part of the harlot's wealth no doubt came as a reward for the immoral services she provided to the kings of the earth, for she is a prostitute! This raises a very important question. How can a city commit immoral acts with kings? The answer to this question is found in the woman's very name. The name on the woman's forehead is "Babylon the Great, the mother of harlots and of the abominations of the earth." In the Bible, the term "harlot" is used to describe a people who outwardly profess allegiance to God yet are unfaithful to Him. The imagery is that of a husband whose wife has broken her marriage vows and prostitutes herself to others. Examples of this can be found in the Old Testament. God said of Jerusalem, "How the faithful city has become a harlot" (Isaiah 1:21). The Jews, being in covenant with God, had fallen into gross sin and error. Alliances were formed with certain surrounding nations that did not worship the God of Abraham, Isaac, and Jacob, but served pagan gods.[2] A city cannot commit adultery. Therefore, God must have been referring to harlotry in a *spiritual* sense. The people of Israel forsook the covenant they had with God, and by forming alliances with other nations that worshipped other gods, committed *spiritual adultery*, or harlotry. The imagery in Revelation 17, thus, portrays a city that publicly claims to have a special relationship with God but is in actuality an unfaithful partner. She must, then, be a religious or spiritual entity!

It is interesting that the New Testament portrays the church of God as the bride of Christ arrayed in "fine linen, white and clean."[3] In direct imitation of God, Satan ensures that his chosen one, the Antichrist, also has a "female" companion. She is a counterfeit bride and a counterfeit church, the religious arm of the Antichrist's kingdom. The fact that she is called a harlot in the Word of God proves that her worldwide influence is not primarily political but religious, for this form of biblical harlotry depicts *spiritual* unfaithfulness. While Rome appears to be her seat, her influence is clearly global. She is extremely wealthy, and finds herself "in bed" with the kings and political leaders of the earth.

But why the name Babylon? Some have mistakenly supposed that the woman represents ancient Babylon, a city in what is now modern-day Iraq. However, some of the key details associated with Revelation 17 seem to rule out the literal, physical city of Babylon. When John received this vision, Rome was a great city, not Babylon. Furthermore, it is the Roman Empire that she rides, not the Babylonian Empire. Interestingly, the apostle Peter seemed to have used the word *Babylon* as a code name for Rome when concluding his first epistle (1 Peter 5:13). Nevertheless, the fact that the woman has the word *Babylon* in her name does in fact suggest a very real association with that ancient city.

**Why Babylon?**

Being a religious system, the relationship between the harlot and ancient Babylon appears to be a religious one. The religion of ancient Babylon was one of self-effort to attain salvation and immortality. Unlike the biblical gospel, Babylonian religious belief taught that immortality was attainable by human will and effort. Salvation in the Bible is through faith in Jesus Christ, accepting His death on the cross as the satisfaction of God's wrath toward sin. Thus, the one who believes in Christ is justified from all sin. The cults of Babylon, on the other hand, taught that human effort accomplished salvation. The religion embraced by the woman in Revelation 17, then, would appear to be a religion of self-effort to attain salvation. She represents an apostate religious system that teaches a different gospel than the one found in Scripture. The biblical gospel states "believe on the Lord Jesus, and you will be saved" (Acts 16:32). The gospel according to this apostate system declares "do this, don't do that, then you will be saved." It is a religion of bondage that places men and women under the burden of trying to earn what God has already freely given!

Ancient Babylonian religious practice also incorporated the belief that an individual could be exalted to become like a god through secret ritual, Gnosticism (secret knowledge), and initiation.[4] It was a system based on esoteric spirituality, incorporating the many pagan beliefs of the ancient world. The word *Babylon* is the Greek form[5] of the name Babel, a city in ancient Mesopotamia believed to have been built by Nimrod, who is described in the Bible as "a mighty one on the earth" (Genesis 10:8). It was here that the famed Tower of Babel was constructed. The Tower of Babel was built in the shape of a ziggurat, (a pyramid-like occult worship tower). The goal of the builders was to construct a monument "whose top will reach into heaven" and to make for themselves a name, to prevent them from being scattered over the face of the earth (Genesis 11:4).

In constructing the tower, these people were defying God's authority by trying to "reach heaven" by their own works. God had commanded man to "be fruitful and multiply, and fill the earth" (Genesis 1:28). Instead of doing as God commanded, they decided to remain in one place and construct a tower, lest they be "scattered abroad over the face of the earth." The result of this ambition was mankind's first united attempt at creating a God-defying world order upon the earth. God responded by confusing the language of the builders, preventing them from completing the work, and scattering them across the entire earth.[6]

What occurred at Babel was the establishment of multiple languages. Up until God confused the language of the people and scattered them, the world was united with one language (Genesis 11:1–2). By confusing their language, God made possible the establishment of many different nations and peoples defined and separated mainly by language. Nations are defined by the culture of a particular people, and that culture is often distinguished by language. For example, the French speak one language, while the English speak another. France, the home of the French, is a separate nation from England, the home of the English. The scattering of the people at Babel contributed greatly to the creation of the nations of the world, and slowed down man's united, global rebellion against his Creator.

As the people of Babel scattered and filled the earth, they naturally took with them their spiritual beliefs, practices, and rituals. As these beliefs began to mix with the various cultures that formed from this mass scattering, many various religions began to emerge. Thus, not only did the scattering give rise to many new nations, but also to the numerous religions of the world. A question often asked is, if there is one God, why are there so many different religions? Many religions in the world today all come from the same root—Babylon! The reason they differ from each other is that each culture that emerged from the scattering at Babel expressed their belief in a slightly different manner, depending on how the particular culture of a specific region affected that belief. So many religions express the same Babylonian concept of working one's way up to heaven. Interestingly, the gospel of Jesus Christ not only opposes the widely held concept of working one's way up to God,[7] but also transcends cultural barriers.[8] It is not an American, Canadian, or European gospel. It is not without significance that the gospel of Jesus Christ reflects the transcendence of the one true God, who is not confined within any one particular race, culture, or time period.[9]

What, then, does the woman named Babylon in Revelation 17 represent? Depicted in this dramatic portion of Scripture is the widespread influence of a global religious system associated with ancient Babylonian paganism. Not only will the world come under the influence of the political Antichrist, but it will also come under the spiritual influence of this Babylonian religious system.

## The Cult of Babylon

Clarence Larkin outlines the trail of the Babylonian cult from its ancient Mesopotamian home to Rome in his masterful work *The Book of Revelation.* Larkin points out that the geographical home of the Babylonian cult—called here "the seat of Satan"—remained in Babylon until the fall of the Babylonian and Medo-Persian empires, at which point it shifted to Pergamos in Asia Minor (see Revelation 2:12–17). When Attalus, the king of Pergamos, died in 133 BC, he left the leadership of the Babylonian religious order to the city of Rome. Consequently, the Babylonian religion began to take root in Rome, resulting in the instalment of a pontiff (high priest) over its pagan priesthood. This pontiff was later accepted by the Roman people as not only a religious leader, but also a civil ruler. Eventually, the Roman political leaders, such as Julius Caesar, inherited the title of pontiff, and became head of the religious order inherited from Babylon. The city of Rome, in effect, became the successor to the city of Babylon.[10]

This dual role of being both the supreme political authority and the supreme religious authority became a distinct mark of Roman emperorship. They held the title Pontifex Maximus, which meant "Supreme Pontiff." They were priest-kings, rulers of both ecclesiastical and civil affairs. The Roman emperors continued to occupy the office of Supreme Pontiff until AD 376, when Emperor Gratian refused to hold that title, apparently due to his Christian convictions. However, the bishop of the church at Rome at that time, Damasus, did not appear to have shared Gratian's convictions and was thus bestowed with the title. As bishop, Damasus' influence over the Roman church was enormous. Ultimately, the head of the Babylonian order became synonymous with the head of the Roman church.[11] Interestingly, the Roman Catholic Church has used the title "Summus Pontifex Ecclesiae Universalis" or "Supreme Pontiff of the Whole Church" in conjunction with its Popes.

Ancient Babylon was also associated with certain pagan beliefs that are often referred to as the ancient mysteries. These mysteries are traced back to Nimrod, who is regarded as the "father of the gods" and the "first of deified mortals,"[12] and to Semiramis, who according to ancient lore was his wife.

The Bible does not mention that Nimrod was married to someone named Semiramis, and some have doubted whether Nimrod can even be linked to a Semiramis of Babylon. Semiramis was a legendary queen of Assyria. There may have in fact been at least two Semiramis's. The first Semiramis was apparently the basis for the goddess Ishtar and in this context can be linked to the goddess principle discussed throughout this book. Linking Semiramis with Nimrod was part of an early 20th century work by Christian author Alexander Hislop entitled *The Two Babylons.*

According to Genesis 10:10, the beginning of Nimrod's kingdom was Babel. David Bay of The Cutting Edge Ministries records how Nimrod established a counter-belief system to the worship of the one true God. This belief system served as a foundation for the construction of the Tower of Babel. The nature of Nimrod's counterreligion was one of open idolatry and blatant disobedience to the one true God of Heaven. He was an apostate,[13] spurning the revelation of the one true God. The Tower of Babel was the visible result of Nimrod's apostate and counterfeit spirituality.

Regarding Nimrod's ultimate fate, some researchers have argued the possibility that Nimrod was executed by Shem, a son of Noah. The stated motive for such an act was to make a public example to all that such apostasy and idol worship would not be tolerated. According to the account, Shem had Nimrod's body cut into numerous pieces and sent to many chief cities where his counterfeit religious system had been established.[14] While Shem's actions successfully eradicated the human source of such apostasy, the damage had already been accomplished, as the "mystery" system had spread out from Babylon throughout all the earth.[15] Hislop notes that the preservation of the mysteries derived from Nimrod occurred under a veil of secrecy,[16] as Shem had already made it clear that idol worship and apostasy would not be tolerated. This veil of secrecy gave rise to an underground stream of esoteric and occult thought, intent on preserving the ancient mysteries of Nimrod. These mysteries would include as a goal the restoration of a Tower of Babel–type setup, where all people would be united in one global spiritual system under a new Nimrod who would once again establish in full public view the ancient pagan mysteries.

The deification of Nimrod was largely the doing of Semiramis.[17] Notable Bible commentator H. A. Ironside notes that it was actually Semiramis who founded the Babylonian mysteries.[18] There are certainly some intriguing aspects to the story of Semiramis. First, she, being the widow of Nimrod, became the high priestess in Babylon of what is referred to as the "mother-child" cult and was often depicted as a woman holding a baby in her arms. The baby was her son, Tammuz, from whom the Babylonian "sign of the cross" originated (in honor of the *T* in his name). Legend states that after Tammuz's death, Semiramis established a forty-day fast for the members of her religious order. At the end of the forty days, Tammuz was supposedly miraculously resurrected. The resurrection of Tammuz was then celebrated by the exchange of colored eggs. Interestingly, Tammuz was also symbolized by an evergreen tree, which was usually displayed during midwinter celebrations.

Semiramis is said to have united with some of Nimrod's followers, helping to establish the underground movement of occultism and esoteric philosophy that would ultimately seek to avenge the death of her husband. According to Bay, this new underground stream created a system of satanic mysteries designed to ultimately spread over the entire world, leading men and women back to pagan worship. This apostate path was made attractive by its offer of secret (esoteric) knowledge to initiates, as well as "enlightenment" into the deep mysteries of the pagan system. Immortality was also promised. Sacred oaths and secret handshakes were employed to ensure that the mysteries were indeed kept secret.

The ultimate ambition motivating the initiates was the overthrow of God's established order, to be replaced by the counterfeit system based on the story of Nimrod, his dismemberment, and his wife Semiramis is linked to legends and myths regarding Babylon. The death of Nimrod and the termination of Babel had two crucial effects. First, it forced the adherents of the ancient mystery beliefs to carry out their work in secret. They were fully aware that the devotees of the one true God would not tolerate a conspiracy to overthrow all existing government in favor of a system based on a belief system that opposed God's revealed will. Shem's treatment of Nimrod made this abundantly clear. The global kingdom sought by those who upheld the ancient mysteries was to be based, not on God's revealed will, but on satanic and idolatrous mysteries. Second, the termination of the Tower of Babel forced the men and women of Babel to spread out across the world, with the confusion of their language necessitating the maintenance of separate, identifiable nations.

Evidence of the global spread of the ancient mysteries can be found when one examines the early belief systems of various cultures. The story of Nimrod, his dismemberment, and his wife Semiramis is found in Babylonian history and legends. Yet, when one looks at certain myths and legends of other regions, the story is strangely familiar. In Egypt, for example, one finds the legend of Osiris, an ancient god-king. Osiris is said to have been murdered by his enemy Set, with his body being cut into fourteen pieces. This, of course, is virtually identical to the story of Nimrod and Shem. Isis, Osiris's wife, begins to search for all the missing pieces of her murdered husband. Legend has it that a miraculous resurrection would occur should all of Osiris's missing pieces be located. Interestingly, the only piece that she could not find was his phallus, which was represented in ancient Egypt by a towerlike object known as an obelisk. In this story, the Babylonian Nimrod is replaced by the Egyptian Osiris, while Semiramis is replaced by Isis. Shem, meanwhile, is replaced by Set.

The Egyptian version of the story becomes even more intriguing when one considers the role of Horus, the son of Isis and the Egyptian equivalent of the Babylonian Tammuz. According to the legend, Horus's ambition is to avenge the death of Osiris, much in the same way that Nimrod's followers sought to avenge the destruction of their god-king. It is said that the battle between Horus and Set goes on forever, and that only when Horus wins will Osiris once again be able to take his rightful place as king of Egypt.[19] Again, the goal is to reestablish what was lost at the hands of Shem/Set. In this regard, the role of Horus is vital. He is the one responsible for reestablishing the kingdom of Osiris/Nimrod, which, in the Egyptian story, would triumph over Set, and in the Babylonian story would triumph over Shem—Set and Shem being symbolic of God's kingdom and order. Horus, then, represents the "savior" of the ancient occult mysteries—the one who restores the lost occult wisdom and kingdom of the ancient world. Curiously, the "eye of Horus," a key symbol of Freemasonry, adorns the US one-dollar bill under the guise of the "eye of Providence," with the phrase *New Order of the Ages* in Latin underneath an Egyptian-like pyramid. More will be said on this later.

The mother-child cult of Semiramis/Tammuz and Isis/Horus can also be found in various other cultures outside of Babylon and Egypt. For example, in Greece, the mother and child were identified as Aphrodite and Eros. In

Assyria, they were Ishstar and Tammuz. The Phoenicians knew them as Astarte and Baal, while pagan Rome identified the mother and child as Venus and Cupid. One key aspect found throughout the ancient mysteries is the veneration of the sacred goddess, the "Queen of Heaven," as she is called. In the Babylonian account, the queen was Semiramis. Hislop writes:

> This Babylonian queen was not merely in *character* coincident with the Aphrodite of Greece and the Venus of Rome, but was, in fact, the historical original of that goddess that by the ancient world was regarded as the very embodiment of everything attractive in female form, and the perfection of female beauty.[20]

He goes on to state that "The mother, in point of fact, became the favorite object of worship. To justify this worship, the mother was raised to divinity as well as her son."[21]

Both the mother and the son in her arms were venerated and regarded as divine. It is not difficult to see in this a strange parallel to the Virgin Mary and infant Jesus of Roman Catholicism, and to a lesser extent, Orthodox Christianity. Often, in Catholic art, Mary and Jesus are depicted in virtually the same manner as the Queen of Heaven and the divine child of paganism—a woman holding a baby in her arms! The fact that this mother-child cult concept is found in so many different cultures and settings stresses the fact that the ancient mysteries had a common geographic root, and then spread out to various regions. Ironside states:

> From Babylon this mystery-religion spread to all the surrounding nations. . . . Everywhere the symbols were the same, and everywhere the cult of the mother and child became the popular system; their worship was celebrated with the most disgusting and immoral practices. The image of the queen of heaven with the babe in her arms was seen everywhere, though the names might differ as languages differed. . . . Within one thousand years Babylonianism had become the religion of the world, which had rejected Divine revelation.[22]

In recent times, a new manifestation of the sacred goddess principle has been found in Mary Magdalene, who is believed by some to have been the wife of Jesus Christ. Here, Magdalene is associated with Semiramis/Isis/Aphrodite/Ishtar/Astarte/Venus. She serves as a "consort" to the king, who in this instance would be Jesus, who in turn is associated with Nimrod/Osiris. The Queen of Heaven is indeed usually presented in the mysteries as the widow of an ancient deceased king, be it Nimrod, Osiris, or Jesus. The resurrection of Jesus can then be seen as the resurrection of the ancient king, even as Osiris is said to be awaiting resurrection.

Babylon the Great is not limited to Revelation 17. She also makes an appearance in the very next chapter, giving us a deeper understanding of this intriguing character. While some commentators believe that the entity in Revelation 18 is a separate one altogether from the Babylon of Revelation 17, others, including this author, feel that both chapters indeed point to the same entity. This view certainly seems to be supported by the way the final verses of Revelation 17 transition into the first few verses of Revelation 18. In Revelation 18:7, we read a remarkable statement: "I sit as a *Queen* and am not a *widow*, and will never see mourning" (emphasis added).

Be it coincidental or not, the language in this verse reminds us of the goddess principle rooted in Semiramis and found in so many other cultures. Here, the woman admits she is a queen and denies her widowhood, possibly implying that she is called a widow by others but does not regard herself as one. By denying her widowhood, is she proclaiming the rebirth of her deceased king? Indeed, Babylon the Great represents the final end product of the ancient mystery religion of Babylon, teamed up with the Antichrist, who can be representative of a resurrected Nimrod/Osiris—Nimrod being the very first of deified mortals. In a sense, Osiris's phallus has been found, bringing him back to life. Horus has triumphed over Set and the occult kingdom of Osiris has been restored. It is as if Queen Semiramis (the woman) has been reunited to her Nimrod (the beast) and, thus, is no longer a widow. Babylon the Great—"Babylon of the Apocalypse," as Ironside calls it— is the religious system that originated at Babel, brought back into a position of prominence during the times of the Antichrist:

> Babylon became the fountainhead of idolatry, and the mother of every heathen and pagan system in the world. The mystery-religion that was there originated spread in various forms throughout the whole earth and is still with us today.

> . . . It will have its fullest development when the Holy Spirit has departed [at the Rapture] and the Babylon of the apocalypse gains control.[23]

## The Conflict of the Ages

What is the ultimate force behind the emerging kingdom of the Antichrist? If God is sovereign and loving and just, why would He allow such a tyrannical system to develop in the earth? The motivation to create a new order in the earth under the leadership of one man does not stem from modern-day politics, economics, or religion. And while the Tower of Babel represents the original, visible attempt at a one-world order, it was not at Babel where the *motivation* for such a system began. The motivation for a new order apart from God's rule was born in the distant past within the heart of Satan, that wicked angelic entity who initiated the first known rebellion against divine authority! This adversary of God is widely believed to be one and the same with the "Lucifer" mentioned in Isaiah 14 of the King James Version of the Bible. *Lucifer* is a Latin word for the phrase *morning star*. It is also a translation of the Hebrew word *helel*, which means "bright one."[24] Concerning Lucifer, Isaiah 14 states:

> How art thou fallen from heaven, O Lucifer, son of the morning! How art thou cut down to the ground, which didst weaken the nations! For thou hast said in thine heart, I will ascend into heaven, I will exalt my throne above the stars of God: I will sit also upon the mount of the congregation, in the sides of the north: I will ascend above the heights of the clouds; I will be like the most High. (Isaiah 14:12–14 KJV)

Note the phrases used in this passage: "I will exalt my throne above the stars of God," "I will ascend into heaven," and "I will be like the most High." While Isaiah 14 in its entirety seems to, in the immediate context, deal with an earthly king, it is obvious that the rebellious ambitions laid out in this passage could ultimately derive only from Satan.

Many also feel that Ezekiel 28 refers to Satan when it refers to the "anointed cherub who covers"—referring to the role of "guardian" or "protector" of the throne of God.[25] The Bible describes this anointed cherub as "blameless" since the day that he was created, until "unrighteousness" was found in him.[26]

Understanding that the rebellion and sin described in Isaiah 14 and Ezekiel 28 seem to reflect Satan's prideful ambition, it is clear that this adversary's chief objective is to dethrone God and establish his own kingdom and system of worship.

Jesus testified of Satan's fall in Luke's gospel when He stated, "I was watching Satan fall from heaven like lightning" (Luke 10:18). This implies a definite moment where Satan, through revolt against God's established order, fell from heaven. He was not alone in his rebellion, as several heavenly angels actually followed his lead. Thus, a rival kingdom and assembly was established consisting of Satan and the angels that fell with him. It is this fall of Satan that gave rise to the great conflict of the ages, in which the kingdom of Satan has been struggling against the kingdom of God for control of heaven and earth.

Satan's futile struggle to wrest control of this world away from God can clearly be seen in numerous events throughout history, including events recorded between Genesis 3:15 and Revelation 20:10. These would include the temptation and failure of Adam and Eve in the garden of Eden (Genesis 3); the conflict between Cain and Abel (Genesis 4:1–16); Noah's Flood, which followed the unholy alliance between the "sons of God" and the "daughters of men" (Genesis 6–9); the episode at the Tower of Babel; King Herod's attempt to kill the newborn Messiah (Matthew 2:16–23); Satan's temptation of Jesus Christ (Matthew 4:1–11); and several others. The Antichrist and apocalyptic Babylon are but further attempts by the Prince of Darkness to dethrone God and replace the divine order of things with his own new world order.

## Pulling It All Together

Satan will temporarily succeed in erecting a counterfeit messianic kingdom—the kingdom of the Antichrist. This kingdom, symbolized by the woman and the Beast in Revelation 17, represents Satan's new universal order established upon the earth in a visible, completed form. The Antichrist will be Satan's messiah, through whom Satan will rule. A careful study of 2 Thessalonians 2 reveals that the actions of the Antichrist closely resemble the stated ambitions of Lucifer in Isaiah 14, including his goal to "be like the Most High":

> Let no one in any way deceive you, for it will not come unless the apostasy comes first, and the man of lawlessness is revealed, the son of destruction, who opposes and exalts himself above every so-called god or object of worship, so that he takes his seat in the temple of God, displaying himself as being God. (2 Thessalonians 2:3–4)

Note the comparison between Lucifer in Isaiah 14 and the Antichrist in 2 Thessalonians:

| Isaiah 14 | 2 Thessalonians |
|---|---|
| For thou has said in thine heart, | |
| I will ascend into heaven | Who opposes and exalts himself . . . |
| I will exalt my throne above the stars of God | . . . above every so-called god or object of worship. |
| I will sit also upon the mount of the congregation | he takes his seat in the temple of God |
| I will be like the Most High | displaying himself as being God |

The first beast of Revelation 13, along with the woman who rides it, represents Satan's established kingdom upon the earth. The woman, representative of Satan's global occult, counterfeit religion, is seated upon the beast, which represents the Antichrist and his global political system. Together, these two represent the initial stages of the kingdom of Antichrist, the final end product of Satan's tireless quest to overthrow and replace the rule of God upon the earth. This setup is a return to the scenario that occurred at the Tower of Babel, where the people of the world were united in one rebellious cause. The Antichrist shall lead a world government, while Babylon the Great—which will take the form of a counterfeit Church—will be concerned with religious matters. Babylon the Great also represents the fulfillment of the aspirations of the secret occult societies throughout history rooted in the ancient Babylonian cult system.

A crucial point to take away from this chapter is the concept of the "severed occult system/kingdom" striving toward restoration. Understanding this concept is vital as we proceed to evaluate the esoteric revelations in the following chapters. In Nimrod and the Tower of Babel we have the occult counterfeit system put in place. In the destruction of Nimrod and the Tower of Babel, we have the defeat and "severing" of both the occult mysteries, and humanity's visible, united effort to overthrow God's authority. In Semiramis, we have the counterfeit religious system set up in an esoteric manner—an underground stream of occultism that has as its goal the restoration of the Babylonian mysteries in a public manner. This concept of the severed occult system/kingdom seeking restoration is a key to understanding the relationship between esoteric philosophy, the kingdom of the Antichrist, and that mysterious object of legend known as the Holy Grail.

# 5

## What Is the Grail?

Asking a question such as "What is the Holy Grail?" is usually met by a familiar answer: "It is the cup used by Jesus at the Last Supper that worked its way into the legends of King Arthur and the knights of the Round Table." While this answer is the most basic definition of the Holy Grail, it merely scratches the surface. The Grail is in fact so much more than just a chalice of legend, and carries a multitude of esoteric implications that go well beyond its traditional association as a cup. For this reason, the Grail can serve as the ideal symbol of the esoteric mysteries that we shall be evaluating.

### King Arthur and the Holy Grail

The first account of the Grail in literature came by way of a twelfth-century priest by the name of Chretien de Troyes. Chretien was a reputable translator and writer, and was also a relative of Hughes de Payen,[1] one of the original nine founders of the Knights Templar. Interestingly, Chretien maintained that the source material for his work, *Perceval, the Story of the Grail,* was given to him by his patron, Count Philip of Flanders, the son of Payen de Montdidier—another original Templar. The Templars themselves have often been referred to as the guardians of the Grail.

The most familiar stories of the Grail come by way of the legends of King Arthur and his knights of the Round Table. The legendary Arthur developed largely through the work of a twelfth-century clergyman known as Geoffrey of Monmouth. Geoffrey's *Historia Regum Britanniae* (History of the Kings of Britain) presents Arthur as a British king who establishes a glorious empire over Gaul (modern-day France), Iceland, and the British Isles. However, it was the work of de Troyes that added the more romantic aspects of the legend, including the Grail. The works that spun off of de Troyes's account then focused on the other well-known elements of the legend, such as the knights of the Round Table. Numerous authors have offered up their own rendition of the Arthurian legends, including Thomas Malory (*Le Morte D'Arthur*); Alfred, Lord Tennyson (*Idylls of the King*); and T. H. White (*The Once and Future King*).

Mysteries abound throughout the legends of Arthur, including the manner in which he is said to have been conceived. According to Geoffrey's account, Arthur is conceived when a magician by the name of Merlin disguises Arthur's father, Uther Pendragon, as the husband of the duchess of Cornwall. Uther then sleeps with the duchess and Arthur is conceived. In typical Grail fashion, Arthur's royal ancestry is inherited through his mother. In Grail lore, the female rather than the male is usually regarded as the true source of kingship.

Another peculiar point to note regarding this story is the meaning of the name "Pendragon." The word is more of a title than a surname, and literally translates to mean "head dragon." Thus, Uther Pendragon, Arthur's father, was a "head dragon." According to Grail researcher Laurence Gardner, the supreme kings (referred by Gardner as "kings-of-kings") in the Gaelic world were known as Pendragons, or Head Dragons.[2] Historically, dragons have often been associated with British and European culture. The dragon is also, according to the Bible, symbolic of Satan (see Revelation 12).

Much mystery surrounds the peculiar magician that lies behind Arthur's conception. In Robert de Baron's rendition, Merlin is conceived by an emissary who is sent forth from hell by demons who are endeavouring to produce an "antichrist" upon the earth. While they do succeed in producing the child, the plan to create an antichrist is thwarted by the child's mother, who baptizes him before evil can take root. Nevertheless, the child is able to retain his supernatural abilities. In Thomas Malory's account, Merlin is regarded as "the Devil's son."

In various accounts, Merlin is presented as having quite a close relationship to King Arthur and the Pendragon line. He is in fact regarded as the guardian of this particular line of kings. He also serves as Arthur's advisor. In Arthur and Merlin we have the dual system of king and priest/prophet.

This setup is quite a common feature, not only in medieval legend but also in European royal history. European monarchs often had spiritual advisors to counsel them. In some cases, the spiritual figure was ultimately the one responsible for making the secular figure king. In the legends of Arthur, it is Merlin who is responsible for the kingship of Arthur.

In the legends, Arthur is presented as a mighty warrior king of incredible renown. He is the ruler of Camelot, a mythic castle/city that represented the perfect state of existence. It is associated with ideals such as truth, bravery, and justice.[3] Camelot is also the location of the famed Round Table, where Arthur and his knights would behold the appearance of the Grail. This Round Table is often depicted as the symbol of societal perfection and equality, with each knight attributed an equivalent rank in the kingdom (hence, a round table with no "head").

The significance of the Holy Grail in the Arthurian legends lies in its identification as a vessel of plenty, healing, and restoration. In Malory's account, the Grail first appears in King Arthur's hall and miraculously produces food and drink for the knights of the realm. Some of the knights, including Bors, Gawain, Lancelot, Percival, and Galahad decide to go questing for the mysterious object. Only Galahad, Percival, and Bors succeed in finding the Grail, as the others are deemed to be unworthy for various reasons.

In another version of the tale, as recounted in Knight and Lomas's *The Second Messiah*, the Grail serves as a source of healing for Arthur and his kingdom. In this account, Lancelot has an affair with Arthur's queen, Guinevere. This transgression naturally leads to a falling out between Lancelot and Arthur, ultimately leading to the decline of the Round Table. Arthur himself becomes sick, and the kingdom is turned into a wasteland. It is believed that the land can only be saved by finding the Holy Grail. This plot is reminiscent of Chretien de Troyes's *Perceval*, where a wounded king—the "Fisher-King"—needs to be restored by the power of the Grail. In order to bring healing and restoration, Arthur sends his remaining knights out in search of the mysterious chalice. In this version, Lancelot is the one to find the Grail. He returns and Arthur is healed. However, the restoration is short-lived, as Arthur is then mortally wounded in a conflict with his traitor-son, Mordred, who had challenged him for the throne.

Legend has it that Arthur did not die but was simply carried away to the mythic land of Avalon, located westward "beyond the western sea."[4] Avalon was portrayed as a place of refuge where Arthur could be healed of his wounds, only to one day return and fight again on behalf of his people. Other accounts, such as that of Thomas Malory and T. H. White, imply a deceased but future manifestation of Arthur, as he is referred to as the "Once and Future King." This reference is derived from an inscription on his assumed tombstone, which states, "Here lies Arthur, the once and future king." According to legend, Arthur's work is not yet complete. A "second coming" is to occur at some point in the future that will feature a restored King Arthur defending and reigning over his people. The coming of this new Arthur would signify the restoration of the rule of the "perfect king."

## The Deeper Mysteries of the Holy Grail

***The Crown Jewel of Lucifer.*** It is clear that in esoteric and pagan spirituality, the Grail represents so much more than a simple cup of legend. There are in fact several "Holy Grails" that collectively reveal the heartbeat of esoteric spirituality. According to some esoteric philosophers, including Masonic author Manly P. Hall, the Holy Grail was actually derived from the *Lapis Exilis*, or the "crown jewel" of Lucifer, which supposedly fell from heaven during a conflict between Lucifer and the archangel Michael. The lost jewel stone was apparently used to make the Holy Grail—the cup of the Last Supper.[5] Wolfram von Eschenbach, in his romantic epic poem *Parzival*, identifies the Grail as this peculiar stone. However, in his account, the stone was left on earth by angels just prior to their ascent high above the stars. Here, the mysterious stone turns out to be the source of all kingship. It also possesses supernatural power capable of bringing the dead back to life.

***The Philosopher's Stone and the Elixir of Life.*** The Holy Grail has also been equated with the philosopher's stone,[6] the mythological object believed to be a source of immortality. This "elixir of life" is again rooted in a stone that is said to have fallen from heaven. Called the Emerald Tablet of Hermes, this Grail stone was supposedly engraved with wisdom by the Greek god of writing that detailed the process by which the philosopher's stone could be created.[7] According to occult researcher Tracy R. Twyman, this elixir of life had the power to grant both enlightenment and immortality to whoever partook of it.[8] This rendering of the Grail is carried further by occultists like the famous magician Aleister Crowley, who draws a parallel between bodily secretions, the Grail or "Sangraal," and the elixir of life. As many researchers have documented, sex, in the occult world, is often practiced as a ritual. According to Crowley, the bodily fluids secreted by sexual activity, when brought together, create the elixir of life—a source of rejuvenation and spiritual enlightenment. Crowley identifies the mixing of male semen and female vaginal secretions as creating the coveted philosopher's stone. He then identifies the vessel (Grail) from which the elixir is consumed as the female vagina.

***Ambrosia, Female Secretions, and the Sacred Feminine*:** According to Laurence Gardner, the Holy Grail is identified with something called the "Rosi-crucis," or "Cup of Waters,"[9] which supposedly carried a particular substance associated with the female womb known by the Greeks as ambrosia.[10] The substance in question is maternal blood—the blood of a royal ancestral line possessed by a female in that line, whom Gardner calls the "Grail Queen."[11] Associating maternal "Grail blood" with ambrosia—a mythical substance linked to the "gods" that was believed to confer immortality upon whoever consumed it—is indicative of the potency believed to be possessed by the female in Grail and occult lore. Female potency is clearly reflected in the Arthurian legends:

> The women of the Arthurian legends are every bit as important as their male counterparts—some might say even more important as they frequently initiate new adventures. They are also, in many cases, the holders of the magical power and secrets of the realm. Thus it is the Lady of the Lake who brings Arthur his magical sword, Excalibur, and who continues to aid him throughout his Kingship. . . . The reason why these otherworldly women are considered so important within the Arthurian cycle is that they were once regarded as goddesses. That this is not immediately apparent is due to the gradual Christianization of the material, and to the changing attitudes of successive generations of storytellers who altered and sometimes suppressed the pagan aspects of the tales they told.[12]

Nicholas de Vere, author of *The Dragon Legacy*, speaks at length about the ritualistic practice of ingesting female blood and hormones in order to heighten one's consciousness and senses. De Vere regards himself as a prince of "dragon blood"—a type of blood that, according to him, can be traced back to Arthur, Jesus Christ, King David of Israel, and Satan/Lucifer. According to de Vere, Lucifer managed to perpetuate a bloodline that contains within its DNA code heightened spiritual sensitivities. This bloodline produced a race of "dragon kings" (synonymous with the Pendragons of the Arthurian legends) that, due to their unique origin, supposedly have the right to rule the earth. The means by which the dragon kings maintain or heighten their supernatural senses is through physically ingesting the menstrual secretions produced by females of the dragon line, a practice called "the Starfire Ritual."[13] Thus, once again it is the female who delivers the potency to the male.

***The Blood Royal*:** As we saw in chapter 1, the Holy Grail is also believed by some to be a royal bloodline that includes the Davidic kings of Israel, and often made to include Jesus Christ and Mary Magdalene. This bloodline is regarded as the true line of kingship—both for the throne of Jerusalem and the world. This rendering of the Grail is a satanically inspired assault on the precious blood of Jesus Christ that was shed for the world for the forgiveness of sin.

***The All-seeing Eye, Atlantis, and the Lost Knowledge of the Ages*:** The Holy Grail can also be identified with the capstone on top of a pyramid, and the all-seeing eye[14] that is often depicted inside a capstone. This is portrayed on the reverse side of the American one-dollar bill. A careful analysis of the dollar-bill pyramid will reveal that it is actually a truncated pyramid, missing its natural capstone. However, the missing capstone is replaced by a glorified one containing the all-seeing eye. Behind this capstone is a radiant blaze of light. Author David Ovason sheds light on the significance of the pyramid. Commenting on a prior work that depicted a flying pyramid inside a roundel or circle, Ovason states:

> The roundel portrays a flying pyramid, even though the text expounds upon the stability of "a true triangled Pyramid," which stands fast against winds and raging seas. The moral is that human virtue should aspire to the same stability that the pyramid offers. . . . Within such a context, the truncated pyramid (that invaluable Stone) is a symbol of virtue as yet incomplete.[15]

In this light, the pyramid is a symbol of virtue and stability, and the truncated pyramid is a means of conveying the belief that this virtue has not yet been attained—and cannot be without the addition of the glorified capstone containing the eye. Regarding this eye, we are told:

> The eye above the pyramid on the dollar-bill roundel is set within a triangle, which reminds one of the capstone of a pyramid. However, this triangle is surrounded by a brilliant aura that seems to represent either the Sun or the spiritual world.
>
> The image of an eye within a triangle was used by Masons likely before the Great Seal of 1782 was designed. It is highly likely that this eye was derived from Egyptian symbolism. . . . The triangle, with its enclosed eye, completes the truncated Pyramid of the dollar bill. . . . The Freemasons were the most influential body to adopt the eye as a symbol of God or the Supreme Being.[16]

We then need to ask: What god or supreme being is represented by the eye?

> The All-Seeing eye is an ancient symbol of deity, though not the Christian one, and has been used as an occult symbol for thousands of years. It is also a Masonic symbol.[17]
>
> Through the influence of Freemasonry in United States history, the Eye of Horus came to be depicted on the reverse side of the paper currency of the U.S. dollar.[18]

The eye within the pyramid has its roots in ancient Egyptian mythology. Specifically, it is the eye of the Egyptian god Horus. While some regard it as the eye of Providence, or God, its widest use is in association with Horus and the occult, esoteric mysteries that are embodied in groups such as the Freemasons. Horus is associated with both the Sun and the underworld, and is said to be keeping a watchful eye as his soul awaits rebirth.[19] He is the son of

Osiris and Isis, and according to *The Concise Dictionary of the Occult and New Age* represents the New Age Christ whose soul waits to be reborn.[20] Interestingly, we are told in the book of Revelation that the Antichrist (referred to as the beast) actually ascends up out of the Abyss, almost as if to be reborn—or perhaps more accurately stated: revived.[21] Horus is also said to be the source of enlightenment, as occult leaders urge their "initiates" to meditate on the eye in the hope of attaining this enlightenment.[22]

Like the chalice of legend, the jewel from Lucifer's crown, the philosopher's stone, and the female secretions, the eye of Horus is said to be a source of enlightenment. Thus, it can be identified with the Grail as a source of the spiritual evolution sought after by esoteric adherents. The quest for the Grail can be related to the quest for this missing capstone—the "thing" that will complete the human aspiration for virtue. Interestingly, in this context the Grail is directly associated with a messiah-type figure—"the New-age Christ." Thus, the completion of the pyramid by this "capstone of Horus" seems to be symbolic of the advent of the New Age/occult Christ. Additionally, Tracy R. Twyman notes that the Masonic design of the all-seeing eye is meant to symbolize the world order envisioned by the Freemasons, which would be a return to the world empire that supposedly existed during a former golden age overseen by "gods."[23]

Recall that in chapter 4 we saw how a counterfeit spirituality has run down through the ages from Nimrod's Tower of Babel to this very day, seeking to restore "paradise" and what was lost through Nimrod's demise. From an occult perspective, the Christian church stands in the way of this restoration. Esoteric adherents vehemently despise the teaching of the Christian gospel—that there is only one way to salvation through faith in Jesus Christ. To them, this represents a narrow-minded, destructive, and limited understanding of mankind's "true destiny" and has restricted the emergence of true enlightenment and a new age. However, they also believe that the Christian age has run its "destructive" course, and has given way to a new age— Aquarius:

> The concept of occultism dates at least as far back as ancient Babylon. A worldwide interest in esoteric knowledge and practices continues. This is especially true among new age adherents who believe the era of traditional Christian religion has ended, and the Aquarian Age has dawned.[24]

According to Gardner, this tension between the Christian church and the esoteric mysteries is symbolized by the pyramid and the all-seeing eye. The truncated pyramid represents the loss of old esoteric wisdom, which we are told was forced underground by the church. However, the rays of light associated with the all-seeing eye represent hope that what was lost will be restored.[25]

The symbol of the pyramid and all-seeing eye, then, is an esoteric method of conveying the ambition of those who have adhered to the occult mysteries throughout the ages. The truncated pyramid can be associated with the lost occult wisdom, the unfinished Tower of Babel, and the unfinished work of creating the perfected man and the perfect civilization. The capstone represents the restoration of this lost wisdom, which in turn will result in the arrival of the golden age—a sort of rebuilt Tower of Babel, all under the watchful eye of the New Age Christ, symbolized by the eye of Horus. Thus, the Holy Grail can be identified with a particular type of "wisdom" that must be found and restored in order for humanity to attain its ultimate potential. This is in agreement with Manly P. Hall, who notes that the incomplete pyramid of the Great Seal represents imperfect and incomplete human society that is striving toward a common aspiration, as symbolized by the converging angles and faces of the pyramid.[26]

There is also an apparent connection between pyramids and lost Atlantis. According to Hall, Atlantis possessed a great pyramid-shaped university back to which most of the arts and sciences used now can be traced.[27] Interestingly, Atlantis is integral to the philosophy of all esoteric, secret societies,[28] serving as a blueprint for the creation of a philosophic new world order. According to occult sources, Atlantis represented the perfect society and the perfect government. However, due to rampant wickedness and the abuse of their knowledge, the Atlanteans were severely punished by God, who sent a great flood to destroy their civilization. Here, we have the "truncation" of the pyramid, the wounding of the Fisher-King, etc. The Grail in this Atlantean context can be equated with knowledge—the esoteric knowledge and wisdom that made Atlantis the model for the perfect society. The quest for the Grail can then be equated with the quest to discover lost Atlantis—or more specifically, the *knowledge* of Atlantis.

While most regard Atlantis as a myth, some regard it as the model of the perfect civilization. Some researchers have, for good reason, identified it with the pre-flood society mentioned in the book of Genesis. Just prior to the great flood, we are told that the "sons of God" took the "daughters of men" as wives and produced offspring known as the Nephilim, the "mighty men who were of old, men of renown."[29] If the view held by many biblical commentators that these Nephilim were the offspring of supernatural entities and human women is correct, then it is almost certain that the Nephilim would have been privy to exceptional spiritual knowledge and demonic wisdom. This may also be the basis for the association of the Grail with a "jewel from Lucifer's crown" that fell from heaven. Here, the Grail is knowledge and symbolized by the jewel. Its fall from heaven can be symbolic of the descent of the fallen angels who brought the occult wisdom and imparted it to mankind. Interestingly, it was the *daughters* of men who provided the fertile womb for the supernatural offspring. The potency comes through the woman. God's response to the corruption of mankind was to flood the earth, destroying all but Noah and his family. One must wonder if the Nephilim society is indeed what occultists see as lost Atlantis.

***Why a Chalice?***: By now it should be clear that the Grail is so much more than a mere chalice. To say that the Grail is simply a cup of medieval legend is to miss the entire point. Having said that, there must be a reason as to why a chalice serves as the primary identifier of the Grail. Authors Philip Gardiner and Gary Osborn may have the answer. Gardiner and Osborn's *The Serpent Grail: The Truth Behind the Holy Grail, the Philosopher's Stone, and the Elixir of Life* identifies the Grail originally as a "mixing bowl" used to create the elixir of life. According to the authors, this elixir was made up of a mixture of snake venom and blood, and produced inside a bowl that came to be known as the Grail:

> At this first level, the Grail is a physical mixing bowl, in which is mixed an elixir used to heal the physical body. . . . Our research led us to discover that the original Elixir of Life was a combination of snake venom and blood. The blood used is either that of the snake or blood taken from a mammalian host (e.g. a horse, or a human being) that had been subjected to a series of snakebites or injections of venom. When the two elements were mixed together, the unique properties of the blood not only rendered the venom harm-

> less but also produced a powerful elixir. It was believed that if this was taken repeatedly it could boost the body's immune system, cure most diseases and even extend life. . . . What makes snake venom so deadly and yet also gives it its unique capacity for healing are its high levels of protein. Western science is currently doing all it can to break down the elements of the venom and use them individually in the treatment of specific diseases. However, for the ancients, it may well be that it was the dilution of the venom with the blood which made it a virtual cure-all. Indeed, a Chinese herbalist told us that the blood of a snake is added to soup and other foods to "extend a good life."[30]

In light of this, it is fascinating that the medical establishment in the Western world often incorporates a serpent as a symbol for health and medicine. Interestingly, the logo for the Ontario College of Pharmacists in Canada is a Grail with a serpent entwined around it whose mouth is directly over the chalice, suggesting that its venom is being poured into the chalice. Also in the logo is an equilateral cross, a symbol that, according to Laurence Gardiner, has long been used as the distinguishing device of the Holy Grail.[31]

Understanding this aspect of the Grail sheds tremendous light on the roots of the Grail legends—specifically its role as a "magical dish" or chalice that contained supernatural powers. Clearly, the aura of mystery surrounding the Grail predates its medieval "Christian" rendering. Its primary manifestation as a chalice of supreme importance is now being traced all the way back to the pagan cults of the ancient world which are said to have used a mixing bowl or Grail to create a potent elixir of life. And from the ancient pagan world came the esoteric mysteries that are found concealed within the many legends of the Holy Grail.

## Pulling It All Together: So, What Is the Grail?

From King Arthur's chalice to the all-seeing eye, a careful reading of the above analysis will reveal a commonality in each case. In its every manifestation, the Grail serves as *that thing which heightens mankind's existence.* It is the elusive *thing* that mankind looks to in order to create both a perfect world and er existence. It can take the form of an elixir that is said to bestow health and immortality. Or it may be an ancient and royal bloodline whose restoration to power will mean the restoration of a true and proper monarchy.

The Grail is that *thing* that brings to mankind the perfect state of being, and the perfect society that it seeks. It is the *thing* that restores what has been lost, dethroned, or ruined. It is the *thing* that restores Atlantis, completes the truncated pyramid, restores the lost esoteric knowledge, restores the Grail kingdoms, returning the "wasteland to fertility." It is the *thing* that, if you will recall from chapter 4, defeats Set, avenging the death of Osiris. The Holy Grail is the *thing* that restores the kingdom and system founded upon the ancient Babylonian mysteries. Here we see, once again, the concept alluded to in the previous chapter—the "severed occult mysteries/kingdom" seeking restoration. The Grail is the *thing* that brings about that restoration.

The important thing to note is not what form the Grail takes but, rather, what it represents in all its forms—the esoteric/occult substitute for the immortality and perfect society that God has given to humanity and will give through Jesus Christ. Thus, in a very real sense, the Holy Grail is that esoteric substitute for the salvation found only in Jesus Christ. It is the means by which humanity is to recover from its current state of deprivation and societal chaos.

Part of Satan's temptation to Eve recorded in the book of Genesis was the suggestion that she could be enlightened and become like God, knowing good and evil, apart God's sovereign will.[32] This is the same principle that lies at the heart of all esoteric teaching and ambition—attaining personal enlightenment *apart* from obedience to the true God. It means to remove God from the equation and strive to heighten humanity's existence apart from His divine will and counsel. The Holy Grail, be it secret knowledge, an elixir to convey immortality, or the "messianic bloodline of Jesus Christ" is that satanic substitute for God's very best—the elevation of human existence and the establishment of a heavenly society in the earth through Jesus Christ. Interestingly, the apple (often associated with Eve's disobedience) factors in to esoteric philosophy and Grail lore. Apples have been linked to Avalon,[33] that mythic place of King Arthur's refuge. Here, the apples are said to be a symbol for the "otherworld" and are said to provide wisdom and vision.[34]

It is said that it was from Lucifer's crown that the gem of the Grail fell. This parallels the fact that it was through Satan that Eve and Adam partook of the forbidden fruit of the knowledge of the tree of good and evil. This act on their part plunged humanity into chaos, and ultimately gave rise to esoteric and pagan mysteries that stand in opposition to God's Word. These mysteries were revived after Noah's flood, and remained part of human civilization from the Tower of Babel right down to today's occult fraternities. These mysteries speak of a greater civilization for mankind and are linked to the advent of the New Age messiah. As the Grail is the substitute for God's means of salvation, so the New Age messiah is the substitute for God's Messiah, Jesus Christ. This is the great quest of the esoteric societies—to "enlighten" humanity about the mysteries of the ancient pagan and occult beliefs, and to produce a new golden age upon the earth through the advent of a counterfeit messiah.

# 6

# The Historical Development of the Counterfeit System

## From Eden to Babylon

As we learned in chapter 4, the establishment of the Antichrist's kingdom is actually the earthly end product of Satan's ultimate, millennia-long quest to dethrone the God of all creation and to establish his own universal order upon the earth. For a short time, God will allow Satan to achieve this goal. Satan's counterfeit system can be detected in some form or another from the days of antiquity right through until today. In his insightful book *The New World Religion: The Spiritual Roots of Global Government*, Christian author Gary Kah traces the development of Satan's occultism/pantheism from the days of Adam and Eve right through to the current drive to produce a one-world order on the earth. The "dots" connected by the counterfeit stream in Kah's assessment include the seduction of humanity in Eden, Noah's flood, the Tower of Babel, ancient pagan empires, Jewish mysticism/kabbalism, "Christian" Gnosticism, the Knights Templar, the Masonic Order/Illuminati, and the coming revived Roman empire/Babylonian world religion. We will rely on Kah's outline in this chapter, expanding on certain points, as we assess the historical development of Satan's counterfeit system.

When Eve took of the forbidden fruit, she did so under the impression that she would attain wisdom not previously known by her. She would thus be enlightened! As a result of Adam and Eve's sin, humanity has been plunged into an experience of sin, sickness, death, decay, and divine judgment. Herein lies the source of the conflict of the ages that has ravaged the human race. When Eve succumbed to the serpent's lies and deceit, the seeds of a counterfeit religious system were sown in the soil of the human race. The serpent's temptation to Eve possessed esoteric-like characteristics: the attainment of privileged knowledge and the possibility of becoming like a god.[1] Here then marks the foundation for Satan's infection of the human race with esoteric philosophy as a substitute for God's revealed truth. God had revealed to Adam that he was not to eat of the fruit of the tree of the knowledge of good and evil. The serpent, meanwhile, suggested to Eve that God did not really mean what He said, and that knowledge to make one wise as gods was to be gained by partaking of the fruit. Eve took the fruit and also gave it to her husband to eat. Thus mankind, quite early on, traded God's already *revealed* truth for an "esoteric" substitute offered by the serpent. Two kingdoms are in view here—the kingdom of God and the kingdom of Satan, the kingdom of light and the kingdom of darkness, the kingdom of Christ and the kingdom of the Antichrist. From the garden of Eden to this very day, these two kingdoms have been in conflict. The gospel of Jesus Christ, which promises eternal life for all who trust in God's Son, is opposed by a "gospel of Satan," which offers secret, hidden knowledge to attain immortality, wisdom, and godhood.

In pagan and occult teaching, things are often reversed. Good is declared evil while evil is declared good. Lucifer is declared to be a "good god" while *the Lord* is the "evil God." The argument posed by esoteric author Laurence Gardner regarding Adam and Eve presents us with an example of how Scripture is often twisted to mean something the opposite of what it says. Gardner claims that the Lord, whom he identifies as "Enlil," actually commanded Adam not to eat of the fruit of the tree of the knowledge of good and evil in order to deliberately keep him in ignorance. The serpent, meanwhile, whom he identifies as "Enki," sought to liberate Eve and Adam by offering them the knowledge that Enlil withheld from them.[2] In this fashion, the serpent appears as the savior. Such twisting of Scripture is typical of esoteric and occult philosophy.

This view makes Eve's obedience to the serpent appear not as sin but as a most wise choice. Notice that it is Eve who "gives enlightenment" to the man by giving him the fruit to eat. In this regard, Eve can be symbolic of the "higher virtues" of enlightenment, wisdom, and godhood—quite similar to the goddess in pagan lore. In giving the fruit to Adam, Eve transfers the enlightenment that she has discovered to him. The power comes through the *woman.* From a proper perspective, both Adam and Eve are guilty of sinning against God. From an occult perspective, Eve can be seen as conveying her enlightenment to Adam.

As mentioned earlier, the apple (probably wrongfully) is the fruit often associated with Eve's disobedience. Interestingly, at the center of the apple (when sliced horizontally) lies a five-pointed star, a symbol associated with paganism, the occult, and the sacred goddess. This symbol—called the pentagram (or pentacle) has also been associated with the planet Venus, which itself is named after the Roman goddess of love. Some researchers have maintained that the path of the planet Venus, when viewed from earth, actually forms an almost perfect pentagram every eight years through a succession of what are known as inferior conjunctions. An astronomical conjunction is when multiple celestial bodies appear from earth as being very close to each other in the sky, virtually in alignment with each other. A *superior* conjunction is when a planet in conjunction with the sun is on the opposite side of the sun than the earth. An *inferior* conjunction is when a planet in conjunction with the sun (in this case, Venus) lies between the sun and the earth. A succession of five inferior conjunctions are formed by Venus and the sun, as viewed from the earth, over a span of eight years, which creates a near perfect pentagram in the sky. The five points of the pentagram are marked by tracing Venus's path (as viewed from earth) around the five points of conjunction over the eight-year span.

As named after the Roman goddess, the planet Venus can also be representative of the Queen of Heaven. This of course associates Venus with Semiramis of Babylon, Isis of Egypt, Aphrodite of Greece, Ishtar of Assyria, Astarte of Phoenicia, the Virgin Mary of Roman Catholicism and Eastern Orthodoxy (who is specifically known in these denominations as the Queen of Heaven), and Mary Magdalene. Interestingly, author Henry Lincoln, who documents the Venus-pentagram astronomical pattern in his book *The Holy Place*, notes that Venus is the heavenly counterpart of the terrestrial Mary Magdalene.[3] Be it coincidence or not, it is highly fascinating that the symbol of mankind's plummet into sin through Eve's beguilement by the serpent—the bitten apple—contains at its core a five-pointed star—the symbol of the goddess, and a symbol associated with the "goddess planet." From an occult/esoteric perspective, Eve could be perceived as the vessel by which Satan conveyed the sacred wisdom to the human race, thus, the elevation of the female principle.

Venus is known to achieve its maximum brightness in the sky shortly before sunrise or shortly after sunset. For this reason, it is also often called the morning and evening star. In this context, Venus has also been linked to Lucifer, a Latin word which means "morning star." Here, the pentagram/pentacle serves not only as a goddess symbol, but also as a symbol for Lucifer. Recall as well from chapter 5 that one of the definitions of the Holy Grail is that it is the "jewel from Lucifer's crown." As we shall continue to see, Lucifer plays a prominent role in esoteric spirituality.

Adam and Eve's disobedience laid the foundation for total human rebellion against God. This rebellion culminated in the corruption of the earth, as detailed in Genesis 6–7. In light of this, God purposed to destroy humanity through water, saving righteous Noah and his family. However, it is clear that the rebellious spirit and curiosity in Satan-inspired spirituality that characterized pre-flood humanity once again took root in the post-flood society of Babylon:

> From the moment the first man and woman partook of the forbidden fruit, Satan's deception grew, and sin increased. By the time of Noah, man had become so thoroughly corrupt and intermingled with the demonic realm that God sent the Flood.
>
> After the flood, it took only a few generations before man had again embraced the occult. This was evidenced by the building of the Tower of Babel, which is believed to have been the first ziggurat, an occult worship tower with a shrine at the top. Throughout the cradle of civilization, the occult mysteries flourished. . . . Although God had scattered the people from Babylon during the building of the Tower of Babel, this did not put an end to occultism; it only slowed its

progress. As new civilizations arose in Egypt, Persia, India, etc., the occult practices of old were revived. The people had merely taken their beliefs and practices with them.[4]

## The Seed of the Woman, Cain, and the Grail

Shortly after Adam and Eve succumbed to the Serpent's lies and deceit, we find the first hint of a future redeemer:

> "And I will put enmity Between you and the woman, And between your seed and her seed; He shall bruise you on the head, And you shall bruise him on the heel." (Genesis 3:15)

This passage pertains to God's judgement on the Serpent for his role in the fall of humanity into sin. God is speaking directly to the Serpent and declares that the seed of the woman shall "bruise" the Serpent on the head, while the Serpent shall "bruise" the seed of the woman on the heel. Here we see an example of the great conflict between humanity—with Christ the Redeemer at its head, and Satan. Satan injures humanity (the bruising on the heel) while humanity through Christ absolutely crushes the serpent (the bruising on the head).[5] Christ Himself, of course, is the ultimate conquering "seed."

Here, then, is the basis for the belief that a woman's male child would be the savior of the human race. It is very possible that the mother-child cult of esoteric thought is actually a pagan allusion to the woman and seed of Genesis 3. Satan often offers perverted counterfeits to virtually everything God does. With this, Ironside is in agreement, stating that Semiramis bore a son—Tammuz—who, in view of God's promise concerning a conquering seed of the woman, was hailed as the promised deliverer.[6] Ironside notes that through Semiramis and Tammuz was introduced the mother-child mystery, which was an attempt by Satan to imitate God's truth so that when the true redeemer came, He would not be known as such.[7]

God has determined to save His creation by means of a divine redeemer who, as revealed by the phrase *seed of the woman*, would also share in Eve's humanity in every way (though without sin), ultimately being born of a woman.[8] Adam and Eve's second son, Abel, was killed by his older brother, Cain, who was then subsequently cursed by God. Consequently, it was through Adam and Eve's third son, Seth, that the conquering seed would ultimately come.[9] Not surprisingly, esoteric thought twists this and maintains that it is through the cursed Cain, not Seth, that the messianic line descends. Nicholas de Vere, in his work *The Dragon Legacy* places Cain in the ancestry of the messianic bloodline. Similarly, Laurence Gardner claims that kingly succession on earth (the hereditary right to reign over the earth) was through Cain and his sons—a notion supposedly ignored by the Hebrews and the church in favor of the line through Seth.[10]

It is important to understand the prominence given to Cain, his believed origin, and his supposed descendants by esoteric and Grail spirituality adherents. Cain's identity in esoteric thought is radically different than that ascribed to him in Scripture. It is believed that the father of Cain is not Adam but Enki, who we have already seen is equated with Lucifer. In this context, Enki is said to have impregnated Eve (called Hawah, or the Lady of Life[11]), conceiving Cain. As the Lucifer of esoteric spirituality is often equated with Satan, Cain, in this context, can be regarded as the offspring of Satan. Satan is called in Scripture the "prince of this world" (John 16:11). Fittingly, it is believed that "divine" kingship was conferred by Satan upon his supposed son Cain, legitimizing the bloodline of Cain as the proper messianic royal line.[12]

Cain's value then, is readily evident. To the Grail adherent, he is the source of legitimate kingship upon the earth, having been given this right directly from Lucifer. We have heard much in recent times concerning a so-called "Holy Grail bloodline" supposedly descending from Jesus Christ and Mary Magdalene. While much controversy is caused by incorporating Jesus into this mythical bloodline, the real source of "legitimacy" is not Christ at all, but rather Enki/Lucifer/Satan, who is said to have bestowed the messianic, kingly title upon this bloodline. In other words, Christ's messianic status is not unique to Him. He merely, as a supposed "descendant" of Enki, is one of many participants in the royal line.

The Bible indicates that after cursing Cain, God marked him, or "appointed a sign" for him (Genesis 4:15) so that no one would kill him. We are not told specifically what this sign is. However, esoteric/occult adherents are keen to suggest that the mark was in actual fact a cross inside a circle.[13] The cross itself is apparently associated with the kingly line of the Holy Grail,[14] which identifies Cain as a significant participant in this supposed messianic bloodline. Interestingly, the most famous symbol of the Knights Templar—the "Knights of the Grail"—was also a cross.

## The Genuine and the Counterfeit through the Ages

An integral part of God's plan to provide humanity with a redeemer was to create a particular nation through which that redeemer could come. This nation is Israel, a nation rooted in the promise given by God to a man of faith named Abram (later Abraham).[15] It is through Israel that mankind has been given the revelation of the one true God who is known by the name YHWH. This sacred name was later rendered YaHoWaH, or, Jehovah, when the medieval Masorete scholars applied the vowel points of the word *adonai* and applied it to the consonants of YHWH. Adonai, which means "the Lord," was used by the Jews in post–Old Testament times. They regarded the name of God too holy to be uttered by the tongues of men. Many translations of the Old Testament simply refer to God as "the Lord" with "Lord" being written in small capitals. When we come across this word in the Bible, we are to understand it as standing for the "proper name"[16] of God.

Throughout the Old Testament, we see YHWH stand in contrast to the many gods and goddesses worshipped by the nations surrounding Israel. This should not surprise us. Throughout the ancient world, paganism, polytheism, and esotericism characterized many peoples and nations. Here we can see the conflict of the ages manifested on a national and international level. Often, ancient Israel succumbed to the temptation of wanting to be like other nations by falling into pagan-idol worship. Israel was often so influenced by these pagan nations that YHWH had to severely punish them for worshiping false gods.[17] Even today within Jewish thought, we find esotericism in the form of Jewish mysticism—the backbone of an esoteric movement blending Jewish theology and esoteric philosophy known as the kabbalah:

> Kabalism was merely a unique version of the ancient mysteries specifically designed to deceive God's chosen people. Unlike other mystery religions, its teachings dealt specifically with Israel, offering occult explanations to the revelations of the prophets—complete with a mystical interpretation of Israel's history.[18]

The modern kabbalistic movement has been embraced by such personalities as Madonna and Demi Moore.

Ultimately, God Himself would come to Israel as the promised Messiah in the person of Jesus Christ—the conquering seed of the woman who would redeem not only Israel but all humanity. He was rejected by Israel's leaders, and as such, the promised kingdom of heaven on earth was postponed. The rejection of Jesus by the Jewish leaders did not take God by surprise. Through the rejection, crucifixion, and resurrection of Jesus, God dealt a crushing blow to the serpent, as it is through Christ's death and resurrection that humanity is redeemed. The "conquering seed" has triumphed *through* death, making it possible for guilty sinners to be declared righteous by a holy God. He will in time bless Israel and fulfill the role of Davidic Messiah over the house of Israel. In the meantime, the Christian church continues its task to take this message of Jesus to the four corners of the earth.

Christianity has grown tremendously over the span of two millennia to become the world's largest professed religion. Its association with the Western world is largely rooted in the conversion of the Roman emperor Constantine. While there is some debate as to the authenticity of Constantine's conversion, there is absolutely no doubt that Constantine was instrumental in the ultimate transformation of Christianity from an outlawed sect in Rome to the favored religion of the empire. While some would also argue that post-Constantine state Christianity was not pure Christianity, the door was nonetheless opened for Christians to worship freely.

We can thus trace the redemptive plan of God from Adam to Seth through the ancient world to Noah, to Abraham, to Israel and the Jewish people, to Jesus—who *is* the revealed Word of God—down to the message of the Christian church. Likewise, the satanic counterfeit system can be traced from the serpent in the garden of Eden, to Cain, through the ancient world to the pre-flood society, where it was severed temporarily by the flood. It then resurfaced at Babylon, and then spread throughout the ancient world to Egypt, Greece, and pagan Rome, etc., even down through to some of God's people in the form of Jewish mysticism.

## The Gnostic Movement

Author and theologian Floyd Barackman provides an insightful glimpse into the activity of Satan in opposing the work and revelation of God through history:

> The primary activity of Satan seems to be to thwart God's judicial sentence against him—his utter defeat by the woman's Seed, or Jesus, the Conqueror-Savior (Genesis 3:15). We can trace his effort against God's sentence throughout human history. First, Satan tried to stop the incarnation of God the Son, as foretold by the OT prophetic Scriptures. He attempted to destroy the human line of descent into which his Conqueror would be born.
>
> The Devil led Cain to slay Abel (Genesis 4:8) but Eve bore Seth (Genesis 4:25). The Devil brought destruction to the human race by unprecedented corruption (Genesis 6:1–13), but God preserved Noah and his family (Genesis 6:8–8:19). Satan influenced the post-flood world to turn to idolatry (Romans 1:21–25), but God appeared unto Abram in Ur, saved him, led him to sojourn in Canaan (Acts 7:2–4; Genesis12:1–4), and promised that he would be the father of the messianic line into which Jesus would be born (Genesis 15:5–6; Galatians 3:16). . . . Satan led Israel into idolatry and other gross sins, which finally brought Judah and David's house into Babylonian captivity (2 Kings 24–25; Isaiah 1:1–9), but God used the Persian conqueror of Babylon, Cyrus, to allow Jews to return to Jerusalem (2 Chronicles 36:22–23). Although Satan had induced Judah's King Jehoiakim to burn God's word, and by this to incur the divine judgment that blocked any of his posterity from ruling on David's throne (Jeremiah 36:30; also 22:30), God circumvented this curse by Jesus' virgin conception and Mary's marriage to Joseph, heir to David's throne (Matthew 1:20, 16). Later . . . the Devil unsuccessfully plotted against Jesus' life (Matthew 2:1–16) and sought to divert Him from the work that He came to earth to do. (Matthew 4:1–10; Luke 4:28–29)[19]

As Barackman astutely notes, Satan's ambition is to try to thwart the "judicial sentence" pronounced upon him in Genesis—that the seed of the woman would "bruise" or crush his head. As such, the focus of Satan's attack is upon the One who brings about His complete destruction—the Lord Jesus Christ! From the moment this sentence was pronounced upon the serpent right up until the conception of the Messiah, Satan has tried to thwart God's plan to bring about the redeemer. From the moment of Jesus' birth right through until today, Satan has sought to destroy, render ineffective, and discredit the Son of God and His name. Satan's only chance of avoiding a total and humiliating defeat by the woman's seed is to definitively defeat the Lord Jesus Christ. Thus, he sets his fury and energy against the Lord Jesus Christ – seeking to discredit His name, and cast doubt upon His claims. We must understand this truth in order to appreciate the source and motivation behind concepts today that contradict the biblical witness concerning Jesus.

The apostle John warns that "every spirit that does not confess Jesus is not from God; this is the spirit of the antichrist, of which you have heard that it is coming, and now it is already in the world" (1 John 4:3). We saw in chapter 3 that John's primary concern in warning of an antichrist spirit was to alert to a false teaching concerning the incarnation of Christ. There were those who were saying that Christ did not take on human flesh but rather was simply a nonphysical spirit. They were denying the literal incarnation into human flesh of the Son of God. This form of teaching is associated with a concept known as Gnosticism. A major tenet of Gnosticism is that the material world is evil, whereas the spiritual realm is pure. Thus, to the Gnostics, Christ could not possibly be both "pure spirit" and "corrupt flesh." Those who rejected the incarnation of Jesus Christ were deemed by John to be antichrists.

Gnosticism represented a rival system of belief to that of orthodox Christianity in John's day. It not only emphasised the superiority of the spirit realm over the physical, but also placed a great deal of emphasis on esoteric/secret knowledge (*gnosis*) in order to attain freedom from the corrupt physical realm. The goal of the Gnostics was to attain so much enlightenment into secret knowledge that they would then be able to be freed from the physical world and evolve into spiritual entities—pure and free from defilement. This was a complete repudiation of the gospel, which declares that salvation is only possible through faith in the person and work of Jesus Christ:

> The goal of the Gnostics was to become free from evil material existence and to enter a pure spiritual life. They believed this liberation came only through gaining knowledge

> of profound and mysterious spiritual truths. Such knowledge is limited to a select group of "initiated," those specially chosen souls entrusted with the secrets of the universe, and who possessed unlimited powers to reunite with the divinity from which they emanated.[20]

Gnosticism shared much in common with mystic Jewish philosophy, and may have indeed derived many of its tenets from it. Furthermore, in typical esoteric/occult fashion, the "true deity" of Gnosticism is one that we have been introduced to before:

> If Kabalism could be viewed as the occult counter-explanation of the Old Testament, Gnosticism . . . taking into account Satan's "new problem" posed by the risen Christ, would serve as the main occult counterattack against the New Testament. Thus, Kabalism and Gnosticism combined composed a type of occult parallel to the Old and New Testaments. . . . Branches of Gnosticism represented the first significant secret societies of the post-resurrection era, with various degrees or levels of initiation and the inner circle of initiates worshipping Lucifer.[21]

Gnostics, in essence, are dualists in that they believe in two divine powers—one good and one evil. The "evil god" is equated with the physical creation (darkness) whereas the "good god" is equated with the spiritual realm (light). In esoteric thought, these two systems of dark and light are constantly in conflict, striving to bring about balance in the universe. This concept of darkness vs. light or darkness in balance with light can be seen in different cultures, symbols, and belief systems. In Chinese philosophy, there is the "yin" and "yang," with the black and white portions pictured in an interconnected fashion. There is the checkered emblem of black squares mixed with white squares from medieval times, often pictured in medieval castles, palaces, and churches. Even in modern pop culture this concept can be seen, such as in the *Star Wars* movies with the "dark side of the force" (the Sith) striving against the "light side of the force" (the Jedi).

Chillingly, a careful study of certain elements of esoteric thought suggests that the "dark/evil god" of Gnosticism is none other than YHWH, while the "light/good god" is none other than Lucifer. This, of course, is no surprise given the esoteric nature of Gnosticism. According to Albert Pike, who produced the important Masonic work *Morals and Dogma*, both Lucifer and Adonai are "God."[22] These two beings are supposedly in an eternal struggle with each other, a great conflict between "light and dark." Pike affirms that YHWH (Yahweh) is "evil" while Lucifer is "good." One is not inferior or superior to the other but equal, and in constant struggle. Pike also affirms that both the Gnostics and the Templars subscribed to this concept of two divine principles in constant struggle.

This assertion by Pike that the God of the Bible is the "evil God" is a significant one, for in it can be seen a possible motive for the bizarre activity by members of secret societies and esoteric fraternities. As noted by Pike, there is this "eternal" struggle between light (Lucifer) and dark (the God of the Bible). And according to Gnostic thought, the only way one can be freed from the dark material world is through *gnosis* (secret knowledge). In this, we can see why secret, esoteric societies place such an emphasis on secret knowledge, for through knowledge is their salvation. We can also see a possible reason why esoteric philosophies and secret societies such as Freemasonry so vehemently oppose orthodox Christianity, for the Christian is worshipping the "dark" and "evil" God, YHWH, while the Gnostic/esoteric philosopher is following the "light" and "good" god, Lucifer. Thus, the Gnostic is doing the right thing, while the Christian is doing the bidding of the wrong God, the "dark" God, who stands against all that the adherents of the "light" god are striving for. To the secret/Gnostic/esoteric societies, the eradication of all that symbolizes YHWH and His redeemer, the Lord Jesus Christ, is a desirable—even admirable—thing, for to do so would be to set Lucifer—the "good" god—free, and with him, all humanity. It would also represent the triumph of the serpent over his judge—the seed of the woman! To borrow from earlier chapters, it would represent finding the Holy Grail, resurrecting Atlantis, avenging Nimrod and Osiris, rebuilding Babel, and restoring the religion of Babylon in the earth.

## The Knights Templar and Birth of the Grail Legends

The Poor Fellow-Soldiers of Christ and of the temple of Solomon, otherwise known as the Knights Templar, may have played a major role in the transmission of ancient esoteric belief to the modern world. Many esoteric societies claim some form of association with this mysterious group. They have often worked their way into popular culture, such as in the case of the *National Treasure* movies and countless books. The actual history of the Templars is often mixed with legend, which makes it difficult to get a firm grip on just what this order really believed.

Established in France in the twelfth century, the Templars may be a medieval bridge linking the esotericism of the ancient world with the New Age/ occult beliefs of the modern world. They themselves have been linked to the Gnostic sects that inherited many of the pagan and mystery beliefs of the ancient world—including a veneration of Satan and the repudiation of Christ:

> At the base of each form of Gnosticism existed this adoration or worship of Satan, as well as a profound hatred of Christ and his teachings. It was perversions such as these, handed down in an unbroken tradition from the earliest Gnostics, that were eventually embraced by the Knights of the Temple (Knights Templar) in the Twelfth century.[23]

Outwardly, the Templars were a band of "Christian" knights whose official role was to protect Christian travellers on pilgrimages to the Holy Land. But as many researchers have pointed out, the knights spent more time excavating the site of Solomon's ancient temple in Jerusalem than they did protecting pilgrims. Indeed, the original band of knights consisted of only nine members—hardly an army capable of defending pilgrims in the potentially hostile environment that was the Holy Land in medieval times. What exactly the Templars were looking for at the site of the temple is a matter of debate. However, it is widely believed that they did find something of such major importance that it had to be guarded, protected, and hidden for centuries at all costs from the civil and ecclesiastical ruling establishments. This find is cited as a major contributor to the Templar's esoteric/Gnostic sympathies, as well as their role as "Guardians of the Grail."

Though the Templars had an apparent Christian origin, it was the church—in collusion with the King of France—that brought about the Templars' demise. There are various reasons for the friction that arose between the Templars and the ruling establishments. One of these reasons may relate to the Templars' apparent possession of knowledge that contradicted orthodox Christian doctrine—even suggesting that the church had misinterpreted both the resurrection of Jesus, and His virgin birth.[24] The information the Templars possessed may also have dealt with genealogies and bloodlines—including the "bloodline of Jesus."[25] The Templars were thought to represent a counter school of thought to that of the Christian church. In the medieval world, adherence to orthodox Christian teaching was often enforced under the threat of death by the Catholic Church. Wilful deviation from official church dogma was to bring upon oneself a death sentence. Some have argued that many of the charges the church brought against the Templars seem to have been trumped up in order to bring the Templars down. Nevertheless, once the church and the French monarch declared that the Templars were to be eliminated, the order no longer had the backing they needed to survive publicly. Many were arrested, while others fled to lands of refuge.

One of the fascinating aspects surrounding the existence of the Templars is their intimate association with the legends of the Holy Grail. We already saw in chapter 5 how some of the early Grail writers had connections with the Knights Templar. Indeed, the Grail romances themselves originally came out of the court of the count of Champagne, who was closely associated with the very foundation of the order.[26] Furthermore, it has been noted that the stories of the Grail surfaced at the time of the Frankish kingdom of Jerusalem and the very peak of the medieval Crusades[27]—in both of which the Templars played a major role. The birth of the Grail legends occurred during the period of greatest Templar influence in medieval Europe. Recall from chapter 5 how we learned that whatever form the Grail takes, at its core, it represents a rival salvation and kingdom to that which is provided by the Lord Jesus Christ. In this light, the Templars, as "Guardians of the Grail," may have served as the custodians of a rival spirituality, which could explain why so many occult and esoteric organizations of today—such as the Freemasons—hold the Templars in such high regard.

Regarding the Grail legends, it is the belief of many researchers that the mythology of the Grail romances so familiar to Western society may actually represent hidden, esoteric, and heretical beliefs of the Templars in coded form. Authors Tim Wallace-Murphy and Marilyn Hopkins write:

> Additional clues to [Templar] beliefs can be found hidden, albeit in allegorical form, within . . . a literary work that still fascinates millions of people today, *The Search for*

> *the Holy Grail*. . . . The grail sagas of the 12th and 13th centuries are a clever amalgam of pre-Christian traditions with a Christian gloss, and containing a coded guide to the true teachings of Jesus. . . . The original romances carry coded clues to a heretical belief system that contradicted the monolithic power of the oppressive Church of that time. . . . The Grail saga is an allegory for an alchemical quest, a heretical guide to a spiritual pathway to enlightenment. . . . The king of the Grail castle, the Fisher King, is wounded. He imperfectly serves his impoverished realm, just as the usurpers of the true teachings of Jesus, those who lead the Christian Church, despoil the spiritual lives of those they claim to serve. When someone pure enough to see the Grail restores the Fisher King to full health, his wasted kingdom will be restored. When the true teachings of Jesus triumph over greed, lies, hypocrisy, and distortion, the realization of heaven on Earth will be made manifest.[28]

When researchers such as Wallace-Murphy and Hopkins refer to the "true teachings of Jesus," they do not mean His teachings as recorded in the Bible but rather "teachings" that are hidden from the common man and were supposedly discovered, guarded, and disseminated in coded form by the Knights Templar and similar groups. Thus, as "Knights of the Grail," the Templars may be a major medieval vessel through which esoteric philosophy became encapsulated in a popular legend known as the Holy Grail. It is ironic, really, that almost all in the West have heard of the Holy Grail, yet so few are aware of its deeply esoteric nature. This is the essence of esoteric philosophy. Things are often placed right in front of our eyes that we cannot understand without the "inside knowledge."

After being chased out of France by Pope Clement V and King Philip IV, some surviving Templars set sail—some say with most of their treasure—for Britain, where they took refuge in Scotland. It is in Scotland where the link is made between the medieval Templars and Freemasonry. Freemasonry, of course, is today's largest and most established esoteric fraternity and has always had very close ties to the political world. Templar ideals can also be found within another modern esoteric society with close political associations—the Rosicrucians. Within these orders can be found preserved the mysteries of the ancient world, guarded for centuries and entrusted only to those who sympathize with and promote their agenda: a new spiritual world order.

## Pulling It All Together

In this chapter, we have spanned a few thousand years of esoteric philosophy, connecting the serpent's lie in the garden of Eden with the esoteric beliefs of modern fraternities such as the Freemasons. We have seen how a rival cult has run parallel to the revelation of the one true God from the time of Eden, right up until this very day. At the heart of the esoteric movement is Satan's tireless and desperate quest to discredit the conquering seed of the woman and prevent His reign. In doing so, Satan seeks to avoid the inevitable judgment pronounced upon him by God. This quest of Satan is visible in the counter-spirituality that has characterized the pagan empires of history such as Egypt and Greece. It is visible in Satan's numerous attempts to seduce God's own people into occult/pagan worship. It is visible in the many Gnostic sects that flourished shortly after the time of Christ, denying the very person and incarnation of Christ. It is visible in the occult mysteries of the mythical Holy Grail, and according to some, the mysterious Knights who are regarded as the Grail's guardians. Finally, it is visible in the many esoteric societies of today—such as Freemasonry, the modern-day custodians of the esoteric mysteries of the ancient world.

# 7

# Mary Magdalene, the Priory of Sion, and the Bloodline of Christ

## Mary Magdalene: "Goddess" of the West

As we have already seen, the female plays a pivotal role in the world of esoteric and occult spirituality. Not surprisingly, esoteric adherents also view the Christian church as a great suppressor of the female side of the human race and the perpetrator of a masculine-dominated spirituality that is out of sync with the belief systems of the ancient world. Elizabeth Clare Prophet, in her book *Mary Magdalene and the Divine Feminine*, remarks how both Judaism and Christianity refer to God simply as Father, rather than make reference to the divine mother-father tandem so prominent in other world religions.[1] To the esoteric and occult community, Christianity is far too "male-centric."

In the occult, balance between opposites is paramount. Black must balance with white, good with evil, male with female, etc. Suppressing one side while favoring the other is to breed chaos and disorder. Thus, bringing opposites into equilibrium is the goal of the occultist. This may help us understand why Mary Magdalene is so important to the esoteric adherent. She can be seen as a symbol of the eclipsed female side of the male-female divine concept. In esoteric Christianity, it is Magdalene who counterbalances the male Jesus. As the "wife of Christ"—a notion made popular in recent times—a Jesus-and-Mary marital union would represent the "divine" sides of male and female in balance.

This male-female scenario calls to mind the Nimrod-Semiramis/Osiris-Isis mythologies. Interestingly, to present a story about Semiramis or Isis might generate interest in Iraq (the location of ancient Babel) or Egypt, but would probably not appeal to the casual Western observer. However, presenting the ancient mystery religion under the guise of Jesus and Mary—as many popular writings and movies have recently done—would instantly intrigue the Christian West. Concerning Mary Magdalene, best-selling author Margaret Starbird remarks:

> For decades, women in universities have searched ancient records and mythologies of the Goddess that survive in the far corners of the Earth. She is Queen of Heaven, giver of bread, the compassionate, the merciful, the immanent. How ironic it is to discover *Her* at the very heart of Western civilization, embodied in the woman whom Christian tradition vilified as prostitute—effectively silencing her voice for nearly two millennia and, with it, the voices of countless generations of her daughters.[2]

The esoteric Mary Magdalene represents Satan's counterfeit mystery religion wrapped in a Christian/Western cloak. Should we be surprised that she has become so prominent in Western pop culture? Until we understand the pagan mysteries that lie behind the esoteric Magdalene mythology, her perceived role as the bride of Christ will appear as nothing more than a romantic and popular alternative to the biblical account.

## The Priory of Sion and the Merovingian Bloodline

Between 2003 and 2006, the world was dazzled by Dan Brown's blockbuster book-made-into-movie *The Da Vinci Code.* Brown's main premise—that Jesus Christ and Mary Magdalene were married and sired a bloodline that is to this day guarded by an esoteric society called the *Prieure de Sion* (Priory of Sion)—is not original. His fictional account borrowed ideas from the 1982 nonfiction work *Holy Blood, Holy Grail.*

In this publication, authors Michael Baigent, Richard Leigh, and Henry Lincoln present the possibility that Jesus and Mary were married, and that their Jewish descendants intermarried with the nobility of France, placing what would become the French Merovingian dynasty in a line of descent from Jesus Christ. The authors also suggested that the Priory of Sion may be the guardians of this dynasty, working behind the scenes to navigate the dethroned Merovingians back to a place of prominence in European affairs.

Why should the Merovingians be "navigated back to prominence"? Aside from the claim that the bloodline may have been linked to Jesus Christ and the throne of David, the Merovingians may have been the most instrumental royal family in the ultimate creation of the Holy Roman Empire, and as some might have it, the rightful heirs to today's European royal thrones. For the purposes of mutual benefit, an alliance was made late in the fifth century between the Roman Catholic Church and the Merovingian king Clovis. Clovis was to champion the cause of Roman Christianity, which was under threat from an unorthodox Christian movement known as Arianism. In return, the church pledged their allegiance to Clovis and his descendants, ultimately allowing the Merovingians to become the chief political rulers of France, Belgium, and parts of Germany. Clovis was in fact regarded as the "New Constantine,"[3] a clear reference to the fourth-century Roman Emperor Constantine, who opened the door for Roman Christianity to become the official religion of the empire. This union between the church and the Merovingians laid the foundation for the formation of the later Holy Roman Empire.

This pledge by the church to Clovis and his descendants was apparently short lived. Following the death of the Merovingian king Dagobert, division arose in the Merovingian realm of Austrasia, ultimately leading to the transfer of power from Merovingian authority to officials known as "Mayors of the Palace," who were said to be under the control of the Catholic Church.[4] One of the mayors, Pepin III the Short, ultimately would depose the Merovingians and go on to create the Carolingian dynasty, a move that met with church approval. The church is in fact suspected as having a hand in Dagobert's death, since Dagobert's killer, Pepin the Fat, had close ties to the church. The idea being put forward by some researchers is that the church, for whatever reason fearing the Merovingians, orchestrated their removal and set up the Carolingian dynasty in their place.

What might have led the Roman church to betray their alliance with Clovis and his descendants? One suggestion is that the supposed Merovingian link to Jesus Christ and the house of David posed a threat to the church. If Jesus' descendants were sitting upon the thrones of Europe, it would mean that the traditional biblical account of a celibate savior Jesus would be "proved" to be a myth. The church, in removing the Merovingians, acted in self-preservation. It is the descendants of these displaced Merovingians that some esoteric researchers, conspiracy investigators, and revisionist historians suggest may be striving to regain the throne of France, and indeed the thrones of all of Europe.

Charged with the task of manipulating the Merovingians back in to power is the Priory of Sion. The supposed Merovingian claim to Europe's thrones may rest on the initial pact made between the Church of Rome and Clovis. This pact was to be in perpetuity, so long as Clovis had descendants. However, as Baigent, Leigh, and Lincoln suggest, Sion's ambitions may have extended far beyond the thrones of mere nations. It is suggested in *Holy Blood, Holy Grail* that Sion may have worked with other esoteric organizations—one known as the *Hieron du Val d'Or*—to create a nineteenth-century version of the Holy Roman Empire, ruled simultaneously by a Merovingian descendant and the Papacy. Such an establishment would certainly represent the revival of the ancient pact between Clovis and Rome. We are told that this grand project would ultimately have given birth to an occult world government—a global theocracy where nations would become mere provinces.[5] According to Baigent, Leigh, and Lincoln, this ambition was thwarted by the advent of WWI, which ultimately resulted in the fall of many of Europe's royal dynasties.[6]

We are told that part of the Priory's vision may have been to see a reunited *theocratic* European federation, to be ruled by, as some would have it, a "descendant" of Jesus.[7] It is fascinating to note that some of what Baigent, Leigh, and Lincoln have stated concerning the possible ambitions of Sion over two decades ago have since come to pass. The creation of a united Europe and the establishment of a European parliament are two specific developments that the authors suggested could be part of Sion's goals. Both of these are now a reality in today's European Union. In their follow-up book, *The Messianic Legacy*, the authors present a photo of a horseman riding into the sunset with the words "Etats-Unis d'Occident,"[8] which in English translates to "United States of the West." The horseman is holding a flag with the Priory of Sion logo encircled by a ring of stars. Today's European Union flag features a ring of twelve stars. Many reputable Bible prophecy authors and teachers have cited the European Union as a possible candidate to produce the Antichrist, due to its historical connection to the Roman Empire. Interestingly, Baigent, Leigh, and Lincoln remark at how the advent of Jesus' lineal descendant would be, to a receptive audience, a sort of second coming.[9]

A "descendant" of Jesus sitting upon the throne of a European-led occult world government would also serve as a candidate for one additional office—the Messiah! In claiming Davidic ancestry, this "descendant" would possess one of the most important requirements to pose as a king of Israel. It is indeed a curious thing that such a bizarre myth (the bloodline of Jesus) appears related to so many issues pertaining to the appearance of the Antichrist: false spirituality, a revived Roman Empire, a world theocracy, an attack on biblical Christianity, and the possibility of a world leader posing as Israel's messiah. The late Bible prophecy teacher David Allen Lewis wrote in 1988 concerning this same Priory of Sion/"bloodline of Christ" myth promoted by Baigent, Leigh, and Lincoln:

> Seldom in a lifetime do students of biblical prophecy see written works coming from our opponents that tend to confirm our views relating to the end times in such a vivid manner.[10]

## The Basis for the Popular Sion/Merovingian Story

There is much debate surrounding the historical reality of the Priory of Sion, as well as any future manifestation of the Merovingian dynasty. Since the publication of *Holy Blood, Holy Grail* and *The Messianic Legacy*, one of the three authors, Henry Lincoln, has distanced himself from anything to do with the Priory, stating that he prefers to stick to that which is verifiable.[11] Proving the reality of Sion is like trying to catch lightning in a bottle. It is extremely difficult (if not impossible), flashy (in that whatever "evidence" is found is often quite spectacular), and intensely dangerous (there have reportedly been bizarre deaths involving individuals apparently associated with or researching this organization).

According to one version of the Sion-Merovingian saga, as recounted at length in *Holy Blood, Holy Grail*, the mystery can be traced back to the late nineteenth century and a small village in the south of France. Berenger Sauniere, the priest of the Rennes-le-Chateau village, decided in 1891 to begin renovations on the village church. This particular church had been consecrated, curiously enough, to Mary Magdalene in 1059. While renovating, Sauniere is said to have stumbled across four parchments that were apparently hidden inside the church. Two of the parchments reportedly contained genealogies, while the other two contained what appeared to be codes of some sort. One of these coded messages, when translated into English, read: "To Dagobert II, King, And To Sion belongs this Treasure and He is there dead."

Dagobert is believed to have been the last true independent Merovingian ruler of Austrasia. Perplexed by the parchments and the codes, Sauniere figured that he should probably present his find to church authorities. As such, he took the parchments to the bishop of Carcassonne, who in turn sent him to Paris to the director general of the Saint Sulpice Seminary. Jim Marrs reports in *Rule by Secrecy* that it was later discovered that this same seminary was, in earlier times, linked to an unorthodox group known as the *Compagnie du Saint-Sacrement*, which was believed to be a front organization for the Priory of Sion.[12]

Somewhere along the way, or perhaps throughout his entire adventure, Sauniere became incredibly wealthy. It was later revealed that this simple priest had spent several million dollars on his church, as well as on the town itself. Sauniere upgraded the village road and water supply, built a garden, a country house, and a tower (interestingly called *Tour Magdala*, which means "Tower of Magdalene.") Within his church, Sauniere set up a statue of a demon known as Asmodeas. Strangely, Asmodeas is also said to have aided in the building of Solomon's temple, the center of Jewish worship. Another title given to this demon is "Rex Mundi," which means "Lord of the Earth."

Regarding Sauniere's wealth, it is suggested that he not only discovered the mysterious parchments but also a treasure of monetary value. It has also been suggested that Sauniere discovered something of non-intrinsic but immense significance that terrified the Catholic Church. Author Martin Lunn raises the possibility that it was the church that paid Sauniere in an attempt to keep him quiet.[13] Alternatively, author Clive Prince raises the possibility that it was actually the Priory of Sion that not only paid Sauniere but was also behind his discovery. One theory suggests that the non-intrinsic "treasure" that Sauniere found involves evidence proving the continuance of the Merovingian bloodline, which was believed to have been extinguished sometime after the death of Dagobert.

Speculative as this may be, there is one curious element that adds intrigue to the scenario put forth by Prince as to the source of Sauniere's wealth. As documented in *Holy Blood, Holy Grail*, it became quite common for Sauniere—a relatively unknown village priest—to entertain rather distinguished guests. One of these guests was the Archduke Johann von Habsburg, a cousin to the Emperor of Austria. The Habsburgs were one of Europe's most powerful royal dynasties, and indeed provided the Holy Roman Empire with most of its sovereigns and all of its formal emperors between 1452 and 1740. Bank statements reported that both Sauniere and Habsburg opened consecutive accounts on the same day and that Habsburg had paid a large sum of money to Sauniere. What makes this curious is not just that an archduke gave a rather generous donation to a lowly village priest, but rather the Habsburg dynasty's supposed connection to the Merovingians. In the eighteenth century, the dynasty became known as the House of Habsburg-Lorraine, or Habsburg-Lothringen (German), as it allied itself with the French House of Lorraine. It is through the Lorraine branch that the Habsburgs are linked by some to the Merovingian dynasty. Interestingly, the current head of the Habsburg-Lorraine dynasty, Otto von Habsburg, is one of a few individuals to presently hold the title "King of Jerusalem." In his book *Charles V*, Habsburg revealed his goal of seeing a united Europe based on both religious and political ideals.[14]

There seem to be mysterious circumstances surrounding Sauniere's death. On January 17, 1917, Sauniere suffered a stroke that would ultimately prove fatal. This date (January 17) is peculiar, as it is the identical date that one Marie Marquise d'Hautpol de Blanchefort died on centuries earlier. Sauniere had discovered Marie's sepulchre buried beneath his church, and for no apparent reason destroyed the inscription on her headstone. Strangely, the inscription was identical to one of the codes in the parchments: "To Dagobert II King and to Sion belongs this treasure and he is there dead." In *Holy Blood, Holy Grail*, the authors present numerous individuals, royal houses, and families with possible Merovingian ancestry. These include the famous medieval Crusader Godfroi de Bouillon, the Gisors, the St. Clairs, the Luisignan family, the Plantards, the House of Habsburg-Lorraine, and the Blanchefort family. The fourth Grand Master of the Knights Templar was also one Bertrand de Blanchefort. These are peculiar coincidences.

The date of Sauniere's stroke is not the only mystery surrounding his death. It is said that on January 12—five days before his stroke, and ten days before his ultimate death—Sauniere's housekeeper, Marie Denarnaud, inexplicitly ordered his coffin! She herself became the benefactor of Sauniere's wealth after his death. Sauniere had in fact transferred his money to her just before he died. But the plot thickens! After WWII, all French citizens were required to exchange their old francs for the new currency the government was introducing. The French government had to account for large sums of money that were gained through fraudulent means. Apparently to avoid having to explain the source of her wealth to the authorities, Marie Denarnaud burned a large portion of the cash she held. She then sold the house to businessman Noel Corbu and managed to live off the proceeds. She also told Mr. Corbu that before she died she would reveal to him a great secret that would make him very rich. However, she also suffered a sudden and ultimately fatal stroke that left her without the ability to speak. Thus, her secret, and by all accounts, Sauniere's secret, went with her to the grave.

It is this Rennes-le-Chateau mystery that caught the attention of Henry Lincoln, who later teamed up Richard Leigh and Michael Baigent to research and write *Holy Blood, Holy Grail.* During the course of their research, the author trio were led to focus in on the Knights Templar, whose history near Rennes-le-Chateau, according to them, seemed filled with strange enigmas.[15] They also cited a series of coincidences and patterns involving the Templars—patterns that, in their minds, required the involvement of planners. They suspected that the excavations the Knights undertook in Jerusalem were indicative of a deliberate quest to locate something, and that they had been deliberately sent on this quest. The authors posed the question: Who sent the Templars to the Holy Land? Interestingly, after their stay in the Holy Land, Bertrand de Blanchefort conferred upon the Templars lands in the region of Rennes-le-Chateau.

Further research suggested to the authors that the mysterious order behind the Templars was the *Prieure de Sion.* As such, they focused their energies on trying to understand this order, and in doing so, eventually found themselves face-to-face with an alleged Grand Master of the Priory, Pierre Plantard de Saint-Clair.

It is Plantard, along with French author Gerard de Sede, who provided the authors with much of the "inside" information concerning Sion. They were also able to locate information concerning the Priory in France's *Bibliotheque Nationale* (National Library of France). Here, they came across what are known as the *Dossier Secrets* (secret documents). These documents were perhaps the single most important source of Priory information. They traced Sion all the way back to the Crusader era, confirmed a link with the Knights Templar, listed Grand Masters, and even disclosed that Sauniere was working for the order while at Rennes-le-Chateau.[16] Thus, the trio of authors had on their hands what was turning into an explosive story. They seemingly had evidence that revealed the existence of a secret, esoteric society that provided many answers to the whole Rennes-le-Chateau mystery, including why the word *Sion* was incorporated on one of the Sauniere parchments.[17]

Eager to delve deeper into the Sion mystery, the authors sought to gain an audience with Sion's modern representative, Pierre Plantard. Initially, they were unable to get a firm grip on the reality of the organization. One journalist warned that those who investigated Sion too closely eventually got killed. They were also told that Sion had existed in the Middle Ages, but yet no longer did. Yet, they were also told that Sion was strictly a modern organization with no historical roots. Eventually, the authors were able to secure a series of interviews with Mr. Plantard.

Perhaps the most revealing bit of information to come out of their meetings with Plantard pertained to the very "secret" of Sion. While Plantard did not reveal exactly what the secret was, he did declare, seemingly quite definitively, that the Priory was in possession of the lost treasure of the temple of Jerusalem. He also stated that this treasure would be returned to Israel at the right time.[18] This, however, appears to have been of lesser importance, as according to Plantard the true treasure was spiritual and involved some secret that would bring about a major social change. He also stipulated that at some point a monarchy would be reinstated in France.

With the ultimate goal of Sion being the restoration of the deposed Merovingian dynasty, the authors then turned their attention to investigating this mysterious French royal bloodline. The main concern for them was one of motivation on the part of Sion. What was it about the Merovingian bloodline that demanded such efforts to place them back on the throne, centuries after their dissolution? The authors suspected that there might be something special pertaining to the *blood* of the Merovingian line. Yet, after reviewing the history of the Merovingians, including Clovis's pact with the church, the authors still could not identify a satisfactory reason as to why the bloodline would matter in the 1980s. It was not until the authors reached further back and began to associate the Merovingians with the house of David, and the Son of David, that the story began to make a bit more sense to them.

The authors note how, in the course of their investigation, the motif of the Holy Grail kept on recurring. For example, the Templars, who appeared to them to be intimately associated with Sion, were hailed as the "Guardians of the Grail." The Cathars, another mysterious group researched by the authors, were also said to be in possession of the Grail. The authors peered through the various Grail legends and noted how in the early Grail stories Mary Magdalene is said to have brought the Grail to France.[19] They also drew a connection between the Grail and Jesus from an analysis of one of the Grail legends known as the *Perlesvaus.* The authors note how, in this account, the Grail consists of a changing sequence of images: a crowned king who is crucified; a child; a man wearing a crown of thorns with a bleeding forehead, side, palms, and feet; and a fourth image that is not specified. It also appears as a chalice. In the *Perlesvaus,* the Grail is also associated with covert secrets that are entrusted to select company, which are in some way linked to "the Savior."[20] From the Grail descriptions in the *Perlesvaus,* the authors suggest that the Grail is many different things, including a bowl or chalice, Gnostic illumination, and a lineage of some sort.

Continuing their analysis of the various Grail legends, the authors comment on how Wolfram von Eschenbach's Grail poem *Parzival* reveals that the Grail somehow has the ability to enlist people into service. They then proceed to associate the Grail itself with a family of some sort whose members are scattered throughout the world. It is this family that enlists certain individuals into service—individuals from outside the family who must be initiated into a mystery of some sort.[21]

They then proceed to hypothesize that the Grail family may be of Judaic origin. This they do by noting the similarities between Wolfram's description of the Grail family suffering the wrath of God at some point in the past and many statements made about the Jews in the medieval period. They support this argument by referencing a book associated with a former Priory of Sion Grand Master, Nicolas Flamel, entitled *The Sacred Book of Abraham the Jew, Prince,*

*Priest, Levite, Astrologer and Philosopher to that Tribe of Jews who by the Wrath of God were Dispersed amongst the Gauls.* The land of the Gauls, of course, is where Mary Magdalene is said to have brought the Grail and where the Merovingian dynasty was to rise to prominence. At this point, the authors were able to draw a possible link between the Grail, Mary Magdalene, Jesus Christ, a lineage of some sort, a secret, a family, and the Jews. But it was the Grail's association with royal blood that would prove to be the most astounding.

In some of the earlier Grail manuscripts, the Grail is referred to as the *Sangraal* or *Sangreal.* As we saw earlier, some argue that when this word is broken down the middle to form *Sang Raal* or *Sang Real,* it translates to mean Royal Blood. Thus, the authors soon found themselves linking the Grail with blood, or more specifically, a bloodline. They also note that the traditional definition of the Grail—a cup that caught Jesus' blood—would seem to reinforce this position. And since, as the authors stress, the Grail legends for the most part are set in Merovingian times, the blood royal of the Grail may perhaps be linked to the blood royal of the Merovingians.

Putting all these factors together, Baigent, Leigh, and Lincoln raised several "possibilities." The royal blood of the Grail can apparently be linked to both Mary Magdalene and Jesus. Perhaps, then, they were united in marriage—a marriage that produced offspring? And perhaps the "Grail" that Magdalene brought to France was a child of the "holy couple"? If so, then the bloodline of Jesus would have taken root in the south of France, where it eventually became allied with the Frankish royal line, spawning the Merovingian dynasty.[22]

Being of the blood of Jesus, this dynasty would also be of Judaic origin, with claim to the house of David. They would also, through King Clovis, eventually become allied with the Church of Rome and serve as the ruling house of a large portion of Western Europe. The dynasty was then displaced by the Carolingians following the death of Dagobert II, robbing them of their rightful, church-sanctioned throne. While remnants of the bloodline would be forced to relinquish all claims to governmental authority, they would eventually be served by an esoteric organization—the Priory of Sion—who would aid them in their quest to return one of Jesus' descendants to the throne of both France and a united Europe.

## The Legitimacy of the Sion/Merovingian Mystery

The Priory of Sion/Merovingian story is clearly a sensational one, so much so that many debate and doubt its authenticity. We may assess the Priory of Sion in light of three basic views: the historical view, the modern hoax view, and the conspiratorial view. The historical view suggests the possibility that the modern Priory of Sion may be connected to the older Order of Sion, a genuine medieval order. This view argues that Sion has existed continuously since the Order of Sion was established in the eleventh century. Some trace it back even further to a Gnostic society led by an Egyptian named Ormus in around AD 46.[23] "Ormus" is also said to be a subtitle adopted by the Priory of Sion in 1188 when its name changed from "Order" to "Priory." As historian Martin Lunn remarks, Sion also referred to itself at this time as the Order of the True Rose-Cross, which he states may indicate that the Priory was the original Rosicrucian Order.[24]

The modern hoax view is by far the most commonly held view—and the most academically accepted one. It argues that while the Order of Sion may have been a genuine organization, the Priory of Sion referred to in *Holy Blood, Holy Grail* and *The Da Vinci Code* is purely modern—tracing its roots back no further than 1956. Esoteric and Grail author Laurence Gardner affirms this view. He supports the bloodline-of-Christ theory, and the messianic heritage of the Merovingians, but regards the Priory of Sion as nothing more than a club created to discuss matters such as bad rental accommodations and low-cost housing.[25] He also states that the organization folded in 1984 with the resignation of its secretary and cofounder, Pierre Plantard.

This view also maintains that the Merovingian association with Sion was a deliberate hoax perpetrated by Plantard and his associates. As Plantard would himself later admit, the parchments associated with the Rennes-le-Chateau mystery, and discovered by Sauniere, were forgeries. This is in agreement with the work of French writer Jean-Luc Chaumeil, who was able to have the Sauniere documents examined by two experts who determined them to be merely approximately forty years old. Chaumeil also claims to have documentation—signed by one of Plantard's associates, Philippe de Cherisey—referring to the Sauniere parchments as a hoax. However, Plantard did also stress that while the parchments were forgeries, real ones—inaccessible ones—did exist.[26]

The whole saga, fascinating as it may be, is actually based on extremely suspicious "evidence." The Priory as a hoax seems to be rooted in Pierre Plantard's fascination with the Rennes-le-Chateau mystery and his desire to present himself as an occult leader descended from a line of kings.[27] To substantiate his claims, he and his associates concocted spurious documents—including the *Dossier Secrets* found by Baigent, Leigh, and Lincoln in the Bibliotheque Nationale. Thus, the hypotheses of *Holy Blood, Holy Grail* and *The Da Vinci Code* appear to be built upon a hoax.

Regarding Rennes-le-Chateau, there is actually a rather simple explanation given for the whole Sauniere saga. Sauniere's estate was purchased by businessman Noel Corbu, who then turned the guest house into a hotel. He also opened a restaurant in the area and sought to gain publicity to attract customers. As such, he began to spread the idea that a priest, Berenger Sauniere, had become extremely wealthy by finding a treasure at Rennes-le-Chateau. The story was first published in 1956 in an article entitled "The Priest's Fabulous Discovery of the Billions of Rennes-le-Chateau." Soon after this publication, many flocked to the village in search of fortune. However, nothing was found. Regarding Sauniere's wealth, many maintain that is was not some astounding find that made him wealthy, but rather fraudulent activity involving the sale of Catholic masses!

After becoming fascinated with Corbu's Rennes-le-Chateau story, Plantard proceeded to embellish it somewhat through a series of forged documents that would make him out to be a Merovingian candidate for the king of France. Baigent, Leigh, and Lincoln then took the story and built their hypothesis around it, suggesting the possibility that the Merovingian dynasty was descended from Jesus Christ and Mary Magdalene, and guarded by the Priory of Sion for an eventual return to power. Obviously, the trio of authors at that time did not have the benefit of hindsight that we now have concerning Plantard and the Priory.

Pierre Plantard died on February 3, 2000. Five years later, Arnaud de Sede—the son of one of Plantard's associates, Gerard de Sede—admitted in a TV documentary that his father and Plantard made up the whole existence of the Priory of Sion. This should obviously put the issue to rest. However, some are not content to leave the Priory in the realm of a total hoax.

The conspiratorial view of Sion can be further subdivided into two categories: the Merovingian conspiracy and the Synarchist conspiracy. The Merovingian conspiracy is related to the historical view of Sion. It is, quite simply, the attempt to place a supposed descendant of Christ back upon the throne of France. This individual would also have claim to the throne of the Holy Roman Empire in a united Europe, as well as the messianic throne of David. The Priory's role is to safeguard this bloodline and work from behind the scenes in the highest levels of politics, religion, and society to bring about a full-fledged United States of Europe, ultimately leading to a world occult government led by a Davidic prince of the blood of Christ.

In *The Da Vinci Code* film, the main character, Robert Langdon (Tom Hanks), remarks on how Philipe de Cherisey exposed the entire Priory story as a hoax in 1967. Sir Leigh Teabing (Ian McKellen) then responds, "and that is what they want you to believe." Some have maintained that this idea factors into the Merovingian-Sion conspiratorial view—that while there are admissions of a hoax, the very admissions were designed to deflect attention away from Sion's conspiratorial activities over the centuries. These activities may have included encrypting esoteric clues in well-known art paintings; manipulating European, British, and American politics; and enlisting some of the most brilliant minds and influential men into Sion's ranks.

Some Christian authors such as Tim Cohen, J. R. Church, and David Allen Lewis have seen in a Merovingian conspiracy a possible fulfillment of biblical prophecies concerning the Antichrist. Without leaning too much toward an over-speculative approach, it is difficult not to see a striking similarity between what the Bible says will transpire in the kingdom of the Antichrist and the stated objectives of the Priory of Sion.

The Synarchist Sion conspiracy, largely promoted by researchers Lynn Picknett and Clive Prince, takes a different approach. Picknett and Prince agree that the entire Plantard saga is indeed a hoax, but one designed to mask the true aim of certain esoteric groups that supposedly lurk behind the Priory:

> The Priory—the alleged upholders of the bloodline of Jesus that is so central to *Holy Blood, Holy Grail* and *The Da Vinci Code*—is a hoax, but in the same way that intelligence deceptions are hoaxes. What really matters are the groups that stand behind it, the network of societies that include the Rectified Scottish Rite and Papus's Martinist Order, with

> their secret interior orders (of which most of their rank-and-file are probably unaware). And behind all this stands synarchy, at whose core is the drive to forge the United States of Europe.[28]

Interestingly, Picknett and Prince maintain that the ultimate goal remains a United States of Europe. However, instead of citing some Merovingian restoration as the motivation for this European project, they identify a network of secret societies working in the shadow of Sion that are driven by an ideology known as synarchy.

The authors liken synarchy to a theocracy—the union of politics with spirituality that involves the rule of priests or priest-king-type leaders.[29] It implies a system of government in which the leaders are driven by occult and esoteric beliefs. According to Picknett and Prince, this implies the rule of an elite group who are considered to be enlightened above common man. They even suggest that these enlightened elite may be in contact with and receive instruction from some other spiritual intelligence. They liken this sort arrangement to the rule of the priest-king pharaohs in ancient Egypt, leaders who served as both secular rulers and spiritual intermediaries between the gods and the people.[30]

It is important to remember that mixing politics with spirituality is by no means unheard of. This sort of arrangement would have been considered the norm in ancient times. Empires such as Rome often consisted of a political emperor who was also worshipped. Since the Bible indicates that it is the Roman Empire as a united imperial force that produces the Antichrist, and that the Antichrist himself will be worshiped, it is not too far a stretch to suggest that the political-occult ideologies of the ancient world will be revived in the days ahead. We may very well witness a synarchistic United States of Europe arise out of the ashes of the Roman Empire. In this light, Otto von Habsburg's goal of seeing a religious-political united Europe may be more significant than we realize.

## Pulling It All Together

Part of the intrigue and appeal associated with the supposed "marriage" of Jesus and Mary Magdalene—and the bloodline that supposedly resulted—is the exalted and erroneous position given to Mary Magdalene as the bride of

Christ. We have seen in this chapter how the exaltation of Mary as the messianic bride is, in reality, a Western incarnation of the goddess sacred feminine principle of the ancient world.

The burden of evidence seems to confirm that the Priory of Sion as revealed in *Holy Blood, Holy Grail,* and *The Da Vinci Code* is a hoax. Pierre Plantard himself declared that the Sauniere parchments—so crucial to the whole story—were forgeries. There is also the de Sede admission—that the whole Priory of Sion was concocted by Plantard and his associates.

Nevertheless, there are some questions surrounding the Sion mystery that remain unanswered. There is, for example, the strange set of circumstances surrounding the deaths of people associated with or researching Sion, such as French Journalist Mathieu Paolio. Paolio published a book in France exposing Sion's apparent interest in the Merovingian bloodline. Shortly afterward, he was executed as a spy. There are also the deaths of Sauniere and his housekeeper. Additionally, there is the death of Antoine Gelis, a priest and close associate of Sauniere who apparently also acquired a large amount of money. Gelis was found beaten to death in his home, with the murder details disappearing from church records, and having to be put together by court and police reports.[31] There is also the strange connection between Plantard and certain people in positions of power. Though Plantard himself admitted to fraudulent activity within the Priory, he apparently was closely connected to former French president Charles de Gaulle as a "secret agent" and may have had a hand in the creation of France's Fifth Republic.[32]

The theory put forth by Picknett and Prince, though far from conclusive, may provide an answer as to why Sion appears to be a total hoax yet also appears to be connected with high-level European politics. Using the Merovingian bloodline myth as a smokescreen, the true Priory of Sion may be a front organization for other esoteric groups intent on building an occult, politically-united Europe. Interestingly, this theory presents a system of government—the union of politics and spirituality—that reflects the way empires were structured in the past, and the way the Roman Empire will be structured in the future.

While I make no speculative or dogmatic claims, we would be remiss to move on without highlighting the many bizarre similarities between this Priory of Sion story and end-time biblical prophecy concerning the Antichrist.

A European prince posing as a "descendant" of Christ would appear to have a crucial requirement should the Antichrist pretend to be Israel's messiah: Davidic ancestry. A prince arising to power over a united, occult, European theocracy also calls to mind what is to occur when the Antichrist arises over a reborn Roman Empire. Furthermore, a restored union between a united Europe under Merovingian rule and the Catholic Church not only revives the pact between Clovis and the church, but also calls to mind Revelation 17, which depicts political Rome (the Beast) united to a religious entity seemingly based in Rome (the woman).

# 8

## Counterfeit Messianic Legacy and the Re-shaping of Christianity

### Counterfeit Messianic Kingdom

What if it were revealed that Christianity was really a ploy by the apostle Paul to appeal to a pagan world that saw no problem in a deified man? What if we were told that the Jesus worshipped by Christians as God was just an ordinary man with no trace of divinity—as "proven" by His "bodily remains" found on earth? And what if it were revealed that the "true" mission of Jesus was not to die for sin but strictly to teach and serve as a political messianic candidate? Similarly, what if it were "revealed" that the most pure form of Judaism was the belief that all gods were equal and under the umbrella of a great, unifying cosmic being? The end result of such "revelations" could be the loss of further credibility of traditional Christianity in the eyes of the world and the creation of a new unified world religion.

Such a scenario involving a new world religion is suggested by authors Christopher Knight and Alan Butler in their book *Solomon's Power Brokers: The Secrets of Freemasonry, the Church, and the Illuminati.* The authors present a scenario that would involve the nations, religions, and economies of the world coming together to form what they regard as "the harmonious union of humankind."[1] The global capital of this world society would be Jerusalem, with God ruling over the unified planet. The ideology behind such a setup would be one that encouraged an ordered and prosperous society, free of depravity and poverty, or any ill will.[2] To Christians and Jews, and perhaps Muslims, this scenario sounds similar to the world utopia expected to be created by the Messiah or the Mahdi. However, Knight and Butler are not Christian, Jewish, or Muslim authors.

The key driving force behind the new world order presented in this scenario is spiritual unity. Knight and Butler hypothesize an ideology that fosters interdependence among the world's religions. Many "gods" would be tolerated, but ultimately made inferior to a greater universal energy.[3] Thus, each religion would have its place, but would be of secondary importance to this universal energy. The great universal energy would be one that could be accessed by the followers of any religion. People could love God under any name.[4]

The Bible reveals that the Antichrist will be worshipped by all the earth. All the earth worshipping one man implies a world that is spiritually united. Hence, any talk of a united world religion—or one great universal energy for all the earth—should raise red flags. Additionally, before humanity is ready to worship a "new supreme god," their faith in their "old god" must be shaken. The old religions must be made to fit with the new Babylonian world system that is coming. Thus, Judaism and Christianity—the underpinning faiths of Western civilization—must be reshaped and made to look more like esoteric philosophies than monotheistic religions. There are several ways this may come about.

## The Bones of the Messiah and the Destruction of Christianity

Richard Andrews and Paul Schellenberger, authors of the number one best seller *The Tomb of God*, have put forth the idea that physical remains of Jesus Christ may actually be located on earth, "proving" that the resurrection never happened. The authors suggest that the "final resting place" of Christ's bones may be Rennes-Le-Chateau in France—brought there by the Templars. The authors also hypothesize that this "true history" of Jesus had to be covered up during the middle Ages when the Catholic Church ruled with an iron fist:

> If these remains were indeed the bones of Jesus of Nazareth, their significance to those who possessed them would

> have been colossal. If it was indeed the Knights Templar who located the remains, why did they not announce the fact, instead of transporting them and concealing them elsewhere? The answer is more obvious to the historian than to the layman. To have declared, in the Middle Ages, that you were in possession, or had knowledge, of the remains of Jesus would lead to immediate execution for heresy. Family and friends would probably suffer a similar fate. The ensuing centuries saw little softening in the Church's attitude to heretics. Although in the nineteenth century Sauniere would not have been burnt at the stake had he declared his findings, he would have lost his post at Rennes, and in any case his "knowledge" was providing him with riches beyond his wildest dreams. . . . We are aware that the consequential issue of the reality of the Resurrection will be of greatest concern to committed Christians.[5]

In light of this apparent connection to Rennes-le-Chateau, it is worth recalling the words of Pierre Plantard—that the secret of Rennes-le-Chateau was *spiritual* and that it would bring about a major social change. Revealing what are believed to be the bones of Christ to the world would indeed bring about a "major social change."

The authors also believe that excavation is needed, despite the overwhelming chaos that may result should Jesus' "bones" be presented to the world:

> At the end of three years of research we also believe the remains to be those of Jesus and therefore, in order to substantiate our findings (overriding moral considerations about digging up sacred remains), we believe that excavation is required. . . . Many will argue that the temporary enlightenment that excavation would offer to the curious would be massively counterbalanced by the spiritual chaos and uncertainty that would be felt by Christians the world over. The only answer to this is that the true message of Jesus was lost with the Resurrection, that many millions of people who might otherwise call themselves Christians have a problem

> with this most fundamental tenet of the Christian faith and that, with the millennium approaching, the time has come for a reappraisal not just of the *life* of Jesus, but of the *death* of Jesus.[6]

Some may be familiar with a "bones of Christ" hypothesis, promoted in 2007 by archaeologist and documentary filmmaker Simcha Jacobovici in his book *The Jesus Family Tomb: The Discovery, the Investigation, and the Evidence That Could Change History*, and subsequent documentary, *The Lost Tomb of Jesus*. The theme is similar to Andrews and Schellenberger's, in that Jesus' mortal remains may be on earth and represent the "true" history and message of Jesus.

I believe it is important to consider the implications should it one day be "proved" that Jesus' remains are on earth. What would happen if a major archaeological dig—financed by top research firms and academic institutions—was carried out in Europe or Israel, resulting in the excavation of the remains of some important individual? Discovering the remains of an important historical figure is nothing new, as this sort of thing has occurred in Egypt for years. What if radiocarbon dating were employed to link this find to the first century? Furthermore, what if DNA testing could somehow be employed to link these remains to another important relic, perhaps the Shroud of Turin or a spear believed to be the one that pierced the side of Christ, "confirming" to all that the remains were those of Jesus Christ? Such a "revelation" would absolutely destroy the Christian message in the eyes of the world concerning a resurrected savior.

William Cooper, a former United States Naval Intelligence Briefing Team member and author of *Behold a Pale Horse*, had this to say concerning the treasure of the Knights Templar:

> The treasure hidden in France is not the treasure of the Temple of Jerusalem. It is the Holy Grail itself, the robe of Jesus, the last remaining pieces of the Cross of the Crucifixion, and, according to my sources, someone's bones. I can tell you that the reality of the bones will shake the world to its very foundations if I have been told the truth. The relics are hidden in France.[7]

Cooper does not reveal whose bones he refers to. However, there is only one person in history whose bones could shake the world's foundations should they be "discovered," and that person is the One whose bones are not supposed to be here. Cooper was shot and killed in November of 2001 by deputies of the Apache County Sheriff's Office. Specific circumstances surrounding his death are somewhat perplexing and uncertain. Interestingly, he himself said ten years before his death that should anything happen to him, look to the Freemasons as the guilty party.[8]

The resurrection of Jesus is the very heart of the Christian gospel. It affirms the total defeat of death and the absolute victory over the grave of, not only Jesus, but also of all those who believe in His name. Without the resurrection, true Christianity falls apart.

## Redefining the Resurrection

How do some of those who deny the literal resurrection of Jesus explain the references to resurrection that are so clearly affirmed in Scripture? Christopher Knight and Robert Lomas, best-selling authors of *The Hiram Key* and *The Second Messiah*, comment on how a "resurrection" did not have to imply a supernatural raising from the dead. They point to an old Gnostic belief that maintained that the term "resurrection" did not necessarily imply *physical* resurrection but rather *spiritual* resurrection. The authors—both of whom are Freemasons—even point to modern Masonry, which uses a symbolic resurrection ritual to make a new candidate a full member of the Masonic Order.[10] The Gnostics apparently used the term "resurrection" to describe what happens when a soul is at the very moment of enlightenment.[11] Thus, to rise from the dead did not mean to physically triumph over death but rather to be elevated from the death of ignorance and be brought through enlightenment into greater *gnosis*, or knowledge. Knight and Lomas actually point to a passage in the *Gnostic Gospel of Philip*, which ridicules Christians who take the resurrection of Jesus literally.[12] According to this view, the church got it wrong, and for almost two thousand years has been propagating the "myth" of Christ's resurrection.

Manly P. Hall, one of the most esteemed esoteric philosophers of the twentieth century, affirms this concept of ritualistic death and resurrection in what he calls the "myth of the dying god." According to Hall, this concept of a dying god—found in many of the pagan cultures of antiquity—has been perpetuated in Christianity in the death and resurrection of the God-man Jesus Christ.[13] Hall identifies the myth of the dying god as an allegory and a key that provides entrance to individual *and* universal redemption. "Philosophic death" he equates with "Lesser Mysteries," while "philosophic resurrection" is equated with "Greater Mysteries." Thus, resurrection is once again a symbol for enlightenment. Hall, much like *The Gospel of Philip*, strongly rebukes those who would fail to perceive this allegory. He regards those who miss the concept as unworthy of considering themselves genuinely religious or wise.[14] Hall also claims that unless this symbolic truth is rediscovered, Christianity will never reach the levels attained by the pagans in the days of their "philosophic supremacy."

Interestingly, we can perceive in Hall's claim the familiar "lost" and "recovered" theme of esoteric spirituality, as Hall speaks of Christianity "recovering symbolic truth." Clearly, the discovery of what are *perceived to be* Christ's bones on earth could be a catalyst to bring Christianity into the fold of a world occult, Babylonian religion.

## Jesus Christ: Lamb of God or Political Warrior?

Was Jesus' mission really to die for the sins of the world? Many influential researchers have presented a far different story concerning early Christianity and the mission of Jesus than what is accepted orthodox Christian teaching. Tim Wallace-Murphy suggests that early Christianity was a collection of small congregations that claimed to follow the teachings of Jesus, who in this scenario was supposedly the leader of an offshoot group of the Essenes.[15] The Essenes were an AD first- to second-century Jewish ascetic religious group known for their extreme discipline and chaste living. They were a desert community, having withdrawn to the Dead Sea area, leaving what they perceived as corrupt city society. The famous Dead Sea Scrolls are often attributed to this mysterious group.

The Essenes are also linked to a wider community also associated with the Dead Sea Scrolls known as the Qumran Community. Qumran is an area to the immediate Northwest of the Dead Sea in Israel. It is worth noting the eschatological beliefs held by this community, as they shed light on why some researchers now believe Jesus' "true" mission had nothing to do with atonement for sin. According to the Dead Sea Scrolls, the ancient Qumran Community of the time had a fervent belief in the coming "end of days" that would involve a great battle between light and darkness. All evildoers would be destroyed while the sect of Qumran would be preserved as the true people of Israel.[16] Associated with this end of days are two messiahs who would preside over an eschatological banquet, a sort of end-of-days new age that would include worship at an end-times temple.[17] One of the two messiahs would proceed from the lineage of the High Priest Aaron and handle religious matters, while the other would be a political messiah. According to some views, the political messiah would be of the blood of David.

In the ancient Jewish temple were two twin pillars that stood at its entrance. These pillars, known as Jachin and Boaz (1 Kings 7:21), have been taken by some to be symbolic of the two-messiah concept. The right-hand pillar is associated with the priestly messiah, while the left-hand pillar is associated with the Davidic messiah, as hinted at by its name. Boaz was the great-grandfather of King David of Israel. The two pillars standing together are taken to symbolize the dual reign of two messiahs in the kingdom of God. When the two messiahs are in place as the two pillars were, then the kingdom of heaven will be established. Interestingly, the high priest of Israel would have to pass in between the two pillars to ultimately get to the Most Holy place where he would meet with YHWH. Thus, the two pillars led to the presence of God, even as the two messiahs are to lead to the kingdom of God. In this context, the temple of Jerusalem becomes symbolic of the great utopian era sought for by humanity throughout the ages.

How does Jesus fit in to this Qumran two-messiah concept? What is now emerging—and in fact has been for some time—is an alternative explanation of what Jesus' mission was that runs in opposition to genuine Christianity. Familiar groups are involved: Gnostics, the Knights Templar, and the Freemasons. It is also being promoted as the *true* Christian story, with its advocates declaring orthodox Christianity to be the counterfeit. As we proceed to assess this alternative account of Jesus, the careful reader will discover that it actually unifies Judaism and Christianity into one belief system, with Jesus Christ, ironically, being the unifying element. However, the redemptive work of Christ is lost in this scenario.

In this account, both John the Baptist and Jesus Christ were messiahs who heralded the coming kingdom of heaven. In their massively successful but controversial book *The Hiram Key*, Knight and Lomas maintain that John served as the priestly messiah, and in fact asked Jesus to be his kingly opposite[18]—the Boaz pillar. In this account, the two pillars—John the Baptist and Jesus Christ—had arrived to usher in the kingdom of heaven as expected by the Qumran community.

Knight and Lomas cite John's messianic status as the cause of his execution at the command of Herod the tetrarch (Matthew 14:1–12), who feared that a revolt could be brought about by John's followers. This, of course, is not the case. John was executed, not because of some messianic threat on his part, but because of Herod's rash promise to a young dancer. With the death of John came the death of the priestly pillar. As such, Knight and Lomas directed their attention to two individuals that had the potential to replace John. One of these was James, the brother of Jesus. The other was Jesus Himself, who the authors proceed to portray in an astonishing light. Indeed, by Knight and Lomas's own admission, the Jesus of their story is one that is vastly different from the Jesus Christians know, and one that is also quite disturbing.[19] They affirm their responsibility to "tell the truth," implying that the Jesus of biblical Christianity is a fake.

The two authors state how Jesus, unlike John the Baptist, was extremely unpopular both in Jerusalem and at Qumran. He supposedly had a radical agenda that did not appeal nor fall in line with accustomed Qumran community traditions. As such, the people supposedly put their support behind James in their attempt to find a successor to John. However, Jesus had other ideas, mainly, to take upon Himself the role of both kingly and priestly messiah. Apparently, Jesus was convinced that the time had come for the final battle against the Romans, and that He had the best chance of leading the people to victory.

The authors maintain that Jesus was on a military mission, attempting to overthrow the power of Rome on behalf of Israel, with the end result being the establishment of a messianic kingdom. Some of the men that Christians know as the disciples of Christ are then, in this hypothesis, made out to be "bodyguards" of Jesus with James, John, two Simons, and Judas as His closest "guards." But the story continues to get even more bizarre. The authors suggest that Jesus "resurrected" common people to an elevated status—a "Qumranian initiate," which supposedly angered the community that felt that their privileged position was being compromised. Of course, by "resurrected," the authors are not referring to a miraculous rising from the dead but rather an elevation to a higher status in the community.

As the time drew near for Jesus' supposed coup on the Romans, a plan was apparently devised in order to demonstrate to the people that He was the king who was to rescue them from Gentile dominion. The triumphal entry, the great event recorded in all four Gospels where Jesus publicly presents Himself to Israel as Messiah, is yet another event twisted and revised to fit an unbiblical hypothesis. It is maintained that the entire event was a deliberate enactment designed to convince the people that the Messiah had come. However, the plan got the attention of both Roman and Jewish authorities. Eventually, the Romans had both James and Jesus arrested, and in doing so, ensured that both pillar claimants were contained. But in the end, only Jesus was executed on the cross, with James being set free.

This account of the life and ministry of Jesus is chalked with revisions to the traditional, biblical account of Christ. Jesus, the Lamb of God, becomes Jesus the political warrior. The one who died for sin becomes the one who died for an earthly kingdom. The triumphant Son of God becomes a mere failed messiah. In effect, He is stripped of His deity with His death on the cross made to look like punishment for a failed coup rather than God's preordained plan to deal with human sin.

Tim Wallace-Murphy and Marilyn Hopkins have presented their research in the form of a hypothesis very similar to that of Knight and Lomas. Stripping Jesus of His deity and resurrection power, these authors present the possibility that the "true teachings" of Jesus were preserved by James, who took over the leadership of Jesus' disciples after His death. These so-called teachings are simply Gnostic or esoteric "truths" hidden behind many of the otherwise literal words of Jesus, together with noncanonical "messages" of Jesus such as those found in the Gnostic gospels. They do not speak of repentance, forgiveness, and atonement through the shed blood of Christ, but rather "enlightenment" and mysticism. Jesus' "true" teachings supposedly used a form of initiation to cleanse the followers of His message in order to motivate them to seek justice among men and brotherhood.[20] His purpose was apparently to create an elite class that would purify Israel, preparing them to be a light to all the world.[21]

According to this alternative account, the true followers of Jesus were those who adhered to these secret teachings, as preserved by a new community of believers led by James and known as the Jerusalem church. It is suggested that the structure of this early church was shaped by Essene teaching, practice, and tradition and actually based on the model of the Essene community.[22]

Some have maintained that the orthodox Christianity we know today was largely a creation of the apostle Paul who, we are told, took the original message of a Jewish rabbi and transformed it into a Gentile-centered message of eternal salvation. This is the view of Barrie Wilson, author of *How Jesus Became Christian.* This view maintains that Paul sought to cover up a Jewish Jesus who was merely human and replace Him with a Gentile god in human form. This "creation of St. Paul" would not just be a mortal Christ but also a divine savior, the literal Son of God. Apparently, St. Paul was motivated by a desire to reach the pagan Greek and Roman civilizations, which had no objections to a deified man, having been used to their pagan gods that quite often mingled with the human race. With the ascendency of Roman Christianity and the imperial church of the Middle Ages, the beliefs of Paul became the accepted and orthodox version of Jesus and Christianity, while all other views were suppressed. The "true" teachings of Jesus, lost for centuries, must be rediscovered, with the result being the transformation and reshaping of Christianity.

According to Tim Wallace-Murphy and Marilyn Hopkins, the leadership of the early church following the death of James was assumed by a group known as the Desposyni, who are described as the "family of Jesus." The priesthood of Israel also continued to play a role in this early messianic movement. However, when the Romans sacked Jerusalem and the temple in AD 70, the Jerusalem church, its priests, and its Davidic-messianic descendants were killed, taken as captives, or scattered abroad. As Roman Christianity became the dominant belief system of the West, those who had taken their Essene-/Qumran-type beliefs with them into Gentile lands were forced to either convert or practice their beliefs in secret. However, as Knight and Lomas reveal, scrolls containing secrets of many in the Qumran community were supposedly safely buried in a vault underneath the foundations of the temple of Jerusalem by those who believed the end of the age was at hand.[23] Thus, a repository of Qumran/Essene beliefs supposedly remained unscathed during the Roman assault on Jerusalem, preserving the mysteries of this sect. It is believed that these secret scrolls remained in Jerusalem beneath the ruins of the temple for centuries until a group of notorious French medieval knights arrived in the Holy Land in the twelfth century to recover them.

## Counterfeit Messianic Legacy

As we have already noted, many researchers feel that the Knights Templars did indeed find something during their excavations in Jerusalem. Though various theories exist as to what they may have found, the hypothesis put forward by Knight and Lomas concerning the Templars' discovery in Jerusalem is intriguing, though debatable. The authors did not deliberately set out to investigate what the Templars discovered. As Freemasons themselves, they simply wanted to investigate the origins of Masonry. What they ended up discovering was a possible link between Freemasonry and the beliefs of the ancient Qumran community. The link would come by way of two bloodlines running through the heart of European civilization. One bloodline supposedly could be traced back to the high priest–related families of Israel, descending from Aaron, while the other bloodline could supposedly be traced back to King David.

According to the authors, the families of the descendants of Aaron and David are known by the name *Rex Deus*, which is Latin for "Kings of God," or "King God." These families are supposedly the remnants of those members of the Jerusalem church that fled Jerusalem during the Roman siege of AD 70. It is suggested that these families are the ones that may have sent the Templars to the Holy Land to recover the scrolls left behind centuries earlier. It is quite fascinating how both the Templars and the Freemasons share a certain affinity toward Solomon's temple in Jerusalem. Indeed, the Knights Templars are named after the temple, while Solomon's temple has been called the most important motif in Freemasonry.[24]

In their book *The Second Messiah*, Knight and Lomas recount their introduction to the Rex Deus hypothesis, which came by way of fellow researcher Tim Wallace-Murphy. During their research for the *The Hiram Key*, Robert Lomas contacted Wallace-Murphy concerning a particular aspect of their investigation. He explained to him how he and Knight came to believe that the Templars knew precisely what they were looking for when they excavated in Jerusalem.

Wallace-Murphy was intrigued, as Knight and Lomas's hypothesis just happened to fit with a curious bit of information that he had had for some time and was about to share with Lomas. He began to explain how he had just finished giving a lecture in London when a mature adult approached him and introduced himself in French. He explained to Tim that he was a direct descendant of Hughes de Payen, a former Templar Grandmaster. When he had reached the age of twenty-one, his father informed him that he was to partake in secret knowledge that would then need to be conveyed to his own son once he reached twenty-one. He had come to realize that a verbal tradition had existed for thousands of years that had been passed down for generations from father to son.[25] Part of this tradition seemed to involve some rather astounding claims regarding the temple of Jerusalem, its priests, and the preservation of the bloodlines of Levi (Aaron was a descendant of Levi), and David. He also made it known that after Jesus was crucified, the main leaders of the Jerusalem church were John, Peter, and James. The Frenchman's testimony concerning the Jerusalem church then begins to take a drastic turn and starts to resemble in striking detail the alternative account of Jesus and early Christianity that we have covered above.

He began to stress to Tim Wallace-Murphy how James, not Jesus, had become the more important figure, and that while not many were too concerned with Jesus' death, most in the city rose up in revolution after James was later executed.

The Frenchman then noted that after James was killed and before the destruction of the temple by the Romans, members of the priesthood—called here the Nazarene Priesthood—fled to Europe. They then briefly returned to Jerusalem to recover the remains of one that they called "the savior," and took these bones to Greece, only to return them six hundred years later to Jerusalem. It was also disclosed that underneath the temple site were many chambers, and on the walls of these chambers were written the genealogies of the children of the priests of the temple, with their lineage being traced back to both David and Aaron. The descendants supposedly adopted the religious practices of the lands in which they settled so long as they were only required to express a belief in the one true God.[26] The bloodlines of David and Aaron were supposedly being preserved for the eventual advent of two new messiahs who would work together to establish on earth the kingdom of heaven, fulfilling the eschatological hopes of the Qumran/Essene community. Possible Rex Deus families are revealed by Knight and Lomas, and include the Counts of Champagne, Lords of Gisors, Counts of Anjou, St. Clairs of Roslin, and the Habsburgs.[27]

Recall from chapter 2 how we saw that John (a descendant of Aaron) and Jesus (a descendant of David) worked together to prepare Israel for the kingdom of heaven. It would appear that the underlying concept of Rex Deus concerning two messiahs is a close (but not identical) mimicry of the biblical scenario. John the Baptist is never referred to anywhere in Scripture as a messiah. Nevertheless, he was a descendant of Aaron and served as a forerunner to the true Davidic Messiah.

Undoubtedly a sensational story, what Knight and Lomas needed, taking into account the information given to them by Wallace-Murphy, was additional evidence to substantiate their hypothesis, linking first-century Jerusalem with the twelfth-century Knights Templars.[28] That evidence would apparently come largely by way of an analysis of the thirty-three degrees of Scottish Rite Freemasonry, which seemed to preserve Rex Deus ideology. In fact, Wallace-Murphy and Hopkins maintain that Freemasonry actually owes its origins to Rex Deus. We will look closely at this evidence when we take a detailed look at Freemasonry in chapter 11.

## Pulling It All Together

We saw in chapter 3 how two world leaders—one political and one religious—will be prominent in the kingdom of the Antichrist. We also saw earlier that the Antichrist will sit in the temple of God, implying a rebuilt temple in Jerusalem (2 Thessalonians 2:3–4). How remarkable, then, that we are now hearing arguments that contradict the biblical witness concerning Jesus and offer instead an ideology that agrees in such a vivid manner with the biblical picture concerning the Antichrist! Now, we must not try to predict exactly how these things will be fulfilled, for we do not yet know how things will unfold. Additionally, some of the claims of Knight, Lomas, Wallace-Murphy, and Hopkins are debatable and difficult to verify (the reality of the mysterious Frenchman appears to rest solely on Tim Wallace-Murphy's testimony). But when something so accurately fits the prophetic picture—especially when it also tears down the person, work, and deity of Jesus—we also must not casually ignore it. The historical reality of Rex Deus has not been definitively proven. Some, including Picknett and Prince, dispute it. However, certain *concepts* associated with the Rex Deus hypothesis were embraced by the Qumran community.

In *Solomon's Power Brokers: The Secrets of Freemasonry, the Church, and the Illuminati*, authors Knight and Butler present the possibility that the idea of a new world order may be rooted in the ideology of an ancient priesthood, seemingly the ancestors of what Knight and Lomas might call the Rex Deus priestly line. They refer to the descendants of this priesthood by the name "Star Families." Interestingly, Jerusalem is hypothesized to be the perfect city to serve as the capital of this new world order, with the United Nations transferring their headquarters to the Holy City from New York. This move, the authors maintain, would be proposed by one individual. However, the ideas he presents would not be his own but would reflect the ideology of the Star families. The fact that God's prophetic picture is mirrored in such striking detail by these scenarios indicates that many of the anti-biblical concepts found in Rex Deus and Star Family ideology will be realized.

Apostate Christianity and apostate Judaism have been fused into one system through this alternative explanation of Jesus and the early church. Be certain that the ideology of Rex Deus does *not* represent genuine biblical Christianity, biblical or Rabbinical Judaism, the State of Israel, or the Jewish people, but rather a counterfeit messianic legacy based on Gnostic and esoteric philosophy. It is an esoteric parallel to God's revealed truth. As we have seen the continuity of Satan's counter-philosophy from ancient times to today, we should not be surprised at this!

Those who do not regard the New Testament as God's revealed, literal truth would see no problem in a mortal Jesus whose *sole* mission was to be a political Messiah. It is even conceivable that by "removing" the divine aspects of Jesus, Israel would have considerably less issue accepting Him as a Messiah (albeit in retrospect). And if it should one day be "proved" that the bones of Jesus are buried on earth, many would certainly approve of a global reformation of Christianity and Judaism, and maybe even Islam. It could be argued that in the place of these three faiths a new religion should be established—based in Jerusalem. And to commemorate this new religion and "kingdom of heaven," a new temple could be erected in Jerusalem as a symbol of peace in the new age between Christianity, Judaism, and Islam, for it is when the two pillars—the prince (Boaz) and the priest (Jachin)—are in place that the kingdom of heaven is to arrive.

Could there be a connection between this two pillar–two messiah (one political, one religious) concept and the beast (political leader) and false prophet (religious leader) of Revelation? The parallels are obvious. However, we cannot know with certainty, and must refrain from definite speculation. What we can say, however, is that any concept, theory, or idea that strips Jesus of His deity and contradicts the biblical witness is to be judged in light of Scripture, and rejected.

# 9

# The Quest for a Philosophic World Empire

With the 2008/09 global financial crisis shaking the very foundations of the world economy, many world leaders declared the need to create a "new world order" and a new financial global system to replace the system that nearly collapsed entirely. Britain's former Prime Minister Gordon Brown was exceptionally keen on calling for this new world order. At the London Summit of April 2009, Brown declared his belief that the "new world order is emerging" and that it will lead to a new era of "international cooperation." In September of 2007, French President Nicolas Sarkozy spoke of building a "new world order of the twenty-first century" during a speech to the UN General Assembly in New York. And on April 3, 2009, Time.com, in partnership with CNN, carried an article entitled "Barack Obama's New World Order." While the main focus of these world leaders may be economics and geopolitics, the phrase *new world order* has, over the years, been intricately associated with esoteric spirituality and esoteric organizations.

## The Plan

A common desire among esoteric philosophers is to see a unified world system of governance established. The heartbeat of this grand project is not politics or money but spiritual and philosophic belief. Apparently, only those trained in the esoteric mysteries can truly accept and understand the relevance and nature of a new global order:

> Only those who have been properly initiated can accept or fathom such ideas as . . . the necessity of uniting humanity under a one-world government and religion, and the certainty that a New World Order will eventually arise.[1]

New Age spirituality adherents refer to something known as "The Plan," which is basically a blueprint for this new world order. Concerning this plan, Lardie writes:

> [The Plan is] an organized agenda for the establishment of the New World Order that will be controlled by the Aquarian Age Christ. The Plan is said to have been revealed first to Alice Bailey (1880–1949) in the 1930s. She was instructed to keep it hidden until 1975, some thirty years after her death. She obtained these mysteries from channelled spirits who proclaimed that this was when the world would be ready to hear the message. . . . The Plan calls for people to be taught their oneness with the impersonal, universal God. . . . As more people come to realize their innate divinity a critical mass will be reached, bringing about a worldwide transformation in consciousness. When this is achieved, the New Age Christ will begin purging the earth of all "negative influences" in accordance with The Plan. Those who oppose the global transformation will be sent to an alternate dimension until they have spiritually evolved enough to return to earth.
>
> Lord Maitreya will establish a one-world religion, a one-world government, and a one-world economy. Through a quantum leap in the spiritual evolution of humanity, the world will become a paradise characterized by peace, love, and unity.[2]

Note that The Plan promotes a "god" that is an impersonal force—a being that can be accessed by anyone, in any fashion. The Plan also refers to humanity's "innate divinity," calling to mind the temptation aimed at Eve by the serpent stating that she could be like God. Notice as well that there is to be some sort of grand spiritual awakening and transformation on a worldwide scale. This "awakening" or "transformation" calls to mind the "resurrection" phenomena that characterizes Gnostic and esoteric thought. According to The Plan, when this awakening occurs, those who fail to "evolve" spiritually will be removed from this earth by the new Christ to some "alternate dimension."

In light of the political, economic, and religious unity called for in The Plan, it is interesting to listen to our world leaders voice their desire for greater political, economic, and religious cooperation. In religion, we have Tony Blair's Faith Foundation, which is aimed at bringing the various religions of the world more closely together. According to Blair, the forces of globalization are bringing the citizens of the world—and all of their diverse religious faiths—closer together.[3] In economics, we have already touched on the call for a new economic world order being made by world leaders. Interestingly, there has even been talk of instituting a new *global* currency system to replace the current system. BBC.com carried an article in March 2009 that reported the call by certain countries for a "new global currency"[4] to replace the US dollar on the world stage. Politically, the world is more united than ever before through international bodies and organizations such as the European Union and the United Nations.

Considering what the Bible states will occur under the Antichrist's reign, we should expect to see greater political and economic unity as we get closer to the appearance of the Antichrist. The stage must be set before the chief actor appears! Many world leaders may not necessarily be deliberately, knowingly promoting a secret agenda but simply acting on a genuine belief that world unity is the best way forward. However, as we shall soon discover, world unity is a notion that lies at the very core of both esoteric teaching and many esoteric societies—some of which have close political associations.

## An Ancient Quest

The renowned esoteric philosopher Manly P. Hall noted:

> Today's thinking toward a democratic world state is neither a new trend nor an accidental circumstance; the

> work of setting up the background of knowledge necessary to the establishing of enlightened democracy among all nations has been carried on for many hundreds of years by secret societies.
>
> Secret societies have existed among all peoples, savage and civilized, since the beginning of recorded history. The esoteric organizations of ancient times were for the most part religious and philosophical. In the medieval world they were philosophical and political. In the modern world, political and social.[5]

This is an astonishing quote! Hall, who was a thirty-three-degree Freemason, reveals that an ambition of the esoteric societies is to create an enlightened democratic world state—a world order characterized by philosophy and democracy. This is in contrast to the medieval world order, which was characterized by ecclesiastical dogma and autocratic rule. Hall also affirms the link between secret esoteric societies and the political world, identifying today's secret societies as "political and social."

According to Hall, the rise of the church brought about persecution against the ideology of esoteric philosophers and secret societies.[6] This necessitated further secrecy among the societies. Many may wonder why esoteric groups have always placed so much emphasis on secrecy. Part of the answer pertains to basic self-preservation. In the Middle Ages, any deviation from church dogma was to mark oneself for death. Those who held views that contradicted the church were often subject to intense persecution. In order to preserve their beliefs, they needed to operate in secret, even clothing their beliefs in a layer of Christian phraseology to hide their true nature.[7] These beliefs were then revealed to those who were initiated into the esoteric schools.[8] It was in this climate of religious persecution that the mysteries of the occult flourished in secret as an esoteric underground stream parallel to, yet directly opposed to, church dogma. In a sense, they formed a shadow church hidden from ecclesiastical authorities.

Eventually, the power of the medieval church waned, largely as a result of the European Renaissance of the late Middle Ages and the Protestant Reformation. As the iron fist of the church began to soften, the opportunities for "free thinking" and intellectual pursuit began to increase. With the Renaissance (a word meaning "rebirth"), men and women began to discover, or perhaps rediscover, classical patterns of learning. Areas of intellectual development included architecture, humanism, art, science, and even religion. With the advent of a more "intellectually free" society, the need for total secrecy by the esoteric fraternities began to evaporate. It is perhaps no coincidence, then, that beginning in and around the seventeenth century, esoteric groups like the Rosicrucians and the Freemasons began to emerge publicly.

A familiar esoteric/occult viewpoint is the belief that Christianity, and the world order that came about in the West as a result of "Christian Europe," is a great hindrance to the development of the new age. Esoteric thought places a great deal of emphasis on enlightenment into sacred knowledge as the means by which regular mortal souls can attain a measure of divinity and immortality. Christianity, on the other hand, maintains that faith in Jesus Christ *alone* saves. The former is based on free thinking and intellectual achievement. The latter, while certainly not devoid of free thinking and intellectual contemplation, is rooted in an *already revealed truth* that must be trusted and obeyed. It should be pointed out that in believing and obeying an already revealed divine truth (Christianity), mankind affirms its dependence on and subjection to God. God sets the standard! In striving toward spiritual evolution and enlightenment into secret and mystical knowledge (esotericism), mankind claims independence from God!

The esoteric philosophers see in Christianity a suppression of human spiritual evolution. Consequently, they do not believe that the sought-after new age can be attained through Christianity but must be achieved through some "awakening" of the soul. Thus, the current Judeo-Christian/nation-state world order must be replaced by an "enlightened" and occult world order, with humanity indoctrinated into esoteric mysteries that were supposedly lost with the rise of the Christian church. The philosophic world system alluded to by Hall, then, is one that disregards the true revelation of God and reacquaints itself with the pagan mysteries of antiquity.

On a political level, the ambition of the esoteric fraternities again reflects their disdain for the Christian church. With the rise of the imperial Roman church and all of its ecclesiastical offshoots (i.e., the Church of England) came political governments and monarchies that were often sanctioned and guided into power by the church. This was the case when the Church of Rome crowned Charlemagne as ruler of the West on December 25, AD 800. We can also see this in Britain today, as the Church of England is intimately associated with the British monarchy. Indeed, the true head of the Church of England is not the archbishop of Canterbury but rather the British monarch, currently Queen Elizabeth II, who holds the title "Supreme Governor of the Church of England."

The esoteric fraternities perceived that the church-sponsored monarchies, and those that ruled with a tyrannical iron fist, hindered the true development of human civilization, since they were basically ruling on behalf of, or in league with, the church. The secret societies strived for the advancement of human civilization, and as such sought to take political power out of the hands of tyrannical monarchs (who they felt prevented such advancement) and place it into the hands of the people![9] The form of government that would advance the cause of the secret societies, then, was not autocracy but democracy!

In a revealing quote by Hall, this affinity toward democracy by esoteric orders like Freemasonry is clearly identified:

> If . . . the modern Freemasonic Order was profoundly influenced by, if it is not an actual outgrowth of [Sir] Francis Bacon's secret society, its symbolism is undoubtedly permeated with Bacon's two great ideas: universal education and universal democracy. The deadly enemies of universal education are ignorance, superstition, and fear, by which the human soul is held in bondage to the lowest part of its own constitution. The arrant enemies of universal democracy have ever been the crown, the tiara, and the torch.[10]

According to Hall, Freemasonry is permeated with the ideals of what he calls "universal education" and "universal democracy." What seems to be implied here is the idea of making enlightenment (education) a worldwide achievement, with democracy being a worldwide system of governance. We can now better understand what Hall meant when he commented on the creation of an enlightened, democratic world state. The dominance of Christianity has to be supplanted by "enlightenment," while the autocratic regimes of church-sponsored governments and repressive monarchies have to be replaced by democratic governments, all in the context of a *world state*! It is a quest for a philosophic, democratic world system to replace the current world order rooted in ancient and medieval Europe.

In his book *The Secret Destiny of America*, Hall writes at length concerning something he calls "the Order of the Quest." Hall remarks how this order is made up of a group of enlightened humans who are aware that civilization has a secret destiny of some sort.[11] Hall seems to link this "secret destiny" to the idea of a universal brotherhood and world democracy—which he says was the secret dream of classical, esoteric philosophers.[12]

## The Atlantean Roots of the World Philosophic Dream

What is this quest for "universal brotherhood" and "world democracy" actually based on? In his book *New World Order: The Ancient Plan of Secret Societies*, Christian author William Still reiterates that the most important mystery of the secret societies—one that has been passed down for thousands of years—involves the establishment of universal democracy, a world government, and a New Atlantis.[13] This identification with Atlantis is a massive clue to understanding the roots of the esoteric plan for an enlightened democratic world state. We have already seen in chapters 1 and 5 how the mythical story of Atlantis greatly factors in to esoteric teaching. Atlantis is believed to have been the ideal human situation in terms of both government and personal evolution. According to legend, Atlantis was governed by ten kings who then submitted to the authority of an overarching eleventh king. Hall refers to the grouping of these ten kings as the "cooperative commonwealth of mankind."[14]

According to Still, the elite class of today's secret societies are still taught the importance of this cooperative commonwealth, and that bringing it to completion is the highest calling that someone can give himself to.[15] Thus, the grand project of the esoteric societies appears to be associated with a quest to create a new Atlantis on the earth. Indeed, Hall noted that the philosophic empire would return in the form of a democracy of wise men.[16] From an esoteric perspective, the new world order appears to be a re-creation of the system and situation of mythical Atlantis:

> The Atlantean legend seems to set the ideological foundation upon which all the secret societies rest. Whether it is the "cooperative commonwealth of the ten kings," the "Philosophic Empire," the "New Atlantic League," the "New World Order," or the "New Atlantis," the meaning is always the same: to establish a so-called "enlightened" world government.[17]

What we have in the eventual establishment of an "enlightened democratic world state" is the continuing development of humankind's rebellion against its creator. The establishment of a philosophic empire can be linked with a re-creation of Atlantis, the discovery of the Grail, a reconstruction of Babel, and the avenging of Osiris's death. The philosophic empire is humanity's attempt to create that which only God can give—an earthly utopia! Interestingly, Hall links the future philosophic empire with several "Holy Grails" of history, identifying the philosophic empire as "that perfect thing," the "perfect order in society"[18] sought for by many groups and individuals. Hall speaks of those chemists who sought the elixir of life, and the European knights who sought the chalice of the Grail, as well as the Illuminati who sought what he refers to as a pearl of great price—possibly a metaphor for wisdom and self-virtue.[19] These quests, according to Hall, were all searching for the same thing under various rituals and symbols—societal perfection![20]

### Democracy, Atlantis, and the Revived Roman Empire of the Antichrist

Could a philosophic, democratic world state such as that sought by esoteric societies have any relation to the coming kingdom of the Antichrist? As we saw in chapter 3, some biblical scholars—commenting on the great image of Daniel 2—have seen in revived Rome an awkward mix of monarchy (the iron) and democracy (clay). Indeed, Clarence Larkin classifies the revived Roman Empire of the Antichrist as a "democratic monarchy." How interesting this is! He sees the great image of Nebuchadnezzar as going from a very effective form of government (the "gold" of an absolute autocracy) to a weak form of government (the iron-clay of a democratic monarchy).[21]

Author Arno Gaebelein (1861–1945) saw in the clay a "foreign ingredient"[22] that did not belong to the rest of the statue. He identified the metals as representative of monarchies and the clay as representing democratic rule—the "rule by the people." Likewise, J. Dwight Pentecost notes that the revived Roman Empire under the Antichrist is one that is weak *and* strong, democratic and autocratic, as symbolized by the clay and the iron.[23]

While the interpretation of the iron and clay given in Daniel does seem to imply more than just the possible influence of democracy,[24] scholars such as Larkin, Gaebelein, and Pentecost could potentially be correct in their association of clay with democracy, as it is only in the final form of Gentile power—the revived Roman Empire—that the clay is present. Democracy, of course, is very prevalent in the world today, and should the esoteric vision of a democratic world state come to fruition and play a part in the development of the Antichrist's kingdom, then democracy will almost certainly—at least initially—be a factor. Interestingly, elements of democracy supposedly characterized the government of Atlantis as well.[25]

Bible prophecy teacher Arno Froese, author of *How Democracy will Elect the Antichrist*, believes that worldwide democracy will usher the Antichrist into power. This is a fascinating viewpoint, especially in light of what we have learned concerning the desire for a philosophic, democratic world empire among esoteric philosophers. But if democracy elects the Antichrist, it will probably not be long before his rule begins to resemble a more dictatorial-type regime. This is not without precedent. Commenting on European royalty, Prince Michael of Greece notes how, in times past, monarchs were elected through an early form of democracy, yet turned themselves into hereditary monarchs once in power.[26] Here, democracy becomes a means to an end, useful only until power is consolidated.

Only time will tell whether or not a philosophic world empire will be established in the earth, leading to the Antichrist's kingdom. But whether or not that is the case, we can, even now, see definite parallels between the esoteric goal and the work and kingdom of the Antichrist.

## The Importance of Atlantis

Atlantis symbolizes a concept that is of critical importance to the esoteric philosopher—the ideal society. Central to Atlantis was its spiritual temple, where Poseidon ruled over the other ten kings. Here we see the familiar union of politics and spirituality, as it was in this *spiritual* temple that the rulers of Atlantis met to set down their laws. It appears that the temple was both a spiritual house and a governmental or judicial house. Some have maintained that Poseidon, also known as the "god of the sea" was worshipped, and that the whole religion of Atlantis was a "water-based" religion based on Poseidon.[27] It is also maintained that the rulers of Atlantis were god-kings—both human and divine. It is these god-kings of Atlantis that supposedly became the mythical heroes and gods of various cultures[28] such as Greece.

Esoteric philosophy places a great deal of emphasis on scientific achievement and spiritual enlightenment, both of which supposedly characterized Atlantis. In this regard, Atlantis is a model for the spiritual development of humanity sought for by esoteric adherents. It is both a political model, with the ten kings being representative of the ideal form of government, and a spiritual model, with its philosophy being retained by the esoteric societies. Interestingly, Freemasonry has been linked to Atlantis, being referred to as a shadow of the Atlantean Mystery School.[29]

As splendid as Atlantis was said to be, it was not immune from moral decay or societal degeneration. An abundance of luxury, an over-preoccupation with material wealth, and the supposed gradual loss of its leader's "divinity" through much comingling with mortals all contributed to Atlantis's corruption and ultimate demise.[30] As a result of this corruption, God (or "the gods") decided to punish and judge Atlantis by burying it in a great flood.

We need to pause here and consider the striking similarity between the myth of Atlantis and various biblical accounts. Some have suggested that the Atlantean account is one and the same with the corruption of humanity and the great flood of Genesis 6 and 7. The god-kings of Atlantis in this context would be equivalent to the Nephilim—the "men of renown" mentioned in the Bible. Interestingly, Clarence Larkin identifies the Nephilim of Genesis 6 as the basis for the gods and god-men myths of antiquity.[31]

The similarities between Atlantis and the kingdom of the beast are too chilling to ignore. There are, of course, the ten kings of Atlantis that mirror the ten kings of the Antichrist's kingdom. The eleventh king of Atlantis, Poseidon, was worshipped, even as the eleventh king of the revived Roman Empire will be worshipped. Poseidon was the god of the sea, and it is from the sea where the Antichrist and his kingdom are depicted as arising from (Revelation 13:1). It was also *by water* that Atlantis was supposedly destroyed, and it is *out of the water* that the kingdom of the Antichrist is depicted as arising from. According to Plato's account, Atlantis dominated the Mediterranean Sea, and it is of course the Mediterranean region that the Roman Empire ruled over. Since the kingdom of the Antichrist is a *revived* Roman Empire, we can be certain that the Mediterranean world will play a major role in the political events of the Antichrist's day. And as the great temple of Poseidon was the center of both religious and legal practice, so a newly built Jerusalem temple will be the site where the Antichrist proclaims himself to be God.

The legend of Atlantis takes on a further twist when we consider the mystique surrounding the Merovingian bloodline. According to legend, Merovee, the founder of the dynasty, was sired by two fathers—a human being and a mysterious sea beast. His name reflects this mythology, with the word mer meaning "sea" in French. From a mythological perspective, one can say that a beast from the sea gave rise to the Merovingian dynasty. Interestingly, occult researcher Tracy R. Twyman links the bloodline of Merovee to Atlantis.32 Many have associated the "sea" in Revelation that the beast arises out of with the Gentile world, with the beast representing the pinnacle of global Gentile authority. It is fascinating, though, how the Bible's depiction of the Antichrist's kingdom in Revelation 13 also bears such striking Atlantean/Merovingian imagery by referring to the abyss, the sea, and the "beast coming up out of the sea with ten horns":

> Then I saw a beast coming up out of the sea, having ten horns. (Revelation 13:1)
>
> "The beast that you saw *was*, and *is not*, and *is about to come up out of the abyss*." (Revelation17:8, italics added)

This is especially fascinating in light of the importance placed on both Atlantis and the Merovingian bloodline by some adherents of esoteric and pagan philosophy. And as we have seen, esoteric and pagan philosophy are closely linked to Satan's counterfeit system. Coincidences all these similarities may be. But they are rather strange and thought-provoking coincidences!

According to some accounts, the wisdom, knowledge, and spirituality of Atlantis were not completely wiped out with the flood. It is believed that before its total destruction, certain enlightened ones fled the doomed continent with their knowledge, settling in Egypt where they became the first god-kings of the Egyptians.[33] Additionally, Hall notes that almost all the myths of antiquity, which form the basis for various religious texts in parts of the world, are based upon the rituals practiced in Atlantis.[34]

## Pulling It All Together

They key to understanding the tireless quest for a new world order by esoteric societies lies, not in what is to come, but what supposedly lies in the past. The legend of the lost continent of Atlantis factors greatly in to esoteric lore. It is believed that the conditions of Atlantis must be reestablished on the earth. From an esoteric/pagan perspective, erecting a new world order would actually be a recovery of what was lost—a rebuilding of what once was. It is believed that there once was a golden age, a perfect civilization in which gods associated with men. This perfect civilization was characterized by peace, prosperity, scientific achievement, spiritual enlightenment, and technological superiority. Due to gradual corruption, Atlantis was destroyed in a flood. It is this type of "ideal" civilization that some seek to recover as a "New Atlantis." Such an achievement would signify the finding of the elusive Holy Grail and a completing of the Tower of Babel. To the esoteric and pagan philosopher, it could symbolize the reassertion of esotericism and occultism over true divine revelation.

As positive as a new world order may seem to some, it is in fact only a patchwork solution to human misery and chaos. It takes care of the external problem—the societal problems—but fails to deal with our most pressing needs: a change of heart, forgiveness for sin, and deliverance from death. The new world order has no true answer for these. Any attempt to create a global society apart from God can only lead to hell on earth, since the most fundamental problem—the heart of mankind—has not been addressed. Only the gospel of Jesus Christ can truly change the heart.

This is not meant to sound narrow-minded or exclusive. Indeed, the salvation Jesus provides is offered to all, regardless of race, nationality, social status, or religious background. True unity must come by way of the One who unifies us in *Him*, that is, Christ. Trying to "glue" humanity together, even through peaceful means, is dangerous. A united world will require one leader *for* the world. That leader is coming, and like so many world leaders before him, his promises of peace, unity, and prosperity will quickly give way to total misery and enslavement.

# 10

# Templars, Rosicrucians, Masons, and Enlightenment

## The Knights of the Grail and the "True History of Jesus"

The Knights Templar seem to be closely linked with most esoteric revelations and theories now being debated and discussed. What is it about these knights that place them at such a foundational level in esoteric/occult/Grail research? Perhaps part of the answer lies in the fact that two of the most influential esoteric orders in history—Freemasonry and the Rosicrucians—have based a great deal of their rituals, beliefs, and symbols on Templarism. Gardner notes that stories of the biblical King Solomon form a legacy integral to modern Masonry, and that before Freemasonry came about as a formal institution, the Templars were the historical link to this legacy.[1] Similarly, Adrian Gilbert, author of *The New Jerusalem*, indicates that the particular brand of Freemasonry known as the "Scottish Rite" claims to derive partly from some inheritance brought to Britain by the Knights Templar.[2] And regarding the Rosicrucians (also referred to as the Order of the Rose-Croix, or Rosy Cross), notable Masonic author Albert Pike indicates that the successors of the Rose-Croix order united with many Templars in one mystical sect.[3] Indeed, the very name of the Rosicrucian/Rosy Cross order reflects the very emblem of the Knights Templar—the red cross.

One of the keys to understanding the Templars' importance to esoteric/occult philosophy pertains to their apparent take on Christianity and the life of Jesus. As we have seen, the Templars apparently had a "Christian" beginning. Yet, the very church that helped create them went to great lengths to eradicate them from Europe. It is believed that one of the reasons the church suppressed the Templars was secret knowledge the Knights supposedly acquired during their stay in the Holy Land. While in the Middle East, the Templars were reportedly initiated into arcane mysteries of groups like the Essenes.[4] Some of what they learned apparently contradicted official church teaching. They were supposedly in possession of the so-called "true history of Jesus Christ," and, as such, were in a position to challenge the supremacy of the Roman church.

It is believed that whatever "treasures" the Templars did or did not find during their stay in the Holy Land, they did, at the very least, come into possession of *information* that represented some of the most foundational elements of esoteric philosophy—some of which blatantly oppose Christianity and speak of a "true new age" to be instituted on the earth. If this is indeed the case, then the Templars may be the most foundational esoteric order of Western civilization, and may be the connection between the anti-Christian and esoteric attitudes of Middle Eastern Gnostic-like sects and the West.

In chapter 5, we saw how the various Grail legends and the many interpretations of what the Grail is, while at times appearing to be Christian, are in reality pagan. Recall as well from the last chapter that we saw that the "pagan intellectuals" often cloaked their esoteric ideas in a layer of Christian "phraseology." The purpose for this is obvious. Open dissemination of pagan and occult ideas in the Middle Ages could not be done without risking one's life. As some researchers seem to now believe, the legends of the Grail represent the anti-Christian, esoteric account of Jesus and true spirituality presented in somewhat of a "Christian" form. And as the Templars were the knights of the Grail, it is they who are considered to have been the medieval custodians of the esoteric mysteries that would eventually come to saturate Western civilization.

Interestingly, as authors Knight and Lomas note, the legends of King Arthur and the Grail sprang from separate authors who could be linked to the Templars. Knight and Lomas also believe that the entire Grail mythology is really a veiled account of the Rex Deus group. In this context, the Grail would symbolize an alternative "Judeo-Christianity" with all of its anti-biblical and anti-Christ elements. Once again, it is the Templars who are supposedly responsible for bringing the "truth" of Rex Deus from the Holy Land to Europe, veiling it in the legends of the Grail. Interestingly, the complete name of the Knights Templar is "The Poor Fellow Soldiers of Christ and of the Temple of Solomon." Perhaps it is strictly a coincidence, but the very essence of Rex Deus—with its dual lineages of David (royal messianic line) and Aaron (high priest) is reflected in the Templar's full title. "Christ" is just the Greek and Gentile rendering of *Messiah*, and could imply the royal line, whereas the "Temple of Solomon," the house where the priests of Israel ministered, calls to mind the priestly line.

According to Gardner, some of the items that the Templars recovered in Jerusalem included documents that were hidden in AD 66–70 during the revolt of the Jews against the Romans.[6] These documents supposedly contained information that would enable the Templars to challenge both church doctrine and the way the New Testament was interpreted.[7] Recall from chapter 8 how we saw that it may have been Qumran scrolls that the Templars were specifically looking for while excavating around the site of Solomon's temple. If indeed the Templars did recover these scrolls, then they would have been privy to the eschatological beliefs of the Qumran community as well as possible counter-Christian beliefs concerning Jesus. Indeed, as Jim Marrs notes, some of the scrolls and artifacts found by the Templars in Jerusalem could have been employed to destroy church traditions.[8]

In addition to the Jerusalem scrolls, it is believed that the Templars also acquired a vast amount of knowledge from books found outside Jerusalem. This would seem to include knowledge from Arabian and Greek philosophers, as well as information pertaining to geometry, music, architecture, and numerology.[9] Additionally, Gardner seems to be convinced of what is often regarded as theory by others—that is, that the Templars did indeed recover intrinsic material treasure from hidden vaults beneath the site of Solomon's temple. Included in this treasure, Gardner affirms, is the lost ark of the covenant.

The alternative Christianity that the Templars are reported to have embraced would include a denial of Jesus' divinity, His virgin conception, His atonement, His resurrection, and His return. This would then be replaced by a belief in a less personal God, and the eventual establishment of the kingdom of heaven on earth—based not on biblical Christianity but on esoteric Christianity. Interestingly, the red cross emblem of the Templars is not the traditional Christian cross, which has a longer vertical bar and a shorter horizontal bar that is placed at a position just above the center of the vertical bar. Rather, the cross of the Templars is equilateral, with both the vertical bar and the horizontal bar being the same length, and intersecting at each bar's respective center. Gardner affirms that the reason for this untraditional cross was that the Templars held to beliefs that challenged traditional New Testament interpretation.

While the Templars were persecuted, scattered, and effectually extinguished, their beliefs and ideals were not. Templar ideals survived the order, and seem to have been preserved by two prominent and influential esoteric societies: the Rosicrucian Order and Freemasonry.

## The Order of the Rosy Cross and Enlightenment

The Rosicrucian Order is an international organization committed to esoteric wisdom, as well as psychic enlightenment.[10] It is also believed by some to be the forerunner of today's occultism.[11] Its emblem is a rose laid on top of a Christian cross, forming a "rosy cross" or a "red" cross. Interestingly, according to author Laurence Gardner, the Rosicrucians were involved in promoting international medical aid for the poor. The most influential and well-known agency in the area of emergency relief today is, of course, the Red Cross.[12]

While the existence of this esoteric fraternity is well known and documented, its origins are somewhat difficult to discern. Information in France indicates that the Rose-Croix Order was founded in AD 1188 by Jean de Gisors, a Knight Templar and the first independent Grand Master of the Order of Sion. Its *formal* inauguration came by way of the Scottish King Robert the Bruce, who selected certain Templars to found the "Elder Brethren of the Rosy Cross" in 1307.[13]

Concerning the red cross symbol, Gardner offers a unique interpretation of this Templar/Rosicrucian emblem. He maintains that the rosi-crucis (red cross) represents a "dew-cup" or "cup of the waters"—an identifier of the Holy Grail[14] as a royal bloodline. In this context, the red cross is a symbol for the Blood Royal or dynastic bloodline of the Grail kings and queens. The supporters of this bloodline were then known as Rosicrucians.[15] Gardner reveals that the Grail is symbolic of the female womb, which supposedly perpetuates the messianic Grail bloodline. Symbolically, the rosi-crucis, then, is interchangeable with the Holy Grail. Thus, the Templars, who were the Knights of the Grail, and the Rosicrucians were apparently both concerned with the same thing: the Grail and what it represented.

A set of documents published in the seventeenth century shed light on the intentions of the Rosicrucian Order. One, reputedly written by somebody named Christian Rosencreutz called *Fama Fraternitatis Rosae Crusis* or "Report of the Rosicrucian Brotherhood," detailed the author's journeys through the Holy Land and Mediterranean, where he gained esoteric knowledge. This tract, which is filled with references to the Knights Templar, speaks of some usurped royal dynasty that is meant to one day be restored. Other documents, known as the Rosicrucian Manifestos, speak of a promised new age of enlightenment along with the unveiling of ancient secrets.[16] According to author Albert Mackey, these documents were concocted in order to kick-start a society that would convert the "dry" theology of the church to a more "civilizing" system.[17]

Key historical Rosicrucians include Dr. John Dee (scientist and spy for Queen Elizabeth I); Robert Fludd, who took part in the translation of the Bible into English for King James I; and Sir Francis Bacon, who wrote *The New Atlantis.* Members also included philosopher/scientist Robert Boyle and Sir Christopher Wren, the renowned architect who did much to rebuild London after its great fire in 1666.

The link between the Rosicrucian Order and Freemasonry seems to be a tight one. Marrs notes that by the time the Grand Masonic Lodge of England was formed in 1717, Rosicrucian leaders Christopher Wren and Elias Ashmole had already established Rosicrucian-based speculative Masonry within the order. It was Ashmole himself who crafted the three introductory degrees of Freemasonry. Indeed, the two orders even shared the same meeting place—Mason's Hall in London—at the time that the Masonic Grand Lodge of England was formed.

According to Manly P. Hall, the objective of the Rosicrucian Order was threefold.[18] First, they sought to abolish monarchical forms of government, replacing them with the rule of a philosophic elect. Interestingly, Hall notes that the democracies in the world are a direct result of the efforts of the Rosicrucians.

Second, the Rosicrucians sought to reform philosophy, science, and ethics, effectively asserting themselves as a rival to Christianity. Here, the familiar theme of esoteric philosophy opposing Christianity can once again be seen. Rosicrucians favored scientific inquiry over church doctrine. They felt that it was not belief in biblical teaching that led to true wisdom but rather scientific exploration. They have been credited as being a major factor in the conflict between church dogma and scientific rationalism, as well as in the European Renaissance.[19] The Rosicrucian Order was concerned with spiritual and scientific enlightenment and learning rather than faith in a personal God. It is important to note that the Bible does not frown upon science, learning, or curious inquiry. All these things are given by God and can be used for His glory. The problem is when God's gifts are used as a substitute for a relationship with Him.

The Rosicrucians were also adepts in the ancient occult mysteries, and in fact sought to reestablish formal organizations of the ancient mysteries as a method of educating humanity in some sort of "eternal" and secret doctrine.[20] Like the Templars, the Rosicrucians were believed to be in possession of information that contradicted and nullified the claims of the church regarding the biblical account of Jesus Christ. According to Gardner, they were also responsible for the creation of a new spiritually aware environment.[21] This was in contrast to the dominance of ecclesiastical dogma that characterized the medieval period. People were becoming less and less comfortable with church dogma and more and more open to the ideas of classical philosophy and scientific inquiry.

The European Renaissance occurred largely between the fourteenth and seventeenth centuries. The early Rosicrucian documents were published in the seventeenth century, and the European Age of Enlightenment reached its height in the eighteenth century. This general time frame (fourteenth to eighteenth century) represents the period in history where European civilization shifted from a predominantly ecclesiastical-led society to a more "enlightened" and "free-thinking" society. During these centuries, the Roman church lost a great deal of its imperial and religious authority. Additionally, it was the work of a sixteenth-century German monk named Martin Luther that lead to the Protestant Reformation, substantially weakening the grip of the Catholic Church on religious and civil matters in Europe. Interestingly, Prince Frederick of Saxony ordered a signet ring to be given to Luther as a gift. On the ring was a seal featuring a red heart, a white rose, and a cross—the rose and cross. Frederick was a member of the House of Wettin, the parent house of what would become the Royal House of Windsor, today's British Royal family.

A further development during this pivotal phase in European history was the publication of Charles Darwin's *The Origin of Species*, advancing the theory of evolution through natural selection, contradicting the biblical account of divine creation. All these factors contributed to the weakening of Catholic Rome's grip on European society, as freethinking and "broad-mindedness" began to replace rigid dogmatic belief. In many ways, the Renaissance, the Enlightenment, and the Reformation led to much good, as they helped strip Rome of some of its abusive powers. However, as so often happens with ideological shifts, the pendulum swung to the other extreme, as many began to completely discard faith in God's Word in favor of rational and scientific inquiry. Whether one chooses to recognize it or not, the increasingly anti-Christian nature of Western society and its growing curiosity in esoteric paganism are exactly what the ancient Rosicrucians and Templars would have wanted.

The third objective of the Rosicrucian Order was the discovery of universal medicine for all forms of sickness. Hall notes that there is sufficient evidence to suggest that the Rosicrucians successfully acquired the "elixir of life." The healing powers of the Rosy Cross Order were also not limited to the physical body. Their greatest curative powers supposedly pertained to the spiritual realm, healing the ignorance of society through the medicine of spiritual understanding.[22] This "medicine" was supposedly for the healing of individuals, races, and nations.[23] Again, we see the provision of God in Christ replaced by an esoteric substitute (Revelation 2:7; 22:1–3).

## The Invisible College and the Crown of Britain

Esoteric societies have often been intimately associated with European nobility. A prime example of this is the Royal House of Stewart, which provided Scotland and Britain with several of their sovereigns. This royal dynasty has also been linked to the "Grail family" and factors in greatly to the history of the Templars, Rosicrucians, and Freemasonry.

The Rosicrucians themselves were said to have been formally instituted by King Robert the Bruce, whose descendants made up the Royal House of Stewart. And it was during the period of Stewart rule in Britain that the Rosicrucians really began to flourish and link themselves with a highly influential scientific organization in Britain known as the Royal Society. This society included the likes of Robert Boyle, Christopher Wren, Isaac Newton, and Robert Hooke, who is known as the "father of microscopy." With the emergence of the Royal Society, the door would be opened wide for the promotion and propagation of scientific knowledge and, inevitably, esoteric philosophy. Many of the society's members were not only Rosicrucians but also Freemasons.

## London and a "New Jerusalem"

Between the second and fifth of September in 1666, the city of London suffered a horrendous fire that began in a bakery on Pudding Lane, not far from where London Bridge stands. The homes of approximately seventy thousand of London's eighty thousand residents were destroyed, along with many churches—including St. Paul's Cathedral. The main layout and historic architectural structures of London today largely reflect the extensive rebuilding projects that ensued in the years following the fire. One of the greatest influences to work on London's reconstruction was Rosicrucian and Royal Society member Sir Christopher Wren.

It was Wren who was given the task of rebuilding the famed St. Paul's Cathedral which, according to some, was purposely rebuilt in a manner and location that would, somewhat esoterically, link it with the temple that once stood in Jerusalem. The church was repositioned in a way that aligned it with the old church of the Knights Templar—Temple Church. This church was modelled after the Church of the Holy Sepulchre in Jerusalem, which is positioned not far from where Solomon's temple once stood. The positional relationship between the Church of the Holy Sepulchre and the Temple Mount in Jerusalem is reflected by the relationship between the new St. Paul's and the Temple Church in London.[24] In this context, St. Paul's Cathedral was built and located to be representative of a new temple of Solomon.[25]

This affinity toward Solomon's temple on the part of the Masonic and Rosicrucian members of the Royal Society was not without significance. Apparently, many of the Society's members believed that in rebuilding London they were actually creating the New Jerusalem,[26] the heavenly city depicted at the end of the book of Revelation. Pagan and occult legend refer to what is known as the phoenix bird, which is said to combust and burn up in its own flames, only to be reborn as something new and better. It is interesting that it was out of the fires of the old London that the new London was reborn as a "New Jerusalem," a pattern that reflects the mythology of the phoenix. Interestingly, on the southern pediment of the new and current St. Paul's Cathedral is a phoenix bird chiselled into the building. It would appear that the builders of the new London were well aware of the phoenix symbolism and the "New Jerusalem" that emerged out of the Great Fire.

In the seventeenth century, London appears to have served as a utopian New Jerusalem dreamed of by the esoteric philosophers, as Britain stood as the major hotbed and source of esoteric activity and propagation. However, in the following century a new nation would be born that would inherit Britain's position as an esoteric lighthouse. In the movie *National Treasure II: Book of Secrets*, which, like its prequel focused on the esoteric Freemasons, there is scene that shows the domed St. Paul's Cathedral in London fading out into the domed Capitol building in Washington D.C. The scene depicts a change in location for the main actors, as they travel to Washington from London in pursuit of additional clues to solve a great mystery. Domes on buildings—particularly churches—are often regarded as symbolic of the celestial realm. This seems to be the case with St. Paul's Cathedral, whose domed roof appears to represent the heavenly "sphere" that God controls.[27] Could there be, as *Book of Secrets* seems to subtly hint, a connection between St. Paul's in London, and the U.S. Capitol in Washington?

The U.S. Capitol building is not a church. It is a government building, yet it employs the heavenly architecture of a dome. Its cornerstone was laid by President George Washington in a ceremony that saw him dressed in Masonic Regalia. To commemorate this event, a plaque was produced—known as the Masonic Commemorative Cornerstone Plaque—and placed at the old Supreme Court chamber entrance in the Capitol complex in 1932. The plaque states: "Laid Masonically on September 17, 1932 in commemoration of the laying of the original cornerstone by George Washington."[28]

One of the paintings found on the inside of the Capitol dome is the *Apotheosis* [deification] *of Washington*, which features George Washington rising into the heavens and becoming a god. He is surrounded by thirteen maidens who represent the original thirteen colonies. The painting also features numerous Greek and Roman gods and goddesses. Additionally, Washington is flanked on either side by the goddesses Liberty and Victory. Some natural questions might be, "Why incorporate such things in a government building? Why include a painting that deifies a mere mortal? Could the domed structure of the U.S. Capitol, so similar to St. Paul's Cathedral, symbolize the transfer of esoteric activity from London to the New World? Could the U.S. Capitol, in a way similar to the mythical temple of Atlantis, be both a spiritual temple and a government temple?"

## Sir Francis Bacon and a "New Atlantis"

We would be remiss to leave this chapter without taking a brief look at perhaps the most influential Rosicrucian in history: Sir Francis Bacon. Bacon (1561–1626) was a highly influential English scientist and philosopher who contributed greatly to the development of scientific inquiry. He served as the Lord Chancellor of England during the reign of King James I, and was also a practitioner of law. He was knighted in 1603. Bacon has been described as the founder of English Masonry, and the guiding light of the order that preserved the "Secret Doctrine of the Ages" during the dark Middle Ages—the Rosicrucians.[29]

Bacon had a profound interest in utopianism. He laid out his vision for the ideal society in his 1627 novel *The New Atlantis.* Much like the sought-after "New Jerusalem" or "philosophic empire," Bacon's utopia represented the best that humanity could conceive of—an ideal state where generosity, piety, dignity, and enlightenment could be found. In the novel there is a university of scientific learning known as the House of Salomon. The novel also features a mythical land by the name of Bensalem. *Ben* is the Hebrew word for "son" while *salem* means "peace." The name, then, means "son of peace". Was Bacon equating the New Atlantis with the New Jerusalem? Interestingly, *The New Atlantis* was not published until one year after Bacon's death. Manly P. Hall states that the reason for this is that Bacon's book revealed too much concerning the pattern that the secret societies would employ in building their new utopia.[30]

Concerning the House of Salomon, there are indications that Bacon's scientific university was really a prophetic (intentionally prophetic, as opposed to something supernatural) allusion to the Royal Society, which would be established officially in Britain after Bacon's death. In a subsequent printing of the 1667 *History of the Royal Society of London*, the introduction states most definitively that the fictional university in *The New Atlantis* was a prophetic reference to the Royal Society.[31] This being the case, one wonders if the New Atlantis and Bensalem were also "prophetic" references to real locations!

Sir Francis Bacon was also quite influential in the European colonization projects of the New World. He has even been referred to as the "founder of modern America."[32] Interestingly, a postage stamp was issued in 1910 out of Newfoundland, Canada, commemorating Bacon's colonization work. About Bacon, the stamp read, "the guiding spirit in Colonization Schemes in 1610." Bacon's influence in the European colonization of North America may lend support to the idea that the New Atlantis was in reality the New World of North America, and more specifically, America itself! As Francis Bacon played such an influential role in the development of European Masonry and the Rosicrucian Order, it is not surprising to see his vision for a utopian world based on science and philosophy at the very heart of these two esoteric orders. And as both these orders exerted a great deal of influence on the construction of the United States of America, it is fascinating indeed that many have identified America as the New Atlantis.[33]

## Pulling It All Together

Two highly influential esoteric societies in particular are often closely linked to the medieval Knights Templar. These are the Rosicrucians and the Freemasons. In understanding these two organizations, we can begin to appreciate the reality and historicity of the esoteric agenda, which is to perfect the human person and construct a utopian civilization. These goals reflect a *right* desire but a *wrong* methodology. These desires for a greater existence reveal the human need for restoration to God and redemption from sin. However, these cannot come about through the philosophies and methods of man, but can only be given by God, through Jesus Christ.

# 11

## Mysteries of Freemasonry

The influence of Freemasonry on the development of the modern West—particularly the New World—is tremendous. Though clearly a legitimate secret society (or a "society with secrets," as some Masons would have it), Freemasonry's origins are disputed and difficult to discern. Some trace them back to 1717, the year that Masonry was officially organized in England. Some trace them back to the builders of Solomon's temple. Others go farther back, pointing to the Tower of Babel as Masonry's true beginning. Still, others look to ancient Egypt as the genuine birthplace of Masonry. In many ways, each of these has contributed to Masonry's development, be it a historical link or a mythical one. We will begin our investigation into Freemasonry with Rosslyn Chapel in Scotland—perhaps the most famous building in the world as it pertains to esoteric spirituality.

### The Chapel of the Grail

Rosslyn Chapel is like an esoteric book carved in stone. Founded by William Sinclair in the fifteenth century, the chapel is filled with symbolism pertaining to Christianity, Judaism, paganism, Templarism, and Islam. Sinclair was obviously not intending to construct a church solely for the propagation of the gospel of Jesus Christ. The chapel is more of a synchronistic structure incorporating elements of various faiths, traditions, and beliefs into one building than a Christian church. According to researcher Kevin Gest, the building is actually regarded as an embodiment of esoteric knowledge.[1]

The chapel has been linked to the Holy Grail, which is no surprise given its medieval history and reputation as a building that conceals something (or some secret). Many have theorized that the chapel is where the Holy Grail—the actual cup of the Last Supper—now resides. Others have proposed that it hides the ark of the covenant. Some believe that the chapel now contains the ancient scrolls supposedly recovered from Jerusalem by the Knights Templar. Interestingly, the chapel has often been protected from excavation, despite requests by various groups to dig beneath Rosslyn to determine once and for all if it is indeed hiding something.

What does seem to be the case is that Rosslyn represents an *ideology*—one that occurs over and over again in esoteric philosophy. Interestingly, according to Tim Wallace-Murphy and Marilyn Hopkins, the very name of the chapel is revealing. When spelled in its alternate form of "Roslin," the name translated from the Gaelic rendering means "ancient knowledge handed down through the generations."[2] Whatever "ancient knowledge" Rosslyn conceals, William Sinclair, who had Templar links, seems to have wanted it preserved in stone. This knowledge/ideology seems to, at the very least, be related to the concept of unity among religions and philosophies. This is evident by the Christian, pagan, Jewish, and other religious elements found blended together in the chapel.

Despite the many mysterious elements associated with Rosslyn, perhaps most bizarre and curious is its association with the ancient Jerusalem temple. When one compares the floor plan of Rosslyn Chapel with Herod's temple that stood in Jerusalem, a virtually identical match is achieved. The western wall of Herod's temple aligns with the western wall of Rosslyn. Rosslyn contains many pillars, but two of them are especially distinct. One is located in the southeast section of the chapel, while the other is in the northeast. These two pillars align with the Boaz and Jachin pillars of the temple.[3] The entire aesthetic design of Rosslyn resembles the Jerusalem temple. It has in fact been called "a Temple of Solomon."[4]

A picture that has emerged among Rosslyn and esoteric researchers is that there appears to be a connection between the temple of Jerusalem, the Knights Templar, Rosslyn Chapel, Freemasonry, and an esoteric philosophy that stands in opposition to biblical Christianity. This philosophy is encoded in the various intricate carvings found at Rosslyn Chapel and includes the concept of one God accessible by all faiths. In light of this, Rosslyn may be the single most important edifice in the conveyance of esoteric wisdom from the Templar-medieval world to the Masonic-modern world. How fitting it is, then, to associate this building with the Grail.

One view maintains that the Templars did indeed recover scrolls from underneath the ruins of the Jerusalem temple. According to Knight and Butler, Rosslyn Chapel was designed to be a new repository for these Templar documents.[5] This might partly explain the chapel's temple-like design, as it may have been deliberately created to supposedly serve as a repository for what was previously held at the temple in Jerusalem.

We must remember that by the time of Rosslyn's construction, the Templars were a fugitive group, condemned and chased out of France. William Sinclair, whose family had Templar connections through Hughues de Payen, may have designed Rosslyn as a means of counteracting the church's persecution of the Templars, preserving Templar beliefs in the process.[6] As Wallace-Murphy and Hopkins note, books, readers of books, and authors could be burnt for heresy, but a stone building could serve as a permanent library of Gnostic instruction. Of William Sinclair, they note:

> The architect, builder and patron of Rosslyn Chapel, he created a storehouse of secret coded Templar information, a superb legacy to all who seek spiritual enlightenment: Rosslyn Chapel is a veritable, three-dimensional "teaching board" of Gnostic, late medieval initiation.[7]

If indeed the Templars recovered scrolls in Jerusalem and reburied them at Rosslyn, then the esoteric and alternative views of Judaism and Christianity that supposedly were contained in these scrolls were also brought to Rosslyn. We can thus see once more how fitting it is that Rosslyn should be linked to the Grail. As we have seen on many occasions thus far, the Grail can be used as a symbol for the stream of esoteric spirituality that runs parallel, yet opposed, to God's revealed truth.

Rosslyn possesses many mysteries, some of which are yet to be revealed. The key to Rosslyn's mystique may indeed lie within Freemasonry. A greater understanding of Freemasonry may provide a greater understanding of Rosslyn. Interestingly, Knight and Lomas state quite definitively that the starting place of Freemasonry was the construction of Rosslyn Chapel.[8]

## What is Freemasonry?

Freemasonry is an international organization supposedly aimed at individual moral self-improvement[9] and service to humanity as a means of worshipping God.[10] It consists of numerous lodges (meeting houses) worldwide that are frequented by men of every race, religion, and social status. It is often presented as a brotherhood that fosters mutual dependence among its members. Women are generally not allowed to become members of Masonic lodges. However, there are numerous Masonic-type organizations for women, such as Job's Daughters, and the Order of the Eastern Star.

Anyone can be admitted to the craft so long as they meet one mandatory requirement: a belief in God. Thus, whether one is a Christian, Jew, Muslim, Buddhist, Deist, or pagan, if they believe that there is a God, they may become a Mason. The God of Freemasonry, however, is clearly not the God of the Bible. Soldier, Confederate military officer, and influential Mason Albert Pike (1809–1891), who also authored *Morals and Dogma*, affirmed that the true philosophic religion is the belief in the one called Lucifer.[11] Pike, whose monument currently stands at Judiciary Square in Washington DC (Fig. 1, see page 140), attributes to Lucifer a divinity equal to that of the God of the Christians, whom he identifies as *Adonay*. He also expressed his belief that Lucifer was in reality that "good" being, while Adonay was the "dark" and "evil" one. In *Morals and Dogma*, Pike also affirms Masonry's role as a unifying agent among the religions of the world, bringing Jews, Christians, Muslims, and others together in prayer to one God. Freemasonry has a motto that states "ordo ab chao" (Fig. 2, see page 140), which means "order out of chaos." This phrase reveals the Masonic hope that people of different backgrounds—assumingly religious backgrounds—will eventually be "enlightened" and come together in peace.[12]

Jack Harris, a former Freemason who became a Christian, notes in his book *Freemasonry* that the order and its teachings are all based upon ancient satanic and pagan rituals.[13] Harris's experience with the order helped him to realize that the God of the Christians was not one and the same with the "god" of Masonry. Prayers in the Lodge were not allowed to be said "in Jesus' name." Certain actions against the promotion of the Lord Jesus Christ were taken in order to not "offend" members of other faiths. This was an indication to Harris that the God of the Bible was not the one embraced by the Masonic Order.

Masons are gradually "enlightened" into esoteric knowledge and rituals through a series of initiatory steps known as "degrees." The higher a Mason advances, the more "light" he is given. The more advanced degrees consist of occult ideas drawn from the pagan religions of ancient Greece and Egypt.[14] Thus, the member who attains these higher degrees is made privy to esoteric knowledge preserved from the ancient world. The total number of degrees a Mason can attain depends on which of the two Masonic streams (Rites) he belongs to—the York Rite or the Scottish Rite.

Freemasonry also has various symbols, each of which is filled with esoteric meaning. Perhaps the most well-known symbol is the square and compass with a letter *G* on the inside. The square is said to represent morality and truthfulness, while the compass symbolizes the use of action coupled with knowledge, restraint, and skill.[15] The *G* has been said to represent God or geometry—possibly a reference to "sacred geometry," which was an art employed by esoteric orders throughout the ages as a means of conveying esoteric belief through geometric shapes and patterns.

Another famous emblem of Freemasonry is the all-seeing eye, which adorns the Great Seal of the United States and is found on the U.S. one-dollar bill. The eye supposedly represents the eye of Providence, or the Supreme Deity. It also reflects Masonry's affinity toward ancient Egyptian paganism, as the all-seeing eye is based on the ancient Egyptian deity Horus.

Central to Masonic teaching is the temple of Solomon. In fact, Freemasonry, while admitting people of all faiths, seems to have a special affinity toward not only Egyptian symbolism but Judaic as well. The House of the Temple in Washington D.C. is a Masonic temple that also serves as the headquarters of Scottish Rite Freemasonry, Southern Jurisdiction, in the U.S. It is also a library and museum and is the home of the "Supreme Council, 33°." In the temple/museum is a Masonic altar with golden Hebrew writing (Fig. 3, see page 141) on the side. There is also a painting of a slightly opened curtain with a Star of David or hexagram behind the curtain (Fig. 4, see page 141). One can also find a sword with the Star of David just below the grip, and an emblem of what resembles a menorah just above the grip. Freemasonry is *not* a Jewish organization. Nor is it a cover for some sort of "Jewish conspiracy," which some have wrongfully (and irresponsibly) claimed exists. This affinity

Figure 1

Figure 2

Figure 3

Figure 4

Figure 5

Figure 6

toward Judaic elements is a curious one and may reflect a self-claimed inheritance of some sort relating to ancient Israel. However, it is clear that Masonry *does not* honor the God of Israel.

Regarding Solomon's temple, Freemasonry uses the construction of the temple as an allegory for the perfecting of the human individual.[16] In this context, the human person is in a sense a "temple" that must be perfected. As the temple was constructed by builders and brick layers, so the "Masons" are supposedly responsible for the building and constructing of the human person. This, then, makes Freemasonry a means by which the human person—and by extension, human civilization—is to be perfected.

There does, however, seem to be more to the story as it pertains to the temple. To Freemasonry, Solomon's structure is not just any building. It is central and integral. Freemasonry even employs the pillar symbolism of Boaz and Jachin—the two pillars located in Solomon's temple that have apparently been mimicked at Rosslyn. According to Masonic legend, these pillars represented the power of the Supreme Being.[17]

Masonic teaching actually traces the significance of the pillars back even further than Solomon's temple. In Masonic lore, the pillars represent an ancient civilization and its lost knowledge. In order to preserve their knowledge of the arts and sciences[18] from an impending catastrophic judgment (either through flood or fire), members of the civilization supposedly carved their knowledge onto stone pillars that were to be able to survive both fire and water. The judgment came but their knowledge was preserved. One pillar was supposedly later found by the Egyptians, while the other was found by Jews on the spot where Solomon's temple was to be built. Perhaps this partly explains why Egyptian and Judaic symbolism abound in Freemasonry.

The twin pillars are also pictured in the House of the Temple (Fig. 5, see page 142). Especially notable are the letters *J* and *B*, referring of course to Jachin and Boaz. There are also two actual pillars standing together in the temple known as the "Pillars of Charity" (Fig. 6, see page 142). Beneath each pillar is the phrase *Sanctum Templi* or "Holy Temple."

Recall that earlier on we saw how the goddess principle factors in greatly to esoteric philosophy. In ancient Babylon, the goddess was Semiramus. In Rome she was Venus. In Grail lore she is Mary Magdalene. The Egyptian counterpart is, of course, Isis. According to Hall, Freemasonry as an institution is Isis.[19] He refers to it as the "womb" in which initiates are born, a birth that he terms the "second or philosophic birth." Figuratively speaking, Hall then regards the initiates—those Masons enlightened into the mysteries—as "sons of Isis." This is important. Recall from chapter 4 how we saw that this goddess has been widowed by the death of her husband-king. In Egypt, this death was brought about by the actions of Set, who, being the Egyptian counterpart to the Babylonian Seth, represented the religion that opposed the esoteric mysteries. Osiris was murdered, which represents the death of the pagan stream. However, it was Isis' son Horus, whose eye has been adopted into Masonic symbolism, who is to avenge the death of Osiris.

Thus, when Hall calls Masonic initiates "sons of Isis," he is, knowingly or not, identifying the Masonic initiates with Horus—the avenger of Osiris's death, bringing about the triumph of esotericism over that which had frustrated its development—the revelation of the true God. He is also equating the school of Masonry with the goddess, the source of esoteric enlightenment and empowerment. As Isis was the widow who sought to restore her husband and king, so the figurative sons of Isis—the Masonic initiates—are on a quest to restore and heal the Masonic institution of its widowhood, a widowhood that came about through the loss of what is called the "living Word."[20] These sons of Isis are now on a quest to discover and restore this lost word.

The "Word" alluded to by Hall appears to be a reference to the so-called missing word of Freemasonry, a concept introduced to Masons during the ritual of the third degree. Hall equates this lost word with the phallus of Osiris,[21] which, if you recall from chapter 4, was the one part of Osiris's body Isis was not able to recover. The legend states that a miraculous resurrection of Osiris would occur should all his body parts be found. Yet, she could not find the phallus. Thus, the missing phallus of Osiris that left Isis a widow is equated with the lost Word of Freemasonry that leaves Masonry, symbolically, a widow. Interestingly, the Egyptian obelisk, according to legend, represents the lost phallus of Osiris. The obelisk is today a Masonic symbol and is often found on Masonic gravestones.

It could be that, as Horus avenges Osiris's death, so the Masonic initiates (the figurative "sons of Isis") are to exact revenge on that which made Masonry a widow. This would imply recovering the lost wisdom and, assumingly, the lost word. Thus, we can once again see the familiar esoteric principle of recovering that which was lost. In this regard, the lost Word can be equated with the Holy Grail, while Freemasonry (the "goddess") can be equated with Mary Magdalene and all the goddess figures before her. Meanwhile, the so-called bloodline of the Holy Grail—the children of Isis/Magdalene—can be equated with the initiates of Freemasonry, who proceed to bring about the restoration of the lost knowledge and the philosophic empire.

As we have seen, the metaphor of the lost Grail, the lost wisdom, the lost city of Atlantis, etc. to be rediscovered typifies the antagonism between the esoteric world and Judeo-Christianity. It symbolizes the hidden nature of the esoteric/occult world in its pursuit to replace Christianity as the religion of the West and create a new philosophic world order. It symbolizes the kingdom of Satan struggling against the kingdom of God for universal and terrestrial supremacy. Masonic author Le Couteulx de Canteleu wrote a book in 1863 entitled *Les Sectes et Sociétiés Secrètes* (Sects and Secret Societies). In this publication, he stated that the aim of secret societies was, is, and has always been the struggle against Christianity and the church.[22] Another author, Vicomte Leon de Poncins, noted that the aim of Freemasonry was to pervert the Christian nature of the West, converting it into a Masonic "religion."[23] Apparently, the destruction of the Christian faith is a must in order to establish what is referred to as the "new political and social city" in its place.[24] De Poncins goes on to note that the conflict against Christianity is one between God and man with reason alone being the thing that leads man in this struggle.[25] This is very revealing. According to de Poncins, the Masonic goal is to replace Christianity, the predominant underlying faith of the West, with a Masonic philosophy led by intellectual reason. This calls to mind the goal of the Rosicrucian Order.

Today, the fundamentals of Christianity are being called into question almost every day through movies, books, documentaries, university lectures, etc. Christianity is increasingly being branded as a hoax. This current trend suddenly takes on a new meaning when we understand that the eradication—or at the very least, the transformation—of fundamental Christianity in the West has reportedly been the goal of the secret fraternities such as Freemasonry for hundreds of years. Today, Freemasonry serves as a reservoir and channel of ancient esoteric knowledge. The Freemasons are the custodians of the ancient mysteries, a present-day organization embodied by ancient esoteric wisdom.

**Operative and Speculative Masonry: The Roots of the Modern Order**

Freemasonry is often described as being either Operative or Speculative. Operative Masonry simply refers to literal stonecraft masonry—the use of brick and stone, etc. for the purposes of erecting structures. The term "Freemasonry" is actually an abbreviation of the phrase "Ancient, Free, and Accepted Masons." The early Freemasons seem to have been closely related to actual stonemasonry. Speculative Masonry refers not so much to literal stonemasonry but to philosophic, metaphoric masonry.

It is through Operative Masonry that a link is made between the esoteric society and the builders of structures such as the Tower of Babel. The art of stonemasonry has been traced back to the Egyptian pyramids, the pyramids of Mexico and South America, and the building of Solomon's temple in Jerusalem.[26] According to Harris, Freemasonry of today bases much of its degree work on King Solomon's temple, with Solomon even symbolically regarded as Freemasonry's first Grand Master.[27]

Operative stonemasonry was employed by many of the castle and cathedral builders of medieval Europe. There was an organization known as the Roman College of Artifices that was made up of craftsmen who were responsible for transmitting stonecutting and setting techniques to cathedral builders throughout Europe.[28] These masons got together in guilds known as lodges. To this very day, the meeting houses used by Masons are known as "lodges." Much of the splendid architectural work found in Europe's many cathedrals is attributed to the skills employed by the medieval stonemasons.

Some have linked the exceptional knowledge of the medieval stonemasons with the Knights Templar, who are believed by some to have acquired geometric skills employed by the masons while they were in the Holy Land. Tim Wallace-Murphy notes that there is a definite link between the Templars' return to Europe from the Holy Land and the sudden rise of what is referred to as Gothic architecture in Europe.[29] It is interesting that one of the fraternities of masonry involved in the European cathedral projects was known as the Children of Solomon—an obvious link to Solomon and his temple. The famous Chartres Cathedral in France, a church with possible Templar connections, was constructed by this group.

Stonemasons were also called upon in the construction of Rosslyn Chapel. William Sinclair was himself the patron of Scottish craft-masonry, even serving as the Grand Master of the Scottish masonry guilds. Of all the cathedrals and churches built by the masons throughout Europe, Rosslyn is regarded as the core church of the esoteric Freemasonic Order.[30]

Rosslyn Chapel may very well be the single most important factor in the transition from Operative Freemasonry to Speculative Freemasonry. William Sinclair was closely associated with stonemasonry, as was another Sinclair—also named William—who became the first elected Grand Master of the Masonic Grand Lodge of Scotland, a more "speculative" brand of Masonry, in 1736.

In *Solomon's Power Brokers*, authors Christopher Knight and Alan Butler affirm the possibility that Rosslyn Chapel, with all of its esoteric carvings and elements, may be a structure of encoded esoteric knowledge, designed intentionally that way by William Sinclair. The purpose for such a structure would be to both preserve and transmit the ancient and medieval esoteric doctrines forward. The authors describe Rosslyn as the "hardware" (the message in stone) and speculative Freemasonry as the "software." When the two are brought together, the program runs.[31] Thus, Freemasonry may be the method by which the esoteric knowledge of the ancient and medieval world—encoded at Rosslyn—is decoded and propagated forward to the modern world and beyond.

Masonic Lodges served as "places of refuge" for those esoteric philosophers who disturbed the church with their unorthodox beliefs. Seventeenth- and eighteenth-century Britain, as we saw in the previous chapter, witnessed a surge of esoteric interest that gained the displeasure of the church. The operative guilds were widespread, and brought individuals together in such a way that fostered fellowship, trust, and potentially, secrecy. As such, these guilds could serve as "underground" meeting places for esoteric adherents, with the operative guilds being a sort of "cover organization" concealing an esoteric network within. As author Jack Driver notes, Masonic records from London dating back to the early seventeenth century reveal that individuals were being admitted to the Masonic guilds that possessed none of the requirements formerly needed.[32] The guilds ultimately became the method of preserving esoteric and mystical belief from the church, transforming themselves from meeting places for actual stonemasons to lodges of esoteric philosophers. Today's esoteric Freemasons are completely of the speculative kind, using the old Operative Masonry metaphorically.

## The Royal Connection

Many see 1717 and the formation of the United Grand Lodge of London as the "official" birth of organized Freemasonry. However, even this is disputed. There does appear to be clear evidence of Masonic activity predating the formation of this Grand Lodge, particularly in Scotland. Part of the dispute may relate to the fact that early Scottish Freemasonry was largely promoted by the Stewarts and their supporters, while later English Masonry was promoted by the rival and newly installed Hanoverian monarchy and their supporters.

It is believed that Freemasonry first came to England from Scotland in 1603, when King James Stewart VI of Scotland acquired the English throne, becoming King James I of England. James was himself a Freemason. When King George I and the House of Hanover acquired the throne, Freemasonry was fervently endorsed. Three years later, the United Grand Lodge of London was formed as an official body of Masonry. However, some Masons felt that this new brand of "official" Masonry had drifted from its original form. As such, a rival Grand Lodge was set up in 1751, with its members being known as "Ancients" or "Antients." The members of the original Grand Lodge were appropriately called "Moderns."

The schism was eventually healed after lengthy negotiations between the two sides, leading to the creation of the United Grand Lodge of England on December 27, 1813. The first Grand Master of this new Masonic body was HRH the Duke of Sussex, Prince Augustus. This Masonic body would grow to become the largest and most authoritative in the world, and remains so to this very day. It is intimately united with the British Crown and must always have a royal prince serve as its Grand Master. The current Grand Master is the Duke of Kent, Prince Edward. While control of reunited world Freemasonry came to rest with the British Crown, it has been suggested that English Masonry may not at all be Freemasonry in its purest form, and that much of Masonry's Scottish origins—and the rituals associated with those origins—may have been lost with the establishment of the Hanoverian monarchy.

By the time of the creation of the United Grand Lodge of England, Freemasonry had already established itself throughout other parts of Europe. Lodges were established in Ireland (1725), Spain (1728), Germany (1737), and various other places. European colonialism also ensured that Freemasonry would spread around the globe,[33] which it did as lodges would eventually be established in Asia, the Caribbean islands, and of course, North America. It would be in America that Freemasonry would find its greatest expression, influencing the founders of what was to become the most powerful country in the world.

**Rex Deus: An Alternative Christianity and a Counterfeit Judaism**

One of the more fascinating explanations given for the establishment of Freemasonry pertains to the Rex Deus hypothesis we explored in chapter 8 involving two supposed messianic bloodlines. Rex Deus researchers have formulated a compelling argument for a link between Freemasonry and the ancient messianic beliefs of the Essene/Qumran community. In this scenario, Freemasonry serves as a "Rex Deus Religion,"[34] preserving and disseminating certain ideals of the supposed Rex Deus family group.

One of the symbols often seen in Freemasonry is the hexagram, which is often equated with the Star of David. This symbol has a multitude of meanings. When the two triangles are *interlocked*, it is said to symbolize the *union* of humanity (the right-side-up triangle) with God (the upside-down triangle). When the right-side-up triangle is *on top of* the other one, it has been said to represent the *triumph* of man over God—perhaps reason over religion. The right-side-up triangle represents humanity because its base is on earth while its point reaches toward heaven. The upside-down triangle represents God because its base is in heaven with its point reaching down to earth. The six points of the star have also been equated with man, who was created by God on the sixth day. We also know from the book of Revelation that the number of the Antichrist is 666, which is the number of man in triple magnification.

The hexagram has also been said to represent the opposites of fire and water. Recall that in the esoteric and occult world, balance is everything. Black must balance with white, while good must balance with evil. Here, the right-side-up triangle of fire (fire points upward) balances with the upside-down triangle of water (water falls from the sky downward). The hexagram has also been said to be an esoteric symbol for the union of male and female, emphasizing balance and union between the sexes. The right-side-up triangle represents the masculine phallic symbol, while the upside-down triangle represents the receptacle of the female and her womb.

According to Knight and Lomas, the symbol may be representative of balance between God and man *through the union* of king and priest. Here, the right-side-up triangle symbolizes the kingly messiah who reigns on earth in God's stead. The upside-down triangle symbolizes the priestly messiah, who represents man before God. The two triangles together in the hexagram symbolize the kingdom of heaven on earth and the two messiahs—the priest and the king.

Recall from above how we saw that with the rise of the house of Hanover in England came the creation of a new Masonic body and the possible distorting of the older Scottish brand of Masonry. Since the Grand Lodge of England exercises authority over worldwide Freemasonry, some, including Masonic authors Knight and Lomas, have wondered what the ancient Scottish rituals may have consisted of. These lost rituals would include many of those behind the thirty-three degrees of the ancient Scottish Rite brand of Freemasonry. As such, they decided to conduct extensive research into these Scottish degrees, which led to some rather astonishing revelations.

Aided by the library of a Balkan scholar by the name of Dimitrije Mitrinovic, the authors were able to reassemble degrees from ancient Scottish Masonry and decode their apparent meaning. What they found was an esoteric belief system that seemed to shed tremendous light on what they had speculated concerning alternative views of Jesus, Christianity, the house of David, the temple, Rex Deus, and God. It seemed to establish a definite link between the so-called "Jerusalem church," the Templars, European royalty, and Freemasonry. It seemed to present pure, original Freemasonry as a counter-Christian movement based on the beliefs of the Qumran community and an esoteric understanding of the Jewish priesthood. I obviously do not agree with the authors' stance on the person of Jesus Christ and the truth of the gospel, as they take a rather revisionist approach to the history of Christianity. However, their research into the origins of Freemasonry and the mysteries of the hidden rituals of the Scottish Rite has produced some intriguing results pertaining to Masonry. What follows is a selective summary of the authors' findings regarding the degrees of Scottish Rite Masonry, as detailed in their work *The Second Messiah.*

The first three degree rituals of the Scottish Rite are identical to those of English Masonry, and did not warrant much attention from the authors. The fourth degree, known as the "Secret Master," is where we begin. This degree involves a ritual whereby initiates are told of the significance of the treasures of the Jerusalem temple, including the altar of incense and the golden candlestick. There is also a certain jewel associated with this degree that bears the letter Z, which we are told stands for Zadok, a priest during the time of King David and King Solomon.[35] Knight and Lomas point out that the Dead Sea Scrolls, along with another ancient document, indicate that a group known as The Sons of Zadok arose to become the Qumran community.

Jumping ahead to the thirteenth degree—the next degree of relevance to Knight and Lomas—we are introduced to an individual known as Enoch who foresees an imminent apocalyptic disaster through either fire or flood. This degree, known as "The Royal Arch of Enoch," is set at the time when Solomon's temple was constructed. According to this degree, Enoch carves onto two pillars—one of brick and one of stone—the secrets of science and of building (constructing). We are told that sections of these pillars survived the disaster, which ended up being a flood. Sections from one pillar were found by the Egyptians, while sections from the other pillar were found by the Jews during the excavations for the foundations of the temple. This degree calls to mind Atlantis, which was supposedly destroyed by a flood. It also suggests that knowledge from the pre-flood civilization was passed on to both the Egyptians and the Jews—two peoples of whom Freemasonry has drawn heavily from in the formulation of its rituals.

The ritual of the fourteenth degree, called "Scotch Knight of Perfection," is carried out in a room in which one sees objects designed to resemble the fragments of Enoch's pillar. The ritual claims that King Solomon established a "Lodge of Perfection" to rule over lower degrees of Masonry, and that the members of this lodge held their initial secret meeting in a vault underneath the incomplete temple. It is also claimed that Solomon's temple was built using the knowledge acquired from the pillar of Enoch. Here, then, a link is made between a pre-flood advanced civilization—possibly regarded to be Atlantis (we are not told what the pre-flood civilization was) and the temple of Solomon. The ritual then goes on to affirm that descendants of these original "perfect masons" accompanied Christian princes during their Crusades to the Holy Land. At this time, the descendants of the Solomon priesthood supposedly elected a Chief and Grand Master of their own. Apparently, the many Christian princes of the Crusader kingdom of Jerusalem possessed admiration for these priestly descendants. Some princes eventually desired to be a part of their order. They were accepted, and the order's secrets spread among the European nobility as Freemasonry.[36]

All this concerning the European nobility, Freemasonry, and the descendants of the temple priesthood (who according to the description given seem to refer to the Knights Templar) appears to be revealed in this astonishing degree. The authors identify this degree as confirmation that a group participating in the first Crusade were believed to have been descended from the Jews. This, of course pertains to Rex Deus and, specifically, the priestly line. This would appear to indicate that Freemasonry came about as a result of Christian European princes being admitted into the order of the descendants of Solomon's priesthood, spreading the hidden knowledge throughout the ranks of European royalty.

The "Knight of the Sword and Knight of the East" is the fifteenth degree and deals with the rebuilding of the Jewish temple after the Babylonian captivity.

Moving ahead to the seventeenth degree, which is known as the "Knight of the East and West," we now come face-to-face with what would appear to be an undeniable reference to the Knights Templar. Knight and Lomas note how the ritual associated with this degree reveals that the degree itself was organized by the knights involved in the Crusades in the year 1118. These knights, who took vows of friendship and secrecy, were eleven in number, which, as Knight and Lomas point out, corresponds precisely to the first eleven Templars. The presiding officer in this degree is known as the "Most Equitable Sovereign Prince Master," who is supported by the high priest. This reference to both a prince and a priest is intriguing.

One of the most revealing degrees is the twentieth degree, which is known as "Grand Master," and pertains to the building of a spiritual temple. A lecture associated with this degree refers to the destruction of the Jewish temple by the Romans in AD 70 and makes mention of "brethren" who were in the Holy Land at the time, grieving the loss of the temple. These brethren then left the Holy Land with the goal of eventually erecting a temple. The degree then reveals that these people, in leaving the Holy Land, divided themselves into various lodges and spread throughout Europe. The degree even notes that one of the groups that fled the Holy Land eventually ended up in Scotland, where they established a lodge. Knight and Lomas suspect that this one group may be a reference to the Sinclairs.

This degree also tells of how the people who settled in Scotland had in their possession the "records of their order"[37] with the intent of storing them in an abbey in 1140. Knight and Lomas suggest that these records may pertain to the documents supposedly recovered by the Templars from underneath the ruins of the Jerusalem temple and may ultimately have been later reburied at Rosslyn.

The next degree, which is known as "Patriarch Noachite" involves a ritual that retells the story of the Tower of Babel. According to the degree, the tower was built by a descendant of Noah named Peleg, who was punished by God for building the tower but later forgiven. Concerning the Tower of Babel and its builders, we read in the Bible:

> "Come, let us make bricks and burn them thoroughly."
> And they used brick for stone, And they used tar for mortar.
> They said, "Come, let us build for ourselves a city, and a tower whose top will reach into heaven." (Genesis 11:3–4)

There is no mention of a "Peleg." However, it is not too difficult to see the operative "Masonic" reference with respect to brick, stone, and mortar.

The twenty-third degree is known as the "Chief of the Tabernacle" and speaks of how the biblical Aaron and his sons formed the Jewish priesthood.

Members of this degree are known as "Levites," which calls to mind the hereditary line of the priests of Israel.

The "Prince of the Tabernacle," which is number twenty-four, is another highly revealing degree. As Knight and Lomas note, this degree tells how God told Moses to build a tabernacle to house the ark of the covenant, and by setting up this tabernacle the royal line of the Jews would be established. Knight and Lomas note that the Masonic candidate in this degree is told that he has now received what is known as the "Masonic science," which was handed down since the time of King Solomon and revived by the Templars. Knight and Lomas were shocked to see a specific reference identifying the Knights Templars as the ones who restored what they refer to as the lost knowledge of the Jews.[38]

The candidate in this degree—now made a high priest—is then told what Knight and Lomas describe as the "Grand Word." This Grand Word seems to be identical to the Lost Word referred to by Manly P. Hall that has "widowed" the Masonic Order. The high priest is told that this mysterious word was discovered by the Templars when they were in Jerusalem. We are also told that the Templars discovered three stones while excavating underneath the ruins of the temple, one of which contained this mysterious word. They then carried these stones with them back to Europe and used them as foundation stones for their first lodge in Scotland.

Moving ahead to degrees twenty-seven and twenty eight, we can now begin to discern a decidedly anti-Christian bent. Known as the "Grand Commander of the Temple," the twenty-seventh degree involves a "court" where its members sit at a round table and interrogate the candidate who is in the middle of the circle. The ritual affirms that the Knights Templar were wrongly condemned by the church. It also affirms, quite blasphemously, the importance of denying the cross of Christ. Interestingly, it was in October of 2007, seven hundred years to the very month that the Templars were persecuted and disbanded by the Roman church, that the Church released information indicating that the Templars were innocent of heresy and blasphemy all along. This suggests a reconciling between the Catholic Church and the Knights Templar, and contrasts the many esoteric ideas to come forward in recent years regarding the Knights Templar

It was the Duke of Sussex, Prince Augustus, who took Freemasonry away from its Scottish form and origin when he became the first Grand Master of the United Grand Lodge of England. As Knight and Lomas note, upon becoming Grand Master, the Duke was initiated into the thirty-three degrees of the Ancient Scottish Rite. However, he was so angered by the contents of these degrees that he set out immediately to have them changed. Today, many of these degrees are conferred upon candidates without the ritual being given.[39] It is, of course, the ritual that reveals the nature and details of the degree. Perhaps it was the blasphemous nature of rituals such as that found in the twenty-seventh degree concerning denying the cross that angered the duke, who had briefly considered joining the clergy of the Church of England.

The twenty-eighth degree, known as the "Knight of the Sun," speaks of the "One True God," which is apparently the essential part of the ancient ceremonies and mysteries.[40] This may at first appear to be a contradiction, considering the esoteric and pagan nature of Masonry. Christianity, Judaism, and Islam also affirm that there is one God. Masonry, however, is dissimilar to these three faiths in that it adopts a deistic attitude toward God. Deism holds the belief that there is indeed one God, but that this God does not necessarily intervene in the affairs of man. Freemasonry, unlike biblical Christianity and Judaism, maintains that this one God can be identified by many names, depending on how different people perceive him.[41] As noted in the *Concise Dictionary of the Occult and New Age*, the deity of Freemasonry is one that represents a unity of all the diverse world religions.[42]

It is very fitting that this degree should be called the "Knight of the Sun," for to the ancients the sun was (or represented) the supreme deity. This was particularly true in ancient Egypt, where Osiris, the great god-king who was said to have been fatally wounded, was represented by the sun in the sky. According to William Cooper, Osiris was the name of a bright star that was believed by the ancients to have been cast down to earth.[43] Of course, as Cooper notes, the Bible indicates that Lucifer—the "morning star" and "bright one" who sought to exalt himself—would be "thrust down to Sheol" (Isaiah 14:15). We also know from the book of Revelation that the dragon, or Satan, will be cast down to earth during the days of God's outpoured wrath (Revelation 12:9–10).

There are a couple of crucial points to gather from this revelation concerning the "God" of Freemasonry. First, the careful reader will have thus far noted that these Masonic degrees are filled with Judaic references. We must not be deceived by this! Again, Freemasonry is *not* a Jewish organization, nor a Jewish belief system. Its incorporation of Jewish elements, such as the six-pointed star (star of David/hexagram), has nothing to do with true Jewish thought. We know this because the deity of Freemasonry is not YHWH, the God of Israel, but a universal "god" accessible by all religions. Second, in uniting the adherents of many religions under one "deity," Freemasonry has preserved an esoteric system of belief that is set up in opposition to the true God of heaven. This may be setting the stage for the ascendency of apocalyptic Babylon—the global religious system that will, at least initially, control the religious affairs in the Antichrist's kingdom.

The thirtieth degree is known either as the "Knight of the Black and White Eagle" or the "Grand Elect Knight K-H." Knight and Lomas note that the ritual in this degree speaks of the Templars vowing vengeance on the ones responsible for the death of their last known Grand Master, Jacques de Molay. This of course calls to mind Pope Clement V and King Philip IV of France—the church and the French nation. Interestingly, there is a legend that states that Jacques de Molay predicted the deaths of his torturers, hinting that both the Pope and the king would meet him at the judgement of God before the year ended. Strangely, both Pope Clement and King Philip died in 1314, shortly after de Molay's death earlier that same year. There is also a legend that claims that during the French Revolution, at the execution of King Louis XVI, an unknown individual jumped onto the guillotine, dipped his hand in the king's blood, and shouted "Jacques de Molay, thou art avenged."

The thirty-second degree, known as the "Sublime Prince of the Royal Secret Master of the Royal Secret" picks up once again on Jacque de Molay. As Knight and Lomas note, the Masonic candidate at this degree is told of something known as "the Royal Secret of the death of Jacques de Molay." Knight and Lomas note that this secret appears to never have been written down. Thus, it appears that it is known only to initiates. Knight and Lomas focused on the word *royal* and strongly felt that it could suggest that de Molay was of the line of David, possibly even regarded as a messiah.

The thirty-third degree, which is the highest in the Scottish Rite and equivalent to the Order of Knights Templar (not necessarily the same as the medieval Knights Templar) in the York Rite, is called the "Sovereign Grand Inspector General." Knight and Lomas don't say too much about this degree other than it had something to do with the secret of the origins of Freemasonry. These origins, the authors feel, relate to some sort of resurrection and star cult of the ancient kings of Egypt.

Knight and Lomas's research into these degrees and rituals was based on a wide volume of sources, the most significant of which was a work published in 1921 entitled *Freemasonry and the Ancient Gods*, by a highly esteemed author—J.S.M. Ward. Ward was himself a Freemason. They also used works written by nineteenth- and early-twentieth-century Masonic researchers. If they have correctly assembled these degrees and rightly interpreted the ritual meanings, the implications are staggering. The authors saw in these degrees confirmation of their suspicion that Freemasonry was a system of beliefs and rituals inherited from the Knights Templar, who themselves believed they had inherited their ideas from the Jewish priesthood. However, the ultimate source of the teachings supposedly dates back to the distant past and a pre-flood civilization that left their intellectual legacy on two pillars found by the Jews and the Egyptians.

This ancient knowledge was supposedly employed in the building of Solomon's temple, and later inherited by the Templars who excavated the site of the temple and brought the knowledge to Europe. Along with this emphasis on knowledge and the priesthood is the royal line of David, which may have been an integral part of the "royal secret" found within Freemasonry. Masonry, according to Knight and Lomas's presentation of these degrees, inherited the legacy of Solomon's temple and the Jewish priesthood following the Roman siege of AD 70, the creation of the Templars, and the Templars' flight to Scotland. And from Scotland Freemasonry proceeded forward, ultimately becoming the world's largest esoteric society, though its rituals were greatly altered from their original form. From the cults of antiquity to the Freemasonic teaching of today, a cable of esoteric thought exists concerning God, history, and what is perceived as the "truth" that actually stands in direct opposition to the true God's revealed truth. Not surprisingly, Knight and Lomas, in light of what they have learned concerning Freemasonry's origins, voice their concern for a revisiting of Christianity's origins.[44]

## Pulling It All Together

Freemasonry represents the channel that has carried forward to the modern era the esoteric mysteries of both the medieval world and antiquity. It is a deistic organization, with its members professing a belief in one true "God" who unites all of the "national" or "cultural" gods. Quite plainly, the supreme being of Masonry is in reality Satan.

While Masonry's origins are shrouded in mystery, it does appear that Rosslyn Chapel in Scotland maintains a rather important link in the development of Freemasonry and its transfer of esoteric knowledge from the medieval world to the modern world. Rosslyn also serves as an example of Operative Masonry, which involves actual craft and stonemasonry as opposed to Speculative Masonry, which is more metaphoric and esoteric.

Freemasonry has been likened to the widowed goddess of pagan lore. This is a most fitting description of the order, as it truly does serve as a great school of the esoteric arts. In the ancient mystery religions, it was the goddess who was largely responsible for the conveyance of esoteric knowledge, power, and wisdom. In this context, Masonry possesses the Grail—the thing that can supposedly bestow that which only God can give—personal and societal perfection. There are only two systems—the genuine, and the counterfeit. A counterfeit messiah is coming, and Freemasonry, perhaps more than any other organization, is setting the stage for his soon coming arrival.

# 12

## The New Order of the Ages

### The Baconian Plan

The goal of the esoteric fraternities has been the creation of a society built, not upon the truth of God's Word, but rather upon reason, intellect, and esoteric philosophy. Coupled with this is the desire to build a civilization that is governed by or created by "enlightened democracy." For much of the Middle Ages, and through to the early modern period (approximately AD 1500–1800), European civilization was the "home base" for societies and organizations linked to esoteric spirituality. The Knights Templar were established in Europe. Rosicrucianism developed in Europe. Though Freemasonry's origins are blurry, it was in Britain that the craft firmly established itself as a visible "official" esoteric society. Another esoteric order established in Europe is the Order of the Illuminati. The word *illuminati* is the plural of the Latin *illuminatus*, which means "enlightened." The Illuminati were established on May 1, 1776, in Bavaria by Adam Weishaupt, a German professor of law at the University of Ingolstadt.

They had five main goals:[1]

1. The abolition of monarchies and all ordered government
2. The abolition of private property and inheritances
3. The abolition of patriotism and nationalism
4. The abolition of family life and the institution of marriage, as well as the establishment of communal education for children
5. The abolition of all religion

The order was effectively dissolved in 1784 when Karl Theodor became the ruler of Bavaria, though many believe that "Illuminism" continues to this day within the ranks of Freemasonry.

Europe in the Middle Ages and early modern period was a society governed by both church and crown. On continental Europe there was the dual leadership of the Pope and various monarchs. In Britain, following English Christianity's break from Rome, there was the Church of England and the British monarchy. These ruling powers of the medieval/early modern period are often regarded as "Christian establishments," and in some ways proved to be a hindrance to the esoteric societies. How were the esoteric societies to achieve their long-cherished dream of enlightened democracy and a philosophic empire? For the esoteric agenda to move forward, a civilization would need to be established free from the restrictive hand of the church and church-sponsored monarchies.

Six decades after Christopher Columbus discovered the New World, Sir Francis Bacon was born, a man who would eventually do more in his time to further the esoteric agenda than perhaps any other. Bacon's *The New Atlantis* spoke of a utopian society based on principles that Bacon believed to be associated with the legendary civilization of Atlantis.[2] According to occult researcher Andre Nataf, Bacon's novel describes the utopian vision that underlies many secret societies, including that of modern Freemasonry.[3] Bacon himself was the head of both the Rosicrucian Order and Freemasonry of his time.[4] As such, he exerted tremendous influence over these two orders.

Regarding Bacon's utopian vision, it is widely believed that the New Atlantis spoken of by Bacon would ultimately find fulfillment in the New World, and specifically America. Sir Walter Raleigh, a British explorer who would ultimately prove to be a great influence in the British colonization of America, was a member of a secret society known as the Baconian Circle. This society believed that America was to be the New Atlantis promised by secret societies.[5]

The discovery of North America by its European colonizers provided an open door for the secret societies to move their agenda westward. The ultimate goal, of course, was a philosophic empire along the lines of what Francis Bacon envisioned in his *The New Atlantis*. According to Manly P. Hall, Bacon was the head of a certain secret society consisting of men united together for the cause of world democracy, and saw in the New World an opportunity to establish this sought-after philosophic empire.[6] Unlike Europe, the New World was free from political tyranny and religious intolerance,[7] providing the secret societies with the perfect opportunity to lay the foundation for a global democratic commonwealth.[8]

Charles A. L. Totten (1851–1908), military officer, professor, and writer, affirms the notion that Bacon's New Atlantis has been fulfilled in America. Author David Ovason writes:

> Totten equated the birth of the United States with the beginnings of what he called the New Atlantis—a title given to a work by Francis Bacon, one of the mysterious financial backers of the Virginia colony, in the early seventeenth century. Totten's vision was both mystical and vast, for it stretched from the mythological beginnings of America into the distant future, when, he believed, the spiritual achievements of the United States will be recognized by the world.[9]

Author Nicholas Hagger makes a similar statement and hints that the role of America as a New Atlantis was to affect not just the New World but the world as a whole:

> [Accepted Masons] received the secret universal knowledge of the oneness and brotherhood of mankind and the Secret Doctrine of the Ages that America would become a Utopian New Atlantis and create a better world. . . . In this paradise, men would follow a religion of reason and become gods and work for a universal world republic that would replicate the Utopian conditions in Atlantis throughout the world. Meanwhile the secret knowledge would be passed on from generation to generation in the Freemason's Temple.[10]

Note that the two quotes above by Ovason and Hagger hint that America's purpose was not strictly domestic but had a global reach. Its "spiritual achievements" were to be recognized by the world, while its inhabitants were to work for a "universal world republic." This world republic can be equated with the philosophic world empire we learned of in chapter 9. As we shall continue to see, it appears that America's purpose was to serve as the catalyst that would bring about this global philosophic empire. With this Hall agrees:

> In America shall be erected a shrine to Universal Truth, as here arises the global democratic Commonwealth—the true wealth of all mankind, which is designed in the foundation that men shall abide together in peace and shall devote their energies to the common cause of discovery.[11]

Author Gary Kah sheds more light on this from a Christian perspective, acknowledging his belief that America's purpose in the overall plan of secret societies was to lay down the groundwork for a coming world government and then to lead humanity to the very threshold, if not into, the new world order.[12] Interestingly, Henry Kissinger, former American secretary of state and national security advisor, commented in January 2009 that the global situation at that time was such that a new world order could be established, and pointed to President Obama as the one whose task it is to develop a strategy for America during a unique time when a new world order could be formed.[13]

## The New World and the New World Order

By the time the new colonies in the land that would become America grew to thirteen in number, the mother country of Great Britain had undergone a royal transition from the House of Stewart to the House of Hanover. It was during Hanoverian Britain that Freemasonry largely evolved from a Scottish-based society to an English-based social club–type society. It was also during Hanoverian rule that the American Revolution took place, as the colonies sought to free themselves from the harsh treatment and heavy tax burden laid upon them by the British Empire.

Britain not only imposed heavy taxes on the colonies but also implanted various other laws designed to maintain British sovereignty. As the colonies did not have any representation in the British Parliament, many in the colonies perceived Britain's behavior as unjust. Other measures were taken by Britain that also affected the emerging economy of the colonies and limited how much the merchants of the colonies could earn. Eventually, the colonies began to reject British sovereignty, ultimately leading to the Revolutionary

War. A major component of the American Revolution was the infamous Boston Tea Party of 1773, an event that was designed to protest the "taxation without representation" policies of the British. Many have noted that the event itself was carried out by members of a Masonic Lodge. Which lodge is a matter of debate, as some have cited St. John's Lodge, while others point to St. Andrew's Lodge.[14]

The Revolutionary War officially began in 1775 and ultimately led to the July 4, 1776 Declaration of Independence, which officially severed the colonies from British rule. With this declaration was born the United States of America. The colonies had severed themselves from the tyranny of Hanoverian rule. However, they had also, wittingly or unwittingly, accomplished another goal that actually lay at the very heart of esoteric philosophy. They had effectively opened the door for the rise of a democratic republic among the nations of the world, free from both church and crown. This might not seem too significant, except for the fact that, by the time of the American Revolutionary War, Freemasonic lodges had been established quite widely and had already begun to exert a great deal of influence.

According to *New Age*, a Masonic publication, it was members of the Masonic Order who instigated the Revolutionary War, and Masonic generals who carried it through.[15] The Boston Tea Party was apparently itself a recessed Masonic Lodge meeting.[16] The Declaration of Independence was signed by fifty-six representatives from among the thirteen colonies. Of the fifty-six, fifty-three were Master Masons,[17] including Benjamin Franklin, John Hancock, and Thomas Nelson. Though many of America's Founding Fathers were Masons, it is clear that biblical Christianity also came to America very early on in its development. This is made evident by the Mayflower Compact, which was a testimony to the Christian faith of some of America's earliest settlers. To accuse all those involved with the American Revolutionary War, the Declaration of Independence, and the creation of the U.S. Constitution—the latter of which also involved Masons—with deliberately following an occult/esoteric agenda would be wrong.

Many of America's Founding Fathers were likely solely concerned with escaping the tyranny coming from the British crown. There are some ideals that both Christians and Masons would affirm, such as freedom of religion, freedom of conscience, freedom of the individual, and freedom from tyranny. These are noble ideals embraced by Mason and Christian alike.

However, it is clear that while Christianity was indeed very prominent in early American society, esotericism was also seeking to take root, and in fact did exert a considerable measure of influence over America's development.

In order to adequately detect the Masonic/esoteric nature of America's foundation and destiny, we must look beyond individuals to the imprint left on American society by the esoteric societies as a whole. What should concern us most are not so much the political ramifications of Masonic influence but the spiritual. The Masonic influence on the development of the United States has opened the door for the pagan/esoteric belief system to openly permeate American society. While Christianity remains a strong element of American society, the difficult truth is that esoteric paganism—from very early on—has been widely embraced and is rapidly gaining a greater acceptance. That esotericism and Masonry have exerted and continue to exert a great deal of influence on American society is clear, as we shall now see.

***The US Capitol***: We saw in chapter 10 how Freemasonry was involved in the building of the U.S. Capitol building in Washington D.C. George Washington, America's first president, laid the cornerstone on September 18, 1793 dressed in Masonic regalia, an event that has been commemorated through the *Masonic Commemorative Cornerstone Plaque* located in the Capitol Complex. Washington himself was a Mason, though his participation in the lodge after receiving his initial degrees was extremely infrequent.

We have also already seen the overt pagan symbolism designed into the Capitol building and, specifically, the inside of the Capitol dome. One painting on the inside of the dome is called *Apotheosis of Washington*, which means the "deification" of George Washington. This calls to mind the pagan/New Age concept of the deification of the human person—the spiritual evolution to godhood. It resembles the lie spoken of by Satan to Eve in the garden of Eden, that she could "be like God" if she partook of the forbidden fruit. It also calls to mind the Gnostic ideal of being "freed" from the "dark," "evil" material world to become a "pure" spirit. We also saw how the painting incorporates numerous Greek and Roman gods, and how the goddess of liberty and the goddess of victory flank the deified Washington on each side. Such overt pagan imagery displayed at such an important government building in America is intriguing.

***The Statue of Liberty***: Liberty and freedom are both Christian and Masonic ideals. But to adherents of pagan belief, liberty is not just an ideal but a deity. This is perhaps best seen in one of America's most enduring symbols—the Statue of Liberty. Situated in New York Harbor, and holding in her hand a torch of freedom, is Lady Liberty, a spin-off of the ancient Roman goddess Libertas. The first temple of Libertas was built upon the Aventine Hill, one of the Seven Hills of the city of Rome, by Tiberius Gracchus, a Roman politician. Another temple was erected by Publius Clodius Pulcher, also a Roman politician, on the Palatine Hill. Libertas's association with the Seven Hills of Rome is fascinating when we consider Babylon the Great in Revelation 17, who is seated on seven hills.

The official name of the New York monument is "Liberty Enlightening the World." This reminds us of the global influence that American ideals were to have on the world at large. Enlightenment is to occur through liberty, a major value of American society in comparison to other parts of the world that suffer under repressive regimes. Is America to be a torch of freedom, promoting liberty and freedom in a dark world? This, of course, is in and of itself good. However, there is no mention here of YHWH, nor Jesus Christ. The deity exalted is the Roman Libertas. This is another example of good idea/bad methodology.

***Washington D.C.***: Washington D.C. is a fascinating city, filled with esoteric symbols and structures. There is, of course, the Washington Monument (Fig. 7, see page 166), which, as we have already seen, is in reality a giant obelisk. The obelisk is intended to represent the male sex organ, which, according to Egyptian lore, was the one part of Osiris's body that Isis could not locate to bring him back to life. We have seen that the missing phallus can be equated with the lost wisdom of the pagan world, supplanted by the triumph of true divine revelation. The obelisk then can be seen as a symbol pointing to the restoration of the ancient mysteries to a place of prominence over Christianity.

In Egypt, obelisks stood in the ancient temple of Isis.[18] In Washington, it stands in the complex known as the National Mall just west of and in perfect alignment with the Capitol. Though there are buildings and trees lining the northern and southern borders of the mall, an observer standing at the U.S.

Figure 7

Figure 8

Figure 9a

Figure 9b

Figure 10

Figure 11

Figure 12

Figure 13

Figure 14

Figure 15

Figure 16

Capitol, or the Lincoln Memorial to the West, has a virtually un-obstructed view of the obelisk, as a vast open space exists between the Capitol and the monument and the memorial and the monument.

Thirteen blocks directly north of the monument is the Masonic House of the Temple, the headquarters of Scottish Rite Freemasonry, Southern Jurisdiction, USA. It is the Home of the Supreme Council, Ancient and Accepted Scottish Rite, Southern Jurisdiction, USA. According to their official Web site, the name "House of the Temple" is associated with the word *heredom*—a word related to the "Holy House," supposedly pertaining to Solomon's temple.[19] Many symbols, paintings, and structures pertaining to Masonry can be seen within this temple. The House of the Temple also serves as a Masonic museum and library.

Structures and buildings incorporating ancient pagan figures and images into their architecture can also be seen throughout other parts of Washington D.C. The National Archives building, located just north of the National Mall, is one example, having chiselled into its pediments various pagan images. The building also draws several parallels to the design of Solomon's temple. Inside the Rotunda of the Archives, one can find the twin pillars associated with Masonry (Fig. 8, see page 166), and the Jewish temple. There is even what resembles a sealed doorway in the interior of the rotunda, flanked by two additional pillars. The sealed doorway calls to mind the veil guarding the entrance into the Holy of Holies in Solomon's temple. The entrance to the rotunda includes a fenced doorway, almost as if to separate the rotunda from other sections of the building in a manner similar to the way the Holy Place was separated from the porch in the Jerusalem temple.

***The Great Seal of the United States and the one-dollar bill***: Perhaps nowhere else is America's esoteric past and apparent destiny more clearly presented than the Great Seal of the United States. The Seal, first adopted in 1782, is found on the reverse side of the one-dollar bill (Fig. 9a, 9b, see page 167). It was placed on the dollar bill in 1935 when former President Franklin D. Roosevelt ordered a new design to the dollar. Roosevelt himself was involved in the designing of the new dollar, along with the former secretary of agriculture, Henry A. Wallace, and the secretary of the treasury, Henry Morgenthau. Apparently, all three of these men were Freemasons.[20] The seal itself, which has evolved over time, largely came about through the work of Benjamin Franklin, Thomas Jefferson, and John Adams.

When one looks at the reverse side of the one-dollar bill, the most striking feature is the Egyptian-style pyramid with the hovering capstone containing an eye. The pyramid, and the entire roundel that contains it, are part of the reverse side of the Great Seal. The obverse side of the Seal is seen on the right of the reverse side of the dollar bill and includes a roundel containing an eagle.

The reverse side of the Seal is perhaps the more intriguing side. The pyramid and the "eye of Providence" are symbols associated with both the Freemasons and the Illuminati. At the base of the pyramid is a date written in Roman numerals: MDCCLXXVI, which translates to 1776. This date is regarded as a reference to July 4, 1776—the date of America's independence. Some have also linked it to May 1, 1776—the date of the Illuminati's official birth. As the date is on the first step of the pyramid, so the subsequent steps of the pyramid are believed to represent time, with 1776 being the point at which construction of the pyramid began.[21] The thirteen steps in the pyramid (excluding the capstone) may also relate to the initial thirteen colonies of independence. One possible implication here is that the United States is, or represents, a project begun by thirteen colonies in 1776. As the pyramid is unfinished, so the project remains to be completed. The completion of the project is symbolized by the capstone of glory, embodied by the eye of Providence, a symbol that dates as far back to at least ancient Egypt. In ancient Egypt, the "all-seeing eye" was known as the eye of Horus. Some identify it as the eye of Osiris, Horus's slain father who, according to some versions of the Egyptian legend, is to be avenged—symbolically bringing about the triumph of the ancient pagan mysteries over the true revelation of God.

The grand project begun in 1776 and moving toward some future fulfillment appears to be related to the motto found just underneath the pyramid: "Novus Ordo Seclorum." The phrase translates to mean "a new order of the ages" and is an adaptation from a poem written by the poet Virgil. The original words from the poem are "Magnus ab integro seclorum nascitur ordo," which translate to mean "The great series of ages is born anew."[22] George W. Bush seems to have referred to this grand project in his 2005 inauguration speech when he made mention of the "new order of the ages" declared by the Founding Fathers. The context of Bush's statement seemed to suggest that there is some sort of "ancient hope" underlying the New Order of the Ages", and that this "ancient hope" is not yet fulfilled.[23]

That the "New Order of the Ages" is not yet complete can mean one of two things. Either the United States as a nation is not yet complete, or the new order of the ages itself is not to be confined to America alone. What is this grand consummation that America is heading toward, and why does it seem to be in some way linked to Horus, as indicated by the eye of Providence completing the pyramid? Masonic author David Ovason notes that it was Charles Thomson who suggested that this motto be included on the Great Seal. Thomson, who was secretary of Congress at the time, apparently believed that the American civilization would ultimately bring about a new world order.[24]

A new order of the ages is in contrast to an old order. We have already seen enough to know that the new order spoken of here is not the kingdom of Christ promised in Scripture but may be the reemergence of an occult/esoteric society subverting Christianity. According to Gardner, the truncated pyramid is symbolic of the loss of the old wisdom forced underground by the church. The all-seeing eye of Providence on the Great Seal of the United States, then, may represent the reemergence of the "old wisdom" *through* American civilization, a land free from the tyranny of a monarch and the "restrictive hand" of a Pope. As Horus was, we are told, the one who avenged Osiris's death, so the eye of Providence, often identified as the eye of Horus, serves as the perfect symbol for the completion of the new order of the ages—returning the ancient mysteries to a place of prominence over true divine revelation.

Very similar to the pyramid on the U.S. dollar bill is the one found on the roof of the Israeli Supreme Court building in Jerusalem (Fig. 10, see page 167). Though the Supreme Court building is white, the pyramid on the roof is green—matching the green pyramid of the U.S. Seal. The pyramid on the roof even has a dot near the top which, coincidentally, seems to match the eye of Providence in the elevated capstone on the Great Seal. There is one critical difference: the Supreme Court pyramid, unlike the pyramid on the Great Seal, is complete. There is no elevated or missing capstone.

According to the Web site of The Judicial Authority of the State of Israel, the pyramid represents the second temple period[25] when the Jews in captivity returned to Israel and rebuilt the temple. Many Jews today believe that it will be the Messiah who allows for and sets in motion the work to build the next temple in Jerusalem. We have already seen how significant the temple is to Freemasonry. We have also seen how the temple was to be an integral part of the kingdom of heaven on earth in the philosophies of the Qumran community. Biblically, we know that a rebuilt temple will factor greatly in the Antichrist's plans, as the man of sin will sit in the temple claiming to be God. Is it possible that the unfinished pyramid, with the eye in the capstone, is an esoteric message pointing to the rebuilding of the temple as coinciding with the rise of a new world order? For the Masons, who so passionately revere Solomon's temple, could there be a greater symbol to celebrate the birth of their new order than a brand-new temple? Genuine peace is elusive right now in Jerusalem, as both Jews and Arabs regard the Temple Mount as sacred (Fig. 11, see page 168). The birth of any new world order would almost certainly require a peaceful resolution to the Middle East conflict. A new Jewish temple could potentially be part of that resolution.

Above the eye of Providence on the Great Seal is found another Latin motto: "Annuit Coeptis." This phrase translates to mean "He favors our undertaking." This motto was also adapted from a poem by Virgil, where a prayer is said to the god Jupiter requesting aid for some daring enterprise. It is a prayer designed to entreat help from the pagan gods.[26] Christian author David L. Carrico warns that the deity being summoned in this prayer is not the God of the Bible but the ancient Egyptian god Osiris,[27] the father of Horus.

The obverse side of the Seal, seen to the right on the reverse side of the dollar bill features a hexagram made up of thirteen starts. Once again, the thirteen is significant, calling to mind the original thirteen colonies. Note, however, that the hexagram is situated in a cloud of glory. Might this be a veiled reference to Rex Deus and Solomon's temple? The hexagram in general has been said to represent the prince and priest—the pillars of the temple—while the cloud of glory calls to mind the presence of God, which was manifest in the Holy of Holies of the temple. Interestingly, occult researcher Tracy R. Twyman identifies the American Republic as a "New Temple of Solomon" created by Masons.[28]

Carrico calls the hexagram one of the most powerful symbols in the occult.[29] He identifies its pagan use as being traced back to when Solomon forsook the God of Israel and turned to pagan worship. Apparently, magicians who practice black magic and Satanists credit Solomon with originating this symbol.[30] 1 Kings 11:4–8 records Solomon's lapse into idolatry, identifying

Chemosh and Molech as two of the gods he honored. Amos [illegible] records how Israel also honored other gods, and that a certain star was [illegible]ated with these gods. The hexagram is also known as the Seal of Solomon, which obviously links Solomon with this symbol. Some make a distinction, however, identifying the Seal of Solomon as interlocking triangles, whereas the hexagram consists of overlapping triangles. We do not know whether or not Solomon really originated this symbol, or if the star mentioned in Amos is in fact the hexagram. However, it is clearly regarded as a pagan and occult symbol by followers of the occult.

The obverse side of the seal contains one motto: "E Pluribus Unum," which means "out of many, one." This refers to the creation of one nation out of thirteen colonies, though some see it as a reference to one world out of many countries. Just like "Annuit Coeptis," the motto contains exactly thirteen letters. Indeed, sets of thirteen are seen throughout the Great Seal. In addition to the thirteen letters in these mottos, there are the thirteen stars in the hexagram. There are thirteen arrows in the eagle's clutch. The eagle is also clutching an olive branch with thirteen leaves. As a side note, olive branches are a symbol of peace, while arrows are a symbol of war. The eagle has both war and peace in its clutch. There are also thirteen bars and stripes in the eagle's shield. It is difficult to discern why the fascination with the number thirteen. Certainly, there were the thirteen colonies. There is also the fact that the Templars were arrested on the thirteenth. In addition to this, thirteen makes up the number of witches in a coven, while the number thirteen has also been regarded as an anti-Christ number.[31]

The meaning of the eagle on the obverse side of the Great Seal is open to debate. It has been associated with many things, such as spiritual power symbolizing the "chief among the gods."[32] The eagle has also been an emblem of various empires throughout history, such as the Roman Empire and the Holy Roman Empire. Interestingly, according to David Ovason, both the eagle and the motto "Annuit Coeptis" were associated with the chief pagan god Jupiter, who was the equivalent of Zeus.[33] Both appear on the Great Seal.

Some have made a point of mentioning that the eagle on the current version of the Great Seal is an adaptation of an earlier design that featured a phoenix bird, a notable pagan symbol. This has confirmed to some that America is merely a catalyst to bring about a global new order of the ages.

Like the phoenix, America is to "combust" (self-destruct) at some point in the future, and out of its own flames and ashes give way to a new world order. Alternatively, some, such as Hagger, note that the phoenix is symbolic of Atlantis reborn in America.[34]

There is one additional motto found on the one-dollar bill, in between the two roundels of the Great Seal. The motto, written in English, is "In God We Trust." This phrase is vague enough that it can be embraced by Americans of any religious background. No doubt, many Christians identify this motto with the God of the Bible. Nothing in the motto itself necessarily precludes Christians from claiming it as a statement of faith. But in light of the overwhelming Masonic/esoteric elements found on the Great Seal, and the Masonic principle of a Grand Architect of the Ages uniting the worshipers of all "gods," we cannot comfortably state that this motto is directed to the God of Abraham, Isaac, and Jacob.

Tracy R. Twyman notes that Masonic and mystical symbolism has been used on American currency as a means of distinguishing the money of the New World from that of Old World Europe.[35] Rather than follow the European trend of adorning coins and bank notes with an image of a reigning monarch or monarch-type figure, the Founding Fathers agreed that the new American currency should be adorned with emblems reflecting pro-democratic Enlightenment philosophy.[36] Twyman also notes that America was founded by men with a philosophy rooted in the occult to be a potential New Jerusalem or New Atlantis that would guide the rest of the world into a democratic and enlightened new world order.[37]

The United States is not alone in its overwhelming display of pagan/esoteric imagery and symbolism. Canada is another example of a country that features esoteric symbols and subtleties in some of its architecture and structures. Like the United States, many of the early explorers to Canada were Christians. There is a tale—disputed by some—that claims that the phrase *The Dominion of Canada* was coined by a nineteenth-century New Brunswick premier, Sir Samuel Leonard Tilley (May 8, 1818–June 25, 1896). Tilley apparently was inspired by Psalm 72:8, which states "He shall have dominion also from sea to sea, and from the river unto the ends of the earth" (KJV). Canada, bordered by the Pacific Ocean in the west, and the Atlantic in the east, was seen in this regard as a dominion of God Almighty.

It does seem, however, that pagan and esoteric philosophy greatly influenced some of Canada's most powerful leaders throughout its history. Within the Parliament buildings, located in the nation's capitol of Ottawa, Ontario, can be found carved in stone what appear to be several pagan deities. Also visible in stone is the famed trident of Poseidon, or Neptune, the ruler of Atlantis and the seas (Fig. 12, see page 168). This affinity toward Atlantis, or the sea, is intriguing considering what we have seen concerning the desire among esoteric fraternities to establish a New Atlantis. Additionally, located on Parliament Hill is the Centennial Flame (Fig. 13, see page 169), lit in 1966 to inaugurate Canada's centennial celebrations. The flame is situated rather neatly in a fountain—displaying the opposite elements of fire and water. Located in the center of the monument is a Canadian leaf shaped in the form of hexagram missing the bottom point in order to resemble a leaf. Wrapped around the sides of the monument's center are alternating maple leaves and hexagrams. This is significant, as one of the things the hexagram can symbolize is the combination of fire and water. It is peculiar that such a symbol is placed in a monument actually *featuring* fire and water. A complete hexagram can also be seen in the clock of the famous Peace Tower on Parliament Hill (Fig. 14, see page 169).

In June 2005, a giant lawn mural could be seen along the Niagara Parkway in Niagara Falls, Ontario. The mural featured a giant Canadian maple leaf with a giant Masonic square and compass emblem set on top. Underneath the leaf and emblem were two dates, one appearing to be 1855, while the other clearly 2005 (Fig. 15, see page 170), seemingly marking an anniversary of some sort. It is quite possible that the mural was placed there to commemorate the famed Niagara Falls Suspension Bridge, which was the first of its kind in the world. The bridge, completed in 1855, linked Niagara Falls, Ontario, with Niagara Falls, New York. The year 2005 marked the one-hundred-fiftieth anniversary.

Further esoteric/Masonic influence in Canada can be seen at Canada's busiest airport: Pearson International Airport in Toronto, Ontario. Situated atop the Terminal Three building is a Masonic-type pyramid (Fig. 16, see page 170), adorning the roof in much the same way that the Jerusalem pyramid adorns the roof of the Supreme Court.

## Pulling It All Together

From the very beginning, the old esoteric orders of Europe exerted a great deal of influence on the newly developing North American continent. Many saw in America a land of opportunity in which to create their coveted New Atlantis, a civilization that would be built upon philosophy, democracy, and intellectual discovery, as opposed to the ecclesiastical authority that characterized Europe.

In influencing the development of the New World, the esoteric orders were able to establish a "Masonic Republic" in the United States of America, inaugurating a grand project, and a new age (or series of ages) known as the "New Order of the Ages." It is believed by some that out of this grand project is to come forth a global philosophic empire—a new world order! This is the quest of the "sons of Isis," the esoteric philosophers who seek a world with less Christian influence and greater occult influence. Such a world would represent the ultimate triumph of Horus and the reemergence of the counterfeit stream of spirituality initiated by Satan himself. To some it would signal the discovery of the Holy Grail, the rebirth of Atlantis, and the completion of the pyramid adorning the currency of the United States of America.

# 13

## The Coming Holy Roman Empire

As we saw in chapter 4, Revelation 17 presents the astounding imagery of a seductive woman seated upon a dreadful beast. Together these two control the kingdom that is the revitalized Roman Empire. The woman represents a religious system whose influence is global, while the beast represents a global political system. The two are, at least initially, united—a setup similar to the Holy Roman Empire of history that featured a close association between Pope and emperor. The two are so intimately connected that, as author F. C. Jennings notes, the geographic boundaries of one will be directly related to the other, and these boundaries will pertain to "Christendom."[1] There will, consequently, in the days ahead be a revival of both political Rome and religious Babylon, apparently *in* Rome.

### The Revival of Political Rome

The revival of Rome's empire can perhaps be likened to the Humpty Dumpty nursery rhyme. In the rhyme, Humpty falls off a wall, breaking into pieces. It then states that the king's horses and men could not put him back together again. Silly as this example may seem, it is actually a perfect description of the history of the Roman Empire as it pertains to its collapse. Rome was a mighty empire that ruled most of Europe, North Africa, and Eastern Asia, including parts of the Middle East. It was never defeated by an outside enemy, but rather "fell" and crumbled into many pieces through internal decay. Many, including the Roman Catholic Church, Napoleon, and Hitler, have tried in some form or another to rebuild a glorious empire on the territory of ancient Rome. All have failed and will continue to fail until the time God allows Rome to be rebuilt. The "pieces" of Rome that lie scattered like a geopolitical Humpty Dumpty are the various nation-states that sprang up out of Rome's demise: England, France, Italy, Belgium, Spain, Austria, Greece, Turkey, Syria, Egypt, and others. They also, in this author's opinion, include the civilizations that sprang out of Rome through European colonization, such as North and South America.

For over fifty years, Europe has been undergoing a unique transformation from a continent of bloodshed to the most unified continent in the world. Emerging out of the ashes of two bloody world wars is a geo-economic-political entity that is significantly unifying the continent and virtually eradicating the possibility of war between European states. The European Union (EU) is accomplishing what no other individual or entity has been able to do: reunify Europe! Today, the EU has its own anthem, flag, parliament, president, and currency. In many ways, it already acts as a *superstate.*

The vision for a United Europe was heralded by British Prime Minister Winston Churchill, who was selected to chair the Congress of Europe in The Hague from May 7–10, 1948. Churchill called for a United Europe, complete with a physical strength that would dissuade anyone from any sort of threat against it. Ironically, this declaration was made just days before Israel declared its independence.

Perhaps the most significant date in the history of the European Union is May 9, 1950, celebrated today as "Europe Day." On this date, French statesman Robert Schuman gave what is now known as the Schuman Declaration, which was a call to build a new Europe—a "federation of Europe"—out of the ashes of war.

The first step toward creating this new Europe was to pool the economic resources of France and Germany, providing both of these countries with less incentive to attack each other. Out of this pooling of resources came the European Coal and Steel Community (ECSC), which was formally instituted in 1951 by the Treaty of Paris. Signing the treaty along with France and Germany were Italy, Belgium, the Netherlands, and Luxembourg.

Six years later, the six nations signed another agreement—the Treaty of Rome—which formally created the European Economic Community (EEC) and set Europe on a course of complete economic integration. The importance of this treaty toward the ultimate creation of a federated Europe and a new Roman Empire was revealed by one of the EU's founding fathers, Paul-Henri Spaak. During a BBC documentary on the new Europe, Spaak, apparently referring to the date the Treaty of Rome was signed, admitted that on that day they were knowingly reestablishing the Roman Empire, and that they felt like Romans.[3]

Since the signing of the Treaty of Rome, the newly unified Europe has become a twenty-seven-nation geo-economic-political bloc. Of the current twenty-seven member states, sixteen make up the Eurozone, which is the area of the EU that uses the euro currency. Instituted in 1999, this currency has in just a few short years become one of the strongest in the world and serves as the second-most-traded currency in the world after the American dollar. The Eurozone is also the second largest economy in the world. Interestingly, in January 2002, CNN likened Europe's Eurozone to the form of European monetary union practiced in the Roman Empire two thousand years prior.

It is interesting to watch the development of what appears to be the creation of a new empire on the geographic territory of the old Roman Empire. However, unlike the empires of history, this empire is not being built by force but by mutual consent. The incumbent president of the European Commission, José Manuel Barroso, speaking in Strasburg, France, on July 10, 2007, likened the European Union to the organization of empires, albeit one built not by force but by mutual cooperation. Barroso stated that the European Union is unique in the history of mankind and represents what some authors have called the first non-imperial empire.[4] This is astounding! The creation of an empire through peace on the territory of the old Roman Empire can only be a signal pointing to the near appearance of the Antichrist.

It is fascinating to revisit what some of God's servants from decades ago have written concerning the revived Roman Empire before there ever was a European Union. Clarence Larkin, writing in 1919, stated that the nations found in the geographical limits of the old Roman Empire will form some sort of alliance for mutual protection during the wars that occur prior to the appearance of the Antichrist.[5] Larkin's statement is strikingly close to what actually happened in Europe. The unity that has come about in Europe following the two major wars of the twentieth century has been accomplished by mutual submission, not force. Larkin was commenting on the beast of

Revelation 17. J. Dwight Pentecost, writing in 1958, commented on how the empire of the Antichrist is built by mutual consent, not by force[6]—precisely what has occurred in the EU. Pentecost's words are strikingly similar to those of José Barroso's and those who refer to the EU as a non-imperial empire. The great British writer Sir Robert Anderson, commenting decades ago on the tenfold division of the coming Roman Empire, notes that a family of nations living together in peace could not have been hinted at by anything in history.[7] These men were not making psychic predictions. They simply believed what the Bible stated. Of course, while these developments are fascinating—possibly even prophetic—we must wait for the final developments to know with certainty whether or not modern-day Europe represents the embryonic stages of the Antichrist's reborn Roman Empire.

During France's presidency of the European Union in 2008, French President Nicolas Sarkozy implemented his ambitious vision to create a "Union for the Mediterranean." The union consists of all EU nations plus several Mediterranean rim countries, including Israel and Syria. The Mediterranean region is, of course, the exact territory of the old Roman Empire, consisting of Europe, North Africa, and the Middle East. Indeed, Libyan leader Muammar al-Gaddafi, who rejected Sarkozy's invitation, referred to the Med Union as a "new Roman empire."[8] A map of the old Roman Empire and a map of the Union for the Mediterranean placed side by side reveal a striking similarity.

Sarkozy saw the Med Union as a means of fostering peace between Israel and the Arabs. During a major summit held in Paris on July 13, 2008 to kick off the Union, Sarkozy held hands with the then Israeli prime minister Ehud Olmert and Palestinian leader Mahmud Abbas in what appeared to be a major step toward bringing peace to the Middle East.

## The Revival of Spiritual Babylon

It is clear from God's Word that the woman in Revelation 17 identified as Babylon the Great represents first and foremost a *system* of worship. She symbolizes counterfeit spirituality that has run down through many ages. The forty-seventh chapter of Isaiah provides additional clues as to the antiquity and nature of this spiritual entity, using language similar to what is found in Revelation 17 and 18 concerning Babylon the Great. These clues confirm that this entity is not a new thing that comes on the scene during the time of the Antichrist but, rather, has been in existence from ancient times:

> "Come down and sit in the dust, O virgin daughter of Babylon; Sit in the ground without a throne, O daughter of the Chaldeans! . . . For you will no longer be called The queen of kingdoms. . . . Now, then, hear this, you sensual one, Who dwells securely, Who says in your heart, 'I am, and there is no one besides me. I will not sit as a widow, Nor know loss of children.' " (Isaiah 47:1, 5, 8)

> "For she says in her heart, 'I sit as a Queen and I am not a widow, and will never see mourning.' " (Revelation 18:7)

Isaiah also seems to link astrology and counterfeit spirituality to this entity in verse 13 by calling upon those who practice these things to try to save the woman: " 'Let now the astrologers, Those who prophesy by the stars, Those who predict by the new moons, Stand up and save you from what will come upon you' " (Isaiah 47:13).

We see then that the entity named Babylon the Great in the book of Revelation is in fact a system, but one in its final manifestation. As Ed Hindson and Tim Lahaye point out, it was at Babel where the ancient city of Babylon was built and where corporate human rebellion against God first began.[9] It was also at Babel where counterfeit religion and polytheism first originated.[10] Hindson and Lahaye also note that symbolizing the false religion of the last days as a woman calls to mind the ancient Babylonian system of worship, which led many into various occult and pagan practices, including goddess worship.[11]

It is clear then, that the kingdom of the Antichrist, depicted as a political beast and a spiritual woman, will be characterized by the widespread manifestation and endorsement of the ancient Babylonian system of worship and all its occult/esoteric spinoffs. Thus, the coming Roman Empire of the Antichrist is to consist of a spiritual element rooted in ancient Babylonian spiritual belief.

While Babylon the Great is indeed a system, it is clear that she is also an institution. It would not be possible to unite the world spirituality into one system affiliated with the political kingdom of the beast without there being a physical, visible institution to manage that system. Furthermore, we are told in Revelation 17 that the kings of the Roman Empire along with the Antichrist himself will actually hate the woman and utterly destroy her with fire (Revelation 17:16). Some will stand at a distance and cry out when they see her burning, saying "What city is like the great city?" (Revelation 18:18). It is clear from this language that while Babylon the Great is indeed a system, it is a system represented by a visible entity that can be geographically and spatially identified.

As we saw in chapter 4, Revelation 17:18 confirms that this woman is a city, and one that sits on seven mountains/hills. The city in view here is widely believed to be Rome, a city built on seven hills. This has been the view held by leading authors and biblical scholars such as Larkin, Anderson, Ironside, Hislop, Hunt, and many more. In 1 Peter 5:13, Peter uses the word *Babylon* as a substitute for Rome, further establishing a link between the city in ancient Mesopotamia and Rome. The implications here are staggering. There is only one global religious institution in Rome today, and that is the Vatican and the Roman Catholic Church (Fig. 17, see page 186). The fact that the woman is called a harlot indicates her spiritual adultery in defecting from the God she professes to serve. What seems to be presented here is a massive apostasy from true Christianity by the Church of Rome that shall actually aid the Antichrist in his rise to power. For a time, the woman and the beast shall aid each other. The Antichrist and his kings will support the false church, while the false church will support the Antichrist in his rise to prominence. This is oddly similar to the way that the Merovingian King Clovis and the Church of Rome formed an alliance for mutual benefit centuries ago.

Hindson and Lahaye note that if indeed the city of Babylon the Great represents the Roman Catholic Church, then it means that the church and the beast will together control the nations.[12] Where the beast is, there the woman is also, and vice versa.[13] They are inseparable. However, we also know that the beast eventually turns on the woman and destroys her. This is perhaps due to the Antichrist's desire for total worship. He may seek to remove all threats to his authority and adoration by destroying the church, which would be his biggest threat.

Interestingly, vengeance on religious Rome may be a goal cherished by the esoteric groups who suffered under the persecuting hand of the church.

The Roman church for centuries hunted down and persecuted those who followed the pagan and esoteric mysteries. Additionally, if there is to be a Merovingian restoration to political power, the destruction of religious Rome could be retribution for what Rome supposedly did to the Merovingians in endorsing their removal from power and replacing them with the Carolingians. Interestingly, in *Angels and Demons*, the Dan Brown prequel to *The Da Vinci Code*, the esoteric/occult Illuminati aim to exact vengeance on the Roman church by utterly destroying the Vatican by a cataclysmic explosion. The results of such an explosion, if carried out in real life, would be strikingly similar to the results of Babylon's actual destruction as described in Revelation 17 and 18, which is said to involve fire and smoke visible from the sea.

Whatever the practical reason is for religious Rome's destruction, there is no doubt as to the spiritual reason. Revelation 17:16–17 reveals that her destruction is actually God's judgement upon her. God allows the beast and his kings to be of one mind in devouring the woman. In this, God's wrath toward Babylonianism, false religion, and the Great Harlot is executed.

## The Historical Precedent

Part of the history in the creation of the Roman church involves the Roman emperor Constantine, who after his supposed conversion to Christianity issued the Edict of Milan in AD 313, which allowed Christians, previously persecuted, to worship freely. The Roman Empire was officially a pagan empire, which even included emperor worship. The Christians who worshipped the Lord Jesus Christ alone and refused to hail the caesars as Lord were ferociously persecuted for not expressing worship to the emperors. The Edict of Milan removed this threat and opened the door for Roman Christianity to become the official religion of the empire.

Constantine also oversaw the Council of Nicaea, which was convened largely to address divisions in the church. The brand of Christianity that came out of this council[14] was ultimately made the official religion of the empire by Theodosius I late in the fourth century AD. From this point on, Christianity, not paganism, would be the official "imperial" religion of Rome. The resulting union between the political empire and the church would prove to be Roman Christianity's great undoing. Jesus said "My kingdom is not of this world. If My kingdom were of this world, then My servants would be

Figure 17

Figure 18

Figure 19

Figure 20

fighting" (John 18:36). The bloody history of the medieval Roman Catholic Church is both rebuked and judged by this principle set forth by Christ.

When the Roman church became allied to the empire, it ultimately became an imperial institution controlled by political ambitions. Thus, the "servants" of this institution often picked up the sword thinking they were defending the honor of Christ. Imperial Rome and religious Rome became inseparable. This led to a decay of true spiritual fervor within the church, as political ambitions eventually eclipsed spiritual mandate. Later, when the political Roman Empire collapsed, the Roman church carried on the political and temporal mandate of the empire and in fact *was* the religious continuation of the empire.[15] This is evident in both Rome's agreement with the Merovingian Clovis, who was called New Constantine, and the crowning of Charlemagne by Rome as the "emperor of the West."

Spiritually, the new association between the political empire and the Roman church had disastrous consequences on the purity of doctrine and practice in the church. The Roman Empire was officially pagan prior to Constantine. Due to the close association between the empire and the church, many of these pagan elements began to seep into the church and actually formed a large part of Catholic teaching. Even while heading the Christian church, Constantine maintained his headship of the pagan priesthood and held the title Pontifex Maximus,[16] a title which, of course, would be associated with the Roman Popes. Constantine also referred to himself as Vicarius Christi, or Vicar of Christ. Author Dave Hunt raises a fascinating point that Vicarius Christi literally means "Antichrist," indicating that Constantine was a prototype of the coming Antichrist.[17]

Various symbols and practices within Roman Catholicism reveal the pagan elements that crept into the new imperial church through its union with political Rome. We have already seen the case of the mother-child cult. In addition to this, there is the concept of purgatory and prayers for the dead—both of which are found in Roman Catholicism and were characteristics of ancient paganism such as found in Greece and Egypt.[18] Purgatory is a concept that states that one who dies may enter an intermediary state between heaven and life on earth in order to "purge" remaining sins, a concept unfounded in Scripture and one that denies both the sufficiency of Christ's atoning work and the severity of divine judgement against sin (Hebrews 10:10–14; Romans 1:18; 3:23–26).

There is also the role played by Mary in Catholicism. In the Catholic Church, Mary is elevated to a status resembling a deity, with many encouraged even to pray to her. She is also regarded as a mediator between Jesus and humanity, something that the Bible clearly does not support (1 Timothy 2:5). As Alexander Hislop points out in his book *The Two Babylons, or The Papal Worship Proved To Be the Worship of Nimrod and His Wife*, the goddess of Babylon bore the name Mylitta, which means "the mediatrix," the title bestowed upon the Roman church's Mary.[19]

In the Roman Catholic Church, the "sign of the cross" is often made prior to and following prayers. This very sign is not of Christian origin but was practiced in the Babylonian mystery religion.[20] It represented the first letter in the name Tammuz, who was the "divine child" of the Babylonian goddess Semiramis.

Perhaps most severe is the subtle denial of the once and for all completed sacrifice of Jesus Christ on the cross (Hebrews 10:12-13). Roman Catholic theology maintains that in the Mass, and the celebration of the Eucharist, the sacrifice of Jesus is "made present". In other words, the very same sacrifice that occurred on the cross almost 2000 years ago is being continued in the Mass.[21] This is a denial of the completed, all sufficient sacrifice of Christ carried out on the cross, and makes possible the temptation for people to believe that salvation can be found in the "works" of the church, and the "works" of the individual.

Concerning Revelation 17 and 18, there are additional clues that seem to point to religious Rome as being symbolized by the woman. We are told that the woman holds a gold cup in her hand, and that the nations were made drunk with the wine of her immorality. This association with a gold cup and wine is of course strikingly similar to the gold chalice of wine in Roman Catholicism. The woman is also said to be clothed in purple and scarlet (Revelation 17:4), which just happen to be two of the most prominent colors worn by the Roman clergy. The woman is said to reign over the kings of the earth (Revelation 17:18) and to have committed immoral acts with them (Revelation 17:2). It is peculiar indeed that the Roman Catholic Church for a time did "reign over the kings" of Europe, with the elevation of Clovis and the crowning of Charlemagne by Rome serving as two examples. As Alan Butler notes, the pact between Clovis and the church basically meant that the Popes had the right to crown or depose kings.[22] The "immoral acts" committed by the kings may refer to them using the church for their own political gain, which often occurred in medieval Europe.

Finally, we are told that the woman was "drunk with the blood of the saints, and with the blood of the witnesses of Jesus" (Revelation 17:6). One of the most persecuting agents ever to exist is the Roman Catholic Church, which persecuted, burned, and killed many—including Jews and Christians—who did not submit to her authority!

Many may be alarmed—even offended—that the Roman Catholic Church, home to countless faithful followers of Jesus, should be presented in such light. Two important things need to be considered here. First of all, as Scripture reveals, it is very possible for God's people to be seduced by pagan worship. The many examples of the people of Israel in the Old Testament teach us this. Certainly the same possibility exists for a church. Nobody is immune to temptation or sin. Second, while Rome may in the end prove to be the headquarters of this religious system, it would be unfair to single out Catholicism alone in this. Indeed, Babylon the Great may be ecumenical—involving other Christian denominations such as Protestant, Anglican, and Orthodox. One is not a Christian because they are Protestant or Catholic or Orthodox. One is a Christian because they believe in what the Bible says about Jesus and trust Him accordingly. God's true church is made up of individuals out of every denomination, including the Catholic Church. The above analysis is not at all meant to be an "attack" on Catholics.

If you are reading this as a Catholic, let this encourage you to cling to Christ more than ever, not to a church. Churches may fail, but Christ never does. And for those in other denominations, let us not think that we are immune to this temptation, as if paganism can only affect the Catholic Church. Indeed, Babylon the Great will hold sway over all the earth. Babylonianism is a system, albeit one that will have a specific geographic location during the times of the Antichrist. The Vatican and the Catholic Church are not in and of themselves Babylon, since Babylon and its philosophy vastly predate the Church of Rome. However, it appears that it is within religious Rome where Babylon shall have its end-time manifestation.

## Paganism, Catholicism, and the EU

Today's European Union is largely perceived as merely an economic and political entity. However, upon close examination, it soon becomes apparent that this emerging "non-imperial empire" is characterized, somewhat strangely, by an odd blend of Catholicism and paganism. There are indeed various theories regarding the EU and the Catholic Church, some of which are not worthy of much consideration. For example, I think most would object to the claim made by some that aliens from the star Sirius are the real movers and shakers behind the EU.[23] Somewhat more plausible but still difficult to accept is the idea that the Catholic Church is orchestrating political events in Europe to rebuild the Holy Roman Empire.[24] People of such influence as former British Prime Minister Margaret Thatcher actually believed that the EU was a conspiracy orchestrated by the Vatican.[25]

An episode involving author Mathieu Paoli, who we were introduced to in chapter 7, does raise suspicions slightly, though it still lacks any degree of certainty. As previously noted, Paoli published a book revealing the findings of his research into the links between the EU's predecessor—the European Economic Community (EEC)—, the Committee to Protect the Rights and Privileges of Low-cost Housing, the Grand Lodge Alpina of Freemasonry, and former French President General Charles de Gaulle,[26] who apparently had links with the Priory of Sion's Pierre Plantard. Paoli was executed without trial some time after the publication of his book.

The EU has often been linked to the infamous Priory of Sion, either as a grand project to restore the throne of the ancient Merovingian dynasty or to serve as a new United States where the ideology of synarchy—a union of politics and esotericism—finds expression. Evidence definitively linking the Priory of Sion and the EU is sketchy. However, much like the New Atlantis of American civilization, we can detect an esoteric/spiritual influence exerted upon the EU by examining its symbols, mottos, and architecture.

***The European Union Flag***: The European Union flag (Fig. 18, see page 186) features a ring of twelve golden stars on a blue background. The design calls to mind Revelation 12:

> A great sign appeared in heaven: a woman clothed with the sun, and the moon under her feet, and on her head a crown of twelve stars; and she was with child; and she cried out, being in labor and in pain to give birth. . . . And she gave birth to a son, a male child, who is to rule all the nations with a rod of iron; and her child was caught up to God and to His throne. (Revelation 12:1–2, 5)

Some see in this vision a reference to the Virgin Mary, who gave birth to the "male child." Two familiar Catholic images are those of Mary with a garland of twelve stars on her head and Mary holding the baby Jesus. However, Laurence Gardner points out that since the woman in Revelation 12 endured labor pains while giving birth, she could not be the Mary of Catholicism, since Catholic teaching states that Mary felt no pain while giving birth to Jesus. Gardner points out that it was actually Mary Magdalene who was sometimes portrayed as wearing a ring of twelve stars.[27]

According to the October 28, 2004 edition of *The Economist* magazine, the flag reflects the EU's historical ties to Catholicism. In an article entitled "The European Commission and Religious Values," we are told that some of the EU's founding fathers, including Konrad Adenauer, Jacques Delors, Alcide de Gasperi, and Robert Schuman, were devout Catholics.[28] The article then goes on to note that the designer of the flag, Arsene Heitz, admitted to deriving his inspiration for the flag from Revelation 12 and the woman clothed with the sun. The incorrect association by some—linking the woman in Revelation 12 with the Virgin Mary—not only brings Catholicism into the mix in terms of the design of the EU flag, but also brings in the pagan concept of the goddess. As we have seen, the pagan Isis, Semiramis, etc., translates into the over-exalted Virgin Mary of Roman Catholicism. The EU flag then, whether unwittingly or not, reflects the pagan goddess principle.

That the woman in Revelation 12 represents the nation of Israel as opposed to the Virgin Mary is obvious when we consider the full passage in proper context. The passage calls to mind the vision Joseph had in Genesis 37:

> Now he had still another dream, and related it to his brothers, and said, "Lo, I have had still another dream; and behold, the sun and the moon and eleven stars were bowing down to me." (Genesis 37:9)

Joseph, one of the twelve sons of Israel (formerly Jacob) saw a vision that, much like the Revelation passage, involved the moon, sun, and stars. That there were only eleven stars in Joseph's vision is indicative that Joseph himself was one of the stars. The twelve stars together represent the twelve tribes of Israel, seen as a whole in Revelation as part of the woman. The male child birthed by the woman "who is to rule all nations with a rod of iron" is the Lord Jesus Christ who, humanly speaking, was birthed by the nation of Israel. We are then told further along in the chapter that the dragon, or Satan, after being cast down to earth during the times of Antichrist, will persecute the woman. Obviously neither the Virgin Mary nor Mary Magdalene is around today to be persecuted. As such, the woman can only be the nation of Israel, which will be persecuted by the dragon during the Antichrist's reign of terror.

By taking the symbolism meant for Israel and applying it to Europe, the flag of the EU may be an inadvertent declaration that it, not Israel, intends to be the chosen "nation" that will bring forth the male child (the child of the goddess—Horus?) to rule all nations.

Additionally, *Europa*, the official Web site of the EU, states that the circle of stars represents harmony and solidarity among the people of Europe. It also states that the number twelve traditionally symbolizes perfection, unity, and completeness, which is why twelve was chosen as the number of stars. This too is telling, for it reveals that Europe's ambition is to build a perfect and complete society, a goal similar to the vision of the ancient philosophers.

***Europe and the Goddess***: Europe is named after the goddess of Greek mythology known as Europa. Interestingly, she is often depicted as riding the bull-deity Zeus, who seduces her and carries her away. This imagery of Europa on the bull/beast may be subtly hinted at in the Bible's depiction of the kingdom of the Antichrist as a woman riding a beast.

Europa riding the beast is depicted in front of the European Council building in Brussels, Belgium (Fig. 19, see page 187). Much like what we saw in chapter 12 with America, pagan imagery and mythology displayed so openly in the EU betrays the supposed traditional religious heritage of its founding fathers.

In a special winter 1998-99 edition of *Time* Magazine entitled "Visions of Europe," the geographic outline of the continent of Europe is depicted as being embodied by a queen, referred to in this issue as the Virgin Mary.[29] A separate but similar version of the picture identifies the woman as "Queen Europe" (Regina Europa)[30] with no apparent link to Mary. Once again we see mythology blended or interchanged with Catholicism.

A peculiar statue is situated in front of the EU Parliament in Brussels. At the Paul-Henry Spaak building stands a statue of a woman holding up the "e" symbol of the euro currency (Fig. 20, see page 187). The woman, identified as the goddess Europa, is being clasped at from below by others, confirming the place of prominence given to this goddess in European civilization.

***The Tower of Babel***: Several years ago, the Council of Europe, which was one of the divisions of the then EEC, circulated a poster depicting the Tower of Babel. The council's poster illustrated the tower with a modern-day construction crane on the top of it. Above the tower, against the backdrop of the blue sky, were the twelve golden stars from the European flag, suggesting that a united Europe will figuratively complete or restore what God blocked from becoming a reality millennia ago. The anti-Christ, anti-God nature of this poster is obvious. A motto was also printed on the poster which read "Europe: Many Tongues, One Voice," which, even if unwittingly, hints at an attempt to reverse the Babel effect where tongues and nations were divided by God.

As we have seen throughout this book, there is a counterfeit spirituality that has run parallel to God's revealed system of worship throughout the ages. This counterfeit system was manifested at the Tower of Babel, and will be manifested in the kingdom of the Antichrist, which will represent this system's temporary moment of triumph. Europe's affiliation with the Tower of Babel is an indication as to what spirit drives the concept of European integration. Though appearing to be a peaceful and positive development, European integration is in reality setting the stage for the appearance of the Antichrist, who will usher in a new world order with roots firmly in the ancient Roman Empire. This new world order will be Babel rebuilt—the restoration of the ancient occult/esoteric mysteries in a new global monarchy.

The Babel symbolism does not stop with the poster. Europe's Parliament building in Strasburg France architecturally bears a striking resemblance to paintings of the Tower of Babel (Fig. 21, see page 195). It is an apparently unfinished cylindrical structure with what appear to be rings making up the various levels. The building, while it appears to be unfinished (much like paintings of Babel), is complete.

***The European Anthem***: The song chosen by the European leaders as a sort of European anthem is also very telling. The melody chosen is from Beethoven's *Ninth Symphony*. In the final movement of the symphony, Beethoven incorporated Friedrich von Schiller's poem "Ode to Joy," setting it to music.[31] According to *Europa*, this piece was chosen for their anthem because the poem by von Schiller spoke of the brotherhood of mankind—the coming together of the human race.[32] Again, the spirit driving European integration is evident. The ideal society envisioned is a brotherhood of mankind,

Figure 21

which, as we have seen, created apart from God restores the Tower of Babel scenario and can only lead to the enthronement of the Antichrist.

## Pulling It All Together: Europe and Beyond

Many years ago, one of the founding fathers of the EU uttered a most chilling expression to delegates of the UN. Citing the threatening economic conditions of the time, Paul-Henri Spaak called for a man of such stature who could bring them out of the economic chaos they were in, and that whether he was God or the Devil, he would be received.[33] The great Christian writer Sir Robert Anderson relayed words of an article in the *Times* newspaper from December 1876 in his classic work *The Coming Prince* that stated that all Europe is looking for the king of men, a great "Emperor of the East" who could provide escape from the difficulties of the times.[34] Many Christian scholars over the past several decades have maintained their conviction that the fragmented European continent would somehow be reunited, and that this reunification would set the stage for the rise of the Antichrist. These faithful servants of Christ simply trusted the Word of God, which clearly reveals that the Roman Empire will rule the world and produce the Antichrist just prior to Christ's return.

We have seen that both political Rome and religious Rome—seemingly symbolized by the beast and the Great Harlot of Revelation 17 and 18—appear to be two entities that will form a union that will characterize the kingdom of the Antichrist. This union will create a new Holy Roman Empire that promotes the intoxicating false spirituality of ancient Babylon. This new Holy Rome reflects the restoration of Babel, the discovery of the Grail, the resurrection of Osiris, and the temporary apparent triumph of the esoteric/occult stream of spirituality over God's established order. In reality, though, it is God Himself who will allow these things to unfold.

Today's European Union, which is uniting the geographic territory of the ancient Roman Empire, appears to be, spiritually speaking, characterized by an odd mix of Catholicism and esotericism, as seen in its various symbols. This, of course, completely falls in line with what we should expect to see from a restored Roman Empire. The historic Roman Empire was initially pagan, and then "Christianized" into a Catholic empire. The esoteric/pagan elements of the EU only serve to show the grip Satan has on this world, as he strives ever harder to produce his counterfeit messiah and reverse what God did at Babel thousands of years ago.

Surely, if anything in our world *today* can be classified as the embryonic Roman Empire of the Antichrist, it is the EU. However, we know from Scripture that the new Holy Roman Empire will be global, and while Europe may be the heart of ancient Rome, it is the entire planet that shall be the sphere of the Antichrist's authority. The coming system of the Antichrist represents the union of a global government and a global religious institution. Political Europe and religious Rome appear to be two of the main players that will participate in this end-time drama. Time will tell if the destinies of these two entities shall meet in the form of a new world order.

# 14

# The Ten Kings of the New Roman Empire

## The Tenfold Division of Rome

Scripture is clear that the final phase of the Roman Empire will be characterized by a federation of ten kingdoms under the head of a new Roman emperor. The great Christian writer Sir Robert Anderson noted that aside from the restoration of the Jews to the land of Israel, the most prominent feature from a political standpoint in biblical prophecy is this tenfold division of the Roman earth.[1]

What exactly constitutes the "Roman earth"? Broadly speaking, the Roman earth is that part of the globe that has "sprung up" out of the collapse and dissolution of the Roman Empire and that has absorbed Roman culture. Rome's influence is not limited to Europe, though Europe is the heart. Western civilization as a whole sprang out of both Greek and Roman culture. The civilizations of North and South America are largely the product of European settlers and colonizers, who themselves belonged to nations directly related to the old Roman Empire. The worldwide spread and influence of Roman Catholicism has taken Rome's religion to the four corners of the globe. Greco-Roman architecture can be found in the government buildings of various Western nations such as the United States of America. Roman principles in law and government are also part of the ideologies of many Western nations. The Roman Empire, as an imperial unified kingdom, does not exist today. However, the reach of Rome's influence has made large portions of the globe Roman.

There are those who maintain that the Antichrist himself will actually arise from the Muslim world. Some have even identified Syria (for reasons more credible than it at first may seem) as the possible land of his origin.[2] This "Muslim Antichrist" view has gained momentum in light of 9/11, the "War on Terror," and the clash between the West and radical Islam. Indeed, some factions of Islam expect the appearance soon of the twelfth Imam: the *Mahdi*—a type of "Islamic messiah." Iranian president Mahmoud Ahmadinejad has publicly and repeatedly voiced his belief that the Mahdi is about to appear. Parts of the Muslim world—including Syria—did fall under Roman dominion. I do not completely rule out the possibility of the Antichrist arising from the Muslim world. However, should that be the case, his rule, from a purely biblical standpoint, cannot be independent of, nor in opposition to, the Roman Empire, whose historic heart is Europe and whose present day successor is the West.

## The Ten Kings and Atlantis

A new philosophic world empire may very well be underway to being fulfilled in the emerging new world order, and it is the West that is spearheading the effort. A new world order, when fully established, would be the visible manifestation of the parallel system of worship that has run down through the ages in opposition to God's revealed truth. Hindered (as Manley P. Hall noted) by the rise of the Christian church in Europe, it has been the quest of the esoteric philosophers to resurrect the ancient occult system that has for ages set itself up against the true God.

We must remember that we are first and foremost dealing with a system—one that has been in existence from the very moment Satan revolted against God's heavenly order. This system infected humanity when Adam and Eve succumbed to the serpent's lie. We should not be surprised to see esoteric tendencies and sympathies in those who govern this world, since, as the Bible indicates, Satan is the god of this world. We have looked at examples of political and ecclesiastical esotericism, such as sixteenth- and seventeenth-century Britain, the founding of the New World, the European Union, and the Roman church. We have done so to illustrate the fact that esotericism can be found at the highest levels of world governance. Historically, esotericism has been a major component of the counterfeit satanic system that shall culminate in Antichrist worship. In light of this, it is significant indeed that, as we saw in previous chapters, the blueprint for the sought-after philosophic empire is legendary Atlantis, believed to have been ruled by *ten kings.*

The supposed tenfold division of ancient Atlantis was not just a random thing. As Hall notes, a tenfold division of governance is regarded as *the most ideal form.* As a *new* Atlantis is a crucial concept among the secret societies,[3] it is quite fascinating that Scripture presents the Antichrist's kingdom as an empire ruled by ten kings. As we have seen, the ten kings of Atlantis were ruled by an eleventh—Poseidon. Likewise, the Antichrist will be the eleventh king who rules over the other ten. The parallels are astounding and suggest that the esoteric quest for a world philosophic empire modeled on ancient Atlantis may be realized in the kingdom of the Antichrist.

## Monarchy-Republic-Empire

The goal of the esoteric orders and philosophers is world democracy and a philosophical state. However, as history has clearly shown us, despotism can and does often follow democracy/republicanism. Sir Robert Anderson notes that democracy—not despotism—is the goal to which civilization is striving.[4] However, he also notes that fully developed democracy is one of the most certain avenues to despotism.[5] He goes on to note that the transformation from democracy to despotism tends to follow a cycle of revolution, plebiscite (a vote by the electorate to either reject or accept a particular notion) and then despot. The Antichrist's rise to power may very well follow this trend. The quest to create a world democratic/philosophic state is in actuality uniting the world for what will ultimately become an occult global monarchy led by the Prince of Darkness himself.

There is a small, easy-to-miss detail found in Revelation 13 and 17 concerning the ten kings that is quite important to grasp. A close look at Revelation 13:1—and for that matter Daniel 2:44 and Daniel 7:24—plainly affirms that these ten leaders are "kings." The word *kings* in the Daniel passages, when translated from the original language, refers to "royalty." In Revelation 13, the ten horns that represent these kings have ten diadems (royal crowns) on them. These clearly appear to be monarchs of some kind. However, in Revelation 17 the ten horns are not crowned. Furthermore, we are told in the passage that "the ten horns which you saw are ten kings who have *not yet received a kingdom,* but they receive authority as kings with the beast for one hour" (Revelation 13:12, italics added). Comparing all these passages with one another, the prophetic picture seems to indicate that the ten kings receive their kingdom only with the assent of the beast. Perhaps the Antichrist will delegate authority to the ten and will crown them as kings of their respective territory. Interestingly, in Atlantis it was Poseidon who bestowed authority on the rulers of the ten kingdoms.[6] This is yet another astonishing parallel between legendary Atlantis and the kingdom of the Antichrist.

Clarence Larkin notes that Revelation 13, which depicts the kings as being crowned, represents the beast (the Antichrist) at the height of his power, while the uncrowned kings of Revelation 17 represent the early stages of the beast's ascent to power.[7] Interestingly, Larkin, based on the unity between the woman and the beast in Revelation 17, notes that the papal (Roman Catholic) church will likely play a key part in the coming together of the nations within the geographical limits of the ancient Roman Empire. He also hints that it is when the ten kings are crowned that they turn on the woman and destroy her.[8] As was noted in chapter 9, Prince Michael of Greece has stated that in past times monarchs were elected through an early form of democracy. However, once in power, they turned themselves into hereditary monarchs. Such could be the case with the new world order and the coming kingdom of the Antichrist.

It is fascinating to note that ancient Rome is often regarded as having passed through three phases: a semi-legendary monarchy known as the Roman Kingdom[9] (753 BC–509 BC), a republic (509 BC–27 BC) and an empire (27 BC–AD 476 in the West and 1453 in the East). This kingdom/republic/empire scenario seems to be recurring in the West as a whole. Medieval European civilization was largely dominated by kings, queens, and their kingdoms. This ultimately gave way to the rise of democratic republics such as those in France and the United States. And we know from biblical prophecy that the fragmented democratic West will ultimately give way to the *kingdom* of the Antichrist. As positive as all of the current talk of world democracy sounds, it is clear that the ultimate end product of any God-defying quest for a democratic new world order will be the dictatorial rule of a satanic prince.

## Rise of the Grail Kings?

Some authors have raised the possibility that numerous royal houses in Europe are behind the push to create a new world order, resurrecting the glories of the Holy Roman Empire. Some who put forth this idea base their argument on the suggestion that certain key noble houses of Europe are of Merovingian blood. Recall that it was the Merovingian dynasty that was the original "partner" of the Roman church in its dominion over Western Europe. The roots of the Holy Roman Empire can be traced back to the agreement between the Roman church and the Merovingian King Clovis. European royalty has also been linked to both the Templars and the Freemasons—two groups that are often associated with the quest for a new world order.

The implications of this view, if accurate, suggest that a Merovingian conspiracy exists to establish a "throne of Europe." At first this sounds quite laughable. We have already looked at this theory in chapter 7, and have also looked briefly at some of the holes in the argument, not the least of which is the fact that the key organization said to be orchestrating this conspiracy—the Priory of Sion—has been proven to be a hoax. Nevertheless, some have suggested that there are those in very high places who believe that it is their birthright to rule over the rest of mankind. Part of what grants these royals their imagined birthright is their supposed descent from the house of David, the royal house of the Messiah.

Christian author G. G. Stearman, in the book *Europe is Rising*, suggests that as Europe progresses toward forming the last Gentile world empire, there is ample reason to believe that the leaders of this new Europe will be monarchs.[10] Stearman draws attention to an eye-opening article in the November 19, 1989 issue of the *London Sunday Mail* entitled "Heralding a New Age for Europe." The article noted how major changes would be coming to the continent of Europe, and that the leaders of this new Europe, to a large degree, are the sons and daughters of Europe's historical royal families.

One of Europe's oldest and most influential royal families, the House of Habsburg-Lorraine, has been very involved in the European unity movement. Otto von Habsburg, the present head of the dynasty, was apparently a major behind-the-scenes contributor to the formation of the European Coal and Steel Community.[11] He was apparently also involved in convincing Belgium, France, Italy, West Germany, Luxemburg, and the Netherlands to forge ahead with the creation of the European Economic Community—the EU's predecessor. Both he and his son Karl have served at the European Parliament. During a memorial service in November of 1989 for Otto von Habsburg's mother, Empress Zita, Father Charles-Roux, who conducted the ceremony, spoke about the wonders of the Holy Roman Empire, which the Habsburgs ruled intermittently for centuries. He also noted that a few weeks prior, at the European Parliament, Otto von Habsburg proposed the reestablishment of the Holy Roman Empire.[12] In attendance at the service were royals from all across the continent.[13]

Researchers such as J. R. Church, author of *Guardians of the Grail*, have seen in the Merovingian/Grail bloodline theory a possible link between European royalty and the coming Holy Roman Empire of the Antichrist. Recall from chapter 7 how we saw that one of the stated objectives of the Priory of Sion was to forge a theocratic United States of Europe—a new "Holy Roman Empire"—and to place Merovingian descendants on the thrones of Europe. These Merovingian descendants, by virtue of their supposed Davidic heritage, could also be pretenders to serve as the messiah and king of Jerusalem. It is bizarre indeed that, despite the overwhelming evidence suggesting the Priory is a hoax, Europe appears to be following a path leading to the very thing that the Priory supposedly sought after. As author Jim Marrs notes, the European Union seems to be a copy of the united Europe envisioned by the Priory of Sion and "New World Order" leaders—whether planned that way or not.[14]

Leaving the Priory of Sion aside, there is one aspect of this proposed Merovingian-Antichrist link that is just too important to ignore. Christians all over the world for the past few years have had to defend their beliefs in the face of constant attacks suggesting that Jesus Christ married Mary Magdalene, spawning a bloodline that supposedly includes the Merovingians. So much doubt has been cast on the biblical testimony concerning Jesus that many find themselves confused as to who Jesus really was. It is quite significant that such arguments about Jesus, Mary, and the "truth" about Christianity should be coming forth as they are at this time, as without sufficient acceptance by the public of these lies, no royal could assert his or her supposed Merovingian/Grail claim successfully, which they would have to do if there is indeed a Merovingian plan for Europe and Jerusalem.

We do not wish to apply any sort of fanciful line of reasoning here, and we always need to remember that both the existence of the Priory of Sion and the continuation of the Merovingian bloodline are highly questionable. But we also do not wish to totally ignore these issues, as they pertain to matters that are intensely relevant to Christians today, and to all who seek to know the true God. I do not know if the Priory of Sion or any such organization actually exists. In fact, I have my doubts. Likewise, I do not know if all or some of Europe's royalty are truly of Merovingian descent. However, I do know that the stated objectives of the Priory and the Merovingian-Grail scenario concerning a united Europe and the throne of Jerusalem fit the prophetic picture concerning the coming Antichrist so perfectly that to ignore these arguments entirely would be unwise, especially since they also tear down and misrepresent the person and work of Jesus Christ.

Currently there are twelve monarchies in Europe. These include the Vatican—which, though overseen by an elected bishop is considered a monarchy/theocracy—and Andorra, which always has two joint heads of state—the elected president of France (currently Nicolas Sarkozy) and the Roman Catholic bishop of Urgell. The remaining ten monarchies are hereditary monarchies, and include Belgium, Britain, Denmark, Liechtenstein, Luxemburg, Monaco, the Netherlands, Norway, Spain, and Sweden. There are also numerous noble houses in Europe that currently do not occupy any thrones. These include the House of Bourbon (France), the House of Savoy (Italy), and the House of Habsburg-Lorraine (Austria, Hungary, Bohemia). Interestingly, each of these nonreigning royal families, along with the reigning Spanish royal family, are claimants to the title "King of Jerusalem." This title is taken from the Medieval Latin Kingdom of Jerusalem, which was a European Christian kingdom established in the Holy Land after the First Crusade. Interestingly, it was two combatants of the First Crusade—Hughues de Payens and Godfrey de Saint-Omer—who proposed the creation of what would become the Knights Templar.

The first European "king" of Jerusalem was Godfroi de Bouillon, who did not actually use the title "King of Jerusalem" but chose rather to be called "Protector of the Holy Sepulchre." The first to use the royal title was Godfroi's brother, Baldwin I, who reigned for just over seventeen years from December 25, 1100 to April 2, 1118.

The Christian armies from Europe fought through nine Crusades over the span of almost two hundred years against Muslim/Arab armies who also desired to control Jerusalem and the Holy Land. Ultimately, the Europeans failed and lost Jerusalem, never to recover it, with the unsuccessful ninth Crusade effectively ending the European Holy Land crusades. Is it possible that the descendants of the rulers of the Latin Kingdom of Jerusalem (the kingly line through to today's royal families) and the descendants of the Templars (the priestly line through to today's Freemasons) are working to recover their lost throne? We know that Freemasonry has adopted symbols from both Judaism and the Christian Kingdom of Jerusalem while some of today's royals still have the title "King of Jerusalem" associated with their noble houses.

Laurence Gardner, who defines the Holy Grail as the Sangréal—the Blood Royal of the Royal House of Judah—claims that a church and governmental plot has succeeded against the "Messianic" descendants and their inheritance.[15] It is also maintained by some that the true nobility of Europe—the "descendants" of Jesus Christ and Mary Magdalene—are the rightful inheritors of the Messianic legacy of Judah. One of the families that Gardner links to the Grail is the Royal House of Stewart, the former reigning House of Scotland and England. We have already seen the Stewart link to early Freemasonry, and the Scottish link to the Templars. The foreword for Gardner's book *Bloodline of the Holy Grail: The Hidden Lineage of Jesus Revealed* was written by HRH Prince Michael of Albany, the self-styled head of the Royal House of Stewart. The prince is not officially recognized as a legitimate heir to the Stewart legacy. Yet he makes assertive claims, suggesting that the church sought to vanquish the royal dynasty of which Gardner speaks and to manipulate history in order to accomplish its own ends.[16] The "prince," whose real name is Michael Lafosse, hopes to see what he calls the "truth" prevail regarding the deposed bloodline.

Another royal pretender, one whom we have already been introduced to, is Nicholas de Vere. Regarding himself as HRH Prince Nicholas de Vere of the royal house of Vere of Anju, this "prince" claims to descend from Lucifer. In his book *The Dragon Legacy: The Secret History of an Ancient Bloodline*, de Vere provides a detailed genealogical chart establishing a line of kingship that passes through Lucifer and includes Cain, the pharaohs of Egypt, members of the nation of Israel, King David, Jesus, Mary Magdalene, and European royalty—including the Merovingians. He himself is, of course, at the end of the family tree. De Vere's titles and descriptions include "The Prince Drakenberg," "Hereditary Dragon Lord," "Grand Master of the Knights Templars," and "Clan Chief and Head of the Royal House of Vere in England."

De Vere claims in his book to be the Sovereign Grand Master of something called The Imperial and Royal Dragon Court of the Dragon Sovereignty. Regarding this organization, Gardner affirms its existence, stating that it is an ancient fraternity with Egyptian origins.[17] De Vere also claims that there is a species of people in existence who are part of what he refers to as the dragon race. The significance of this dragon race is found in the claim that they are part of a dynastic bloodline linked to Lucifer that has the right to rule over mankind and the spiritual potency to do so effectively. They are the supposed shepherds of the human race, and take part in utterly wicked practices to help maintain their potency, such as blood ingesting. We know from Scripture that the dragon is a symbol for Satan. We need not say much more regarding the inspiration behind this dragon concept.

De Vere's story rings a familiar bell. According to this royal claimant, the true nobility—dragon race—has been supplanted and suppressed by the church and the church-backed establishment.[18] The restoration of this dragon race, then, can be linked to the revelation of the Holy Grail, the rebuilding of Babel, the resurrection of Atlantis, and the rebirth of an occult civilization under the rule of satanically inspired kings. The story is always the same among esoteric and esoteric-related themes: there once was a glorious civilization/kingdom/belief system/ king/treasure/philosophy, etc. These were severed by the rise of true divine revelation/Christianity/the church. The goal is now to subvert the true divine revelation/Christianity and resurrect the ancient occultism. This will occur in the kingdom of the Antichrist.

## Pulling It All Together

It is clear from God's Word that the kingdom of the Antichrist will be a monarchy that features the rule of a sovereign king—the Antichrist—over a revived Roman Empire. This new Roman Empire will consist of ten kingdoms within the empire under the authority of ten kings who will in turn submit to the Antichrist. We have already seen that the great quest of the esoteric orders has been the creation of a new Atlantis—a global philosophic empire. Legendary Atlantis consisted of ten kings, who in turn submitted to the authority of the supreme ruler: Poseidon. That the kingdom of the Antichrist mimics this exact setup suggests that the great quest of the esoteric fraternities will be realized. However, the end result will not be a benevc philosophic global democracy but a tyrannical absolute dictatorship unlike any this world has seen. The ten leaders that shall arise to govern the Roman earth are satanically inspired and set themselves against the Lord Jesus Christ. Following their satanic leader, the kings of the empire will attempt to thwart the establishment of the kingdom of Christ at His second coming.

The intent of this chapter was not to try to predict how the tenfold division will come about but simply to illustrate once again how esoteric philosophy, and the fruits of it, not only contradicts God's Word but seems to correlate with startling precision what shall transpire during the reign of the Antichrist. Many of these scenarios have an esoteric connection and are astonishingly close to what the Bible says will occur with respect to the kingdom of the Antichrist. The goal is not to try to fit these scenarios into the Bible but rather to allow God's prophetic Word help us understand what we are witnessing, and maybe why we are witnessing them at this time.

Why has the world been inundated with theories concerning Jesus Christ marrying Mary Magdalene? Why are we being told over and over again that Jesus is not really God but simply a man who has been misquoted and misrepresented, and why are these arguments being promoted with increasing fervency as we get closer and closer to the Antichrist's appearance? God's prophetic Word gives us a framework with which to judge these things. We cannot know with certainty how God's prophetic Word will be fulfilled, and we must not pretend to know. However, we can know the inspiration behind events, theories, and world developments based on whether or not they affirm the person and work of Jesus Christ, or the person and work of the Antichrist. The arguments put forth by esoteric and occult researchers/philosophers concerning a new Atlantis, a messianic blood-dynasty from Jesus and Mary linked to European royalty, and an ancient and superior "dragon" race all affirm and point to the person, work, and kingdom of the Antichrist.

Esotericism, new age spirituality, and occultism are currently undergoing a period of revival in the West. This, as we shall see in more detail in the final two chapters, is setting the stage for Antichrist worship. Perhaps, like no other time in history, God's prophetic Word needs to be read, taught, and understood, as it is His Word that shines the light on a dark world, enabling us to understand both the inspiration behind certain events and philosophies and their relevance to today's world.

# 15

# Esoteric Philosophy and Christian Apostasy

Esoteric and occult philosophers, as well as apostate "Christian" leaders, are presenting to the world a Jesus that is radically different than the Jesus of the Bible. Sometimes He is presented as a cosmic entity, devoid of any true human experience—an entity, or principle that can come upon an individual for a period of time. Others take quite an opposite approach, seeing in Jesus nothing but a mere human, devoid of a divine nature. This assault on the biblical Jesus is further advancing the cause of many who would like to see Christianity remolded into an esoteric religion, fit for a new world order. In light of this, it is critical that we address some of these unbiblical arguments by reaffirming the great *truths* of Scripture concerning Jesus Christ.

## Denying the Incarnation and the Trinity

If there is one activity that unites occultists and esoteric philosophers, it is denying Jesus' unique divinity. Most believe in God. Many consider themselves to be "spiritual." To say that Jesus is God and that God became a man, however, is to draw the line in the sand. In the Bible, Jesus is called the Word of God (Revelation 19:13), indicating that He is not just another messenger, or prophet, or principle, but is Himself the very revelation of God.[1] This is no small matter! If Jesus Himself is the revelation of God, then He Himself must share in God's nature, otherwise the revelation is not an accurate one. Jesus does not simply *bring* the word of God, but *is* the Word of God. A dog cannot himself accurately demonstrate to others the love between a husband and wife, since the dog does not share their nature. However, the dog can bring in his mouth a love note written from one spouse to the other for others to see as a testament of love between the couple. On the other hand, the couple's son need not bring any such note. He himself is the expression of his parent's marital love for each other. He reveals his parents simply by *being*, as he is of the same nature as they are, and is the visible expression of their love. To identify Jesus as the Word of God is to affirm that Jesus shares God's divine nature. Indeed, we read in John's gospel:

> In the beginning was the Word, and the Word *was* with God, and the Word was God. He was in the beginning with God. All things came into being Through Him. . . . And the Word became flesh, and dwelt among us. (John 1:1–3, 14, italics added)

Clearly, Jesus is not simply just a prophet, or messenger, or spirit. The word translated as *Word* in both Revelation and John is the Greek word *logos*, and implies "expression of thought." To say that Jesus is the Word is to say that Jesus is the expression of God.[2] How is the expression of God manifested and revealed to us humans? "The Word became flesh and dwelt among us"! Jesus is in fact the one true God in human form. He is the incarnate God of all creation.

This truth concerning the deity of Christ is increasingly being called into question. Barrie Wilson's *How Jesus Became Christian*, argues that the *divine* Christ preached to the Gentiles by the apostle Paul was simply a cover-up to mask a purely human Jewish Jesus. In *A New Christianity for a New World: Why Traditional Faith Is Dying and How a New Faith Is Being Born*, John Shelby Spong calls into question key Christian doctrines such as the Trinity, the incarnation (thus, the unique deity of Christ), and the atonement at the cross. In *The Jesus Papers: Exposing the Greatest Cover-up in History*, best-selling author Michael Baigent points to supposedly covered-up documents to suggest that Jesus may not have died on the cross after all. And in *Jesus Interrupted*, Bart D. Ehrman, professor of religious studies at the University of North Carolina, argues that the divinity of Jesus and the Trinity were inventions by theologians.

These are just a few examples of a massive movement throughout the West to reevaluate Jesus and present Him as anything but the incarnate Word of God. Such a reshaping of Christianity not only weakens people's confidence in the truth, but also prepares them to receive a counterfeit messiah. The Spirit of God uplifts and magnifies the true Jesus (John 16:13–14), while the spirit of Satan and the spirit of the antichrist denies and belittles Jesus.[3] To deny the deity of Christ is to deny the incarnation, and to deny the incarnation is to neglect the atoning work of Christ, apart from which no one can be saved.

All of humanity, because of sin, deserves the wrath of God. We are all born under the penalty of sin (which is death and eternal separation from God) and continue to sin all our lives. We have offended an infinite, eternal Being, and as such are subject to an infinite and eternal penalty—one that, as finite humans, we cannot pay. All that remains, then, is to suffer eternally under His wrath. God can pay an infinite penalty since He is infinite. However, God's payment would have no value to humans unless He Himself was human. It was humans who sinned, thus, it was a human that had to suffer. This posed an apparent problem, one that only God could solve. Through the incarnation, the God of all creation wrapped Himself in human flesh and thus became a man, the *God-man* Jesus Christ. As a human, He could now be our representative and pay the sin debt that humans owe, though He Himself was sinless. As an infinite God, He could pay the eternal and infinite penalty that we could not. God, being God, could have saved us any way He so chose. However, He chose to do it this way, and in doing so demonstrated His great love for us (Romans 5:8). To strip Jesus of His deity is to strip Christianity of the gospel.

Naturally, those who deny the deity of Christ also, for the most part, deny the virgin birth. However, for God to become a man and yet be free of the taint of human depravity, there had to be a virgin conception. He could not have had a human father, otherwise He would have inherited Adam's sin nature. Thus, the virgin birth is not some fancy, semimythical concept. It is, rather, evidence of the power, sovereignty, and mercy of a God who cared enough for His creation to stoop down to our level in order to pick us up.

The Bible reveals that God is one, but in three persons: Father, Son, and Holy Spirit. Of course, this is also being called into question by those who seek to promote a more "universal" Jesus compatible with all types of philosophies. However, to detach the Father, Son, and Spirit from each other is to annihilate the Christian God. The one true God *is* the Father, Son, and Spirit. There is no God apart from the relationship between these three.

A close look at Scripture will reveal that the acts of God are all *Trinitarian* acts, in that the Father, Son, and Spirit never act independently of each other. Take for example the baptism of Jesus. On this occasion, the Son was baptized, the Spirit descended, and the Father spoke (Matthew 3:16–17). All three—Father, Son, and Spirit—were involved in this act. How about redemption through Christ? The Father willed it (Colossians 1:19), the Son accomplished it (John 19:30), and the Spirit applies it to human hearts (John 3:5–8; 16:8–11).

Of course, we can never in this life fully understand the mystery of the Trinity. There are, however, examples of "triune entities" in creation that, while not fully explaining the mystery of God, do aid us somewhat in our understanding of the Trinity. The human person is one being—that is, there is only one me and one you. Yet, making up this being is body, soul, and spirit (1 Thessalonians 5:23). My body is 100 percent me (not 100 percent of what I am, but 100 percent me in the sense that my body is not any less Adrian than my soul or spirit is), my soul is 100 percent me, and my spirit is 100 percent me. In other words, each of the three are equally Adrian Isaacs. My being *exists* as all three together. My identity is not split among the three, but exists *as the three.* Yet all three are different and distinguishable. My body, soul, and spirit cannot be separated from each other except by death. Thus, everything I am, everything I do, and everywhere I go involves all three aspects of my being, which are each completely me and in constant relation with one another.

We can somewhat apply this logic to the Trinity. The Father, Son, and Spirit are each 100 percent God—each lacking nothing with respect to divinity. God—the divine Essence—is one, yet in three members that each possess all traits and aspects of this divine Essence. God is not divided among the three, but rather God is the three. Yet, the Father, Son, and Spirit are distinct from each other and in relation to each other, not different forms that God can take. They are *real* and *distinct* parts, yet together make up one God. Finally, the relationship between the Father, Son, and Spirit is unbreakable. To separate these members from each other would imply the death of God, which is impossible. Since these three can never be separated, God can never die.[4] We, however, being mortal, do die upon the separation of our soul and spirit from our body.

How serious, then, is this offense of denying the Trinity and separating Jesus from the eternal God? To deny the Trinity is to philosophically kill God, or to destroy the identity of the one true God, apart from which there can be no life, love, peace, forgiveness, or joy. Esoteric philosophers, scholars, and so-called "Christian" leaders like John Spong who deny the Trinity are not presenting us with an enlightened, modern philosophy. They are in fact philosophically destroying the identity of the one true God, which can only further the kingdom of the Antichrist and prepare the hearts of men and women to accept a new god.

## Denying the Resurrection

We have already to some degree considered the implications of denying the resurrection of Jesus, which is the next logical thing to do after denying His deity. The resurrection affirms that Christ's sacrificial work on the cross was sufficient to atone for human sin. Resurrection is the fruit of redemption. Thus, it is no wonder that this doctrine has come under fire by those who seek to reshape Christianity.

Gnostics and esoteric philosophers see in the resurrection of Jesus a metaphor for spiritual advancement and evolution. Thus, the concept of a literal resurrection is absurd to them. However, the language of Scripture is both clear and direct in affirming that Jesus *literally* and *bodily* was raised from the dead. In Matthew 24, we are given the account of two Marys looking for Jesus, only to find an empty tomb. In Luke 24, the resurrected Jesus shows His disciples His hands and feet. This is significant, as it confirmed to the disciples that what they were seeing was not, as they thought, a "spirit," but a real flesh-and-blood person (Luke 24:36–41). The disciples were so amazed and full of joy that they still could not believe it. Jesus even asked them if they had anything to eat (Luke 24:41–43). They gave Him a piece of fish, and He *ate* it. Thus, from Matthew 28 and Luke 24 we learn that Jesus' body was sought for (Matthew 28:5), Jesus was no longer in the tomb (Matthew 28:6), He had a physical body after being raised (Luke 24:38–40), and He was able to eat after being raised (Luke 24: 41–43). Also note that there was great joy and disbelief among the disciples (Luke 24:41), reactions that would be expected from those looking upon one who was "supposed to be" dead! Clearly, the instances and events outlined in Matthew 24 and Luke 28 affirm a literal, resurrected Jesus, not a Jesus who was elevated (raised) to a new level of spirituality. An empty tomb, hands and feet, and eating fish would be irrelevant to a Jesus who was simply "raised" to a new level of spirituality.

It should also be noted that the historicity of the resurrection can be affirmed when we consider the numerous eyewitnesses of the event. As author Norman Geisler points out, no other event from ancient times possesses the testimony that the resurrection of Jesus possesses.[5] Geisler points out that the resurrected Lord was witnessed by over five hundred people (1 Corinthians 15:5) on one occasion, indicating the reality of the event. He also made appearances to His apostles over a forty-day period (Acts 1:3), which proved that His resurrection was not a strange or abnormal occurrence.[6] Furthermore, the activities he did and the amount of time He spent with those to whom He appeared allowed His witnesses to be certain that they were indeed looking upon Jesus. Geisler also makes an excellent point regarding the scepticism among some who witnessed the risen Lord, suggesting that this scepticism (John 20:25, Matthew 28:17) rules out the possibility of hallucination.[7] The witnesses were rational and in a right state of mind, as is evident by the sceptical behavior.

An excellent point is also made by scientist Ambrose Fleming, emeritus professor of electrical engineering at the University of London. Fleming asks whether it is probable that the biblical account of events surrounding Jesus, including the resurrection, could have been cherished and accepted if the events were false or merely myth.[8] The gospels were written near enough to the date that the events occurred, and as such, would have been detected as false by those who had lived through the events the gospels spoke of. Imagine somebody today trying to create a hoax stating that John F. Kennedy rose from the dead. Such a thing would be impossible. There were no witnesses to such an event, no testimonies affirming such a resurrection, and a sufficient amount of people who witnessed JFK's death are still alive today to refute a resurrection claim and prevent such a hoax from taking root. However, the fact that multitudes accepted the biblical writings concerning the death and resurrection of Jesus, cherished them, died for them, and propagated them successfully argues strongly that there is a tremendous historical basis to the claim that Jesus rose from the dead.

The fastest and most effective way to discredit Christianity in the eyes of the world is to present a Jesus who is still lying in a tomb. If Jesus is still in a tomb, then Christianity is meaningless and humanity is lost in sin (1 Corinthians 15:12–17). This is perhaps a clue as to why the resurrection is so ferociously contested by esoteric philosophers and apostate Christian leaders. Leaving Jesus in the tomb undermines the Christian witness.

## Pagan Origins of Christianity?

Some researchers have maintained that Christianity is simply a new manifestation of the old pagan mystery religions of the ancient world. They equate Jesus with the ancient Egyptian deity Horus, or the Babylonian Tammuz. Sometimes Jesus is equated with Osiris, the Egyptian deity symbolized by the blazing sun.

In his book *The Pagan Christ*, former professor of New Testament at the University of Toronto Tom Harpur draws parallels between the Christ of Christianity and the Horus of ancient Egyptian mythology. Harpur notes that both Jesus' birth and Horus' birth were announced by stars. Horus was apparently baptized in the Jordan River, just as Christ was. It is said that Horus walked on water, healed the sick, cast out demons, delivered a "Sermon on the Mount," was crucified between two thieves, buried, and resurrected.[9] Each of these things were, of course, done by Jesus. Apparently, Horus was even called the Lamb of God, the Bread of Life, the Word, and the Good Shepherd,[10] all titles attributed to Jesus Christ.

By making Jesus and Horus one and the same, Christ is stripped of His uniqueness and distinction as the Word made flesh. He cannot be substituted or equated. He is unique in all of history. Jesus is a particular person who existed at a particular time and place. He is not a concept. He is a person to be dealt with. He is the God of eternity who made His mark on human history *as a man* at a particular time (the first century) and a particular place (ancient Israel). He cannot be equated with an ancient deity. Nor can he simply be a concept. We have already seen that the historicity of the life and events of Jesus is both logical and acceptable. Christianity, then, is not a new manifestation of an old philosophy but rather a faith based on the existence, life, and work of a real, historical person:

> By common confession, great is the mystery of godliness: He who was revealed in the flesh, Was vindicated in the Spirit, Seen by angels, Proclaimed among the nations, Believed on in the world, Taken up in glory. (1 Timothy 3:16)

To equate Jesus with Horus is also to deny the eternal existence of Jesus. While the Son of God came into the world at a point in time, the existence of the Son of God is from eternity. Speaking of Himself, Jesus stated, "Before Abraham was born, I am" (John 8:58). Some who heard this immediately picked up stones to throw at Him, seemingly because His expression "I am" was a reference to the eternal God. By applying this name to Himself, Jesus affirmed not only His deity but His eternal existence. Thus, the Son of God preexisted all things, including Horus and the ancient Egyptian mystery religion.

### A Married Jesus and a Messianic Bloodline?

Thanks to numerous books and documentaries in recent times, the "married Jesus" and "bloodline of Christ" concepts have gained a major following. While adequately refuted by both Christian and non-Christian scholars, these concepts have gained a certain romantic aura about them that has caused many to rethink the traditional biblical account of Jesus. Certainly, the Bible makes no mention of a marital union between Jesus and Mary Magdalene. Even secular scholars will affirm that evidence pointing to a possible marital union—fragmented extra-biblical texts and an esoteric reading of Scripture—is not very strong. Nevertheless, theories abound concerning Jesus' marital status.

Of course, for every counterfeit there is a genuine. The genuine bride of Christ is His blood-bought church (Ephesians 5:22–32), counterfeited by the esoteric Mary Magdalene, who is equated with the pagan goddess concept found in the ancient Babylonian religion. This ancient pagan/occult religion, as we have seen, will be revived as the religious arm of the Antichrist's kingdom, symbolized by the woman in Revelation 17 and 18.

### Denying the Authority and Inspiration of Scripture

In order for the esoteric and occult views of Jesus to be accepted, doubt must be cast on the biblical presentation of who Jesus is. If the Bible is true, then what the Bible says about Jesus is true. If the esoteric/occult view of Jesus is correct, then Christians have it wrong. It is no wonder, then, that the divine inspiration and authority of Scripture is called into question in each and every one of the esoteric revelations we have looked at in this book

The arguments made against the Bible by sceptics are often the same: only those books that supported the view of a power-hungry Roman church were included in the Bible, portions of the Bible have been tampered with, and the Bible is not meant to be taken literally. It is well beyond the scope of this book to explore all the evidences affirming the authority and inspiration of Scripture. Many have done this admirably. However, we can briefly address these three arguments, as it is these that are directly pertinent to esoteric and occult spirituality.

The first argument—that the Bible we have today is a collection of only those books that supported the agenda of the Church of Rome—is incorrect. It is argued that the Bible we have today was established under the watch of Emperor Constantine at the Council of Nicaea in the fourth century, and that only those books that made Jesus look divine were included. Books that seemed to contradict the views of the Roman church, like the Gnostic Gospels, were left out. This is not completely true. In the case of both the Old and New Testament canons (collection of officially accepted books),[11] the Council of Nicaea did not determine Scripture. Jesus Himself affirmed the authority of the Old Testament Scriptures by referring to them on several occasions—centuries before Nicaea. In the gospel of Luke, Jesus refers to all the things written about Him in the "Law of Moses and the Prophets and the Psalms" (Luke 24: 44).

With respect to the New Testament, it is important to note that the church did not determine Scripture but rather recognized it.[12] This recognition came over an extended period of time. One of the main tests for canonicity was whether or not a book fell under apostolic authority or approval.[13] For a book to be considered Scripture, it needed to be approved by the apostles—those who were specifically and deliberately chosen by Christ Himself, and who contributed to the foundation of the church (Ephesians 2:19–20).

The apostles were specifically entrusted with the mysteries of God and were promised by Christ to be guided "into all truth" by the Spirit of God (John 16:13). They were also specifically commissioned by Christ to "go int all the world and preach the gospel to all creation" (Mark 16:15). We are also told that those who believed in Christ through the preaching of Peter in the book of Acts were "continually devoting themselves to the apostles' teaching" (Acts 2:42).

An example of apostolic approval can be seen in 2 Peter:

> Therefore, beloved, since you look for these things, be diligent to be found by Him in peace, spotless and blameless, and regard the patience of our Lord as salvation; just as also our beloved brother Paul, according to the wisdom given him, wrote to you. (2 Peter 3:14–15)

In this passage, the apostle Peter is affirming the apostle Paul's writings. Both Peter and Paul were directly commissioned by the Lord Himself—Paul's commission coming, of course, after the Lord's ascension.

We can apply the rule of apostolic authority to the so-called Gnostic Gospels, which many esoteric and revisionist scholars feel are of equal weight to the biblical Gospels. Most Christian and non-Christian scholars date the Gnostic Gospels to around AD 250–350, with the original translations and material for these gospels dated to around the mid-100s–early 200s.[14] This means that the Gnostic Gospels were written decades after the four official biblical Gospels. Though the Gnostic Gospels are often attributed to people like Thomas, Philip, and Mary, they could not possibly have been written by *the* Thomas, Philip, and Mary of Jesus' time, as they were not alive when these gospels were written. As Richard Banes notes, nobody really knows who wrote these Gnostic texts.[15] Furthermore, no apostles were alive to authenticate the Gnostic Gospels. As such, these books could not be included in the biblical canon, as they lacked apostolic authority/approval. Their exclusion had nothing to do with a "biased selection process."

Another indication that the Roman church did not determine Scripture comes by way of Iranaeus, bishop of Gaul in the second century, well before there ever was a Catholic Church. Iranaeus, a disciple of Polycarp, who in turn
sciple of the apostle John, affirmed several of the books we have
oday as Scripture. His list is strikingly close to the list we have
g that Nicaea did not determine Scripture. Iranaeus's writings
lowing NT books as Scripture: all four Gospels, Acts, Romans,

1 and 2 Corinthians, Galatians, Ephesians, Philippians, Colossians, 1 and 2 Thessalonians, 1 and 2 Timothy, Titus, 1 Peter, 1 John, and Revelation.

Regarding the tampering of Scripture, we first and foremost must have confidence that God is able to preserve His Word. We know that the "Law, the Prophets, and the Psalms" have been preserved, as Jesus Himself, speaking hundreds of years after certain Old Testament texts were written, affirmed them. Jesus also alludes to events described in the Old Testament, such as Noah and the flood (Luke 17:26–27). The Old Testament is also quoted or alluded to by many of the New Testament writers, such as Paul, who contrasts Jesus with Adam in Romans 5. Jesus also fulfilled numerous Old Testament prophecies. Old Testament prophecy—prophecy that we still have intact in our Bibles—fulfilled in the New Testament, centuries after the prophecy was written, affirms that what we see in the Old Testament today is what was written down millennia ago.

Old Testament prophecy fulfilled in Jesus authenticates the Old Testament as well as Jesus' messiahship. We saw examples of these prophecies in chapter 2. Since we know, based in these fulfilled Old Testament prophecies, that Jesus is the promised Messiah, we can be confident in both His words and in the twelve He chose to carry on His work. The New Testament canon is then established upon the testimony and foundation of Christ and the apostles, and as God preserved the Old Testament, so has He preserved the New. Furthermore, New Testament prophecy that is already fulfilled—or in the process of being fulfilled—affirms the reliability and divine inspiration of Scripture. Jesus predicted the desolation of Jerusalem and the Diaspora of the Jewish people in the gospel of Luke. Both of these events occurred decades later as the Romans set siege to Jerusalem in AD 70, ultimately leading to the scattering of the Jews into all nations. Fulfilled prophecy tells us that the words of the Bible we have today are as they were written centuries and millennia ago.

Regarding the literal interpretation of Scripture, most who promote a more esoteric or Gnostic Christianity believe that many of the teachings and events of the Bible—such as the resurrection—are not meant to be taken literally but symbolically. The main problem with this argument is that such an interpretive method has no solid, objective foundation to work from. If there is no literal, definite interpretation based on the historical setting of the text, the people involved, and the issue being addressed, then anyone can come up with their own meaning to anything.

> But know this first of all, that no prophecy of Scripture is a matter of one's own interpretation, for no prophecy was ever made by an act of human will, but men moved by the Holy Spirit spoke from God. (2 Peter 1:20–21)

God has inspired biblical Scripture, God has preserved biblical Scripture, and God gives the interpretation to biblical Scripture. It is no wonder, then, that the Bible should be called into question by those seeking to promote a different Jesus. It is in the Bible that the Word of God—Jesus—is revealed, so it is the Bible that must be discredited.

## Pulling It All Together

Esoteric and occult philosophy presents a Jesus that is radically different from the Jesus of the Bible. Apostate Christian leaders who have drifted away from the conviction that the Bible is the inspired Word of God are also presenting a new Jesus. This double-edged-sword of esoteric philosophy and Christian apostasy is rapidly setting the stage for the enthronement of a counterfeit messiah, as many in the West now find themselves questioning the traditional Christian message. The abandonment of truth only leads to the acceptance of error. Darkness exists when the light is turned off. As we get closer and closer to the advent of the Antichrist, we can expect to see more and more antagonism toward Christianity. This should not discourage us or inspire a defeatist attitude but rather spur us on even more to an earnest pursuit and defense of the truth. The Antichrist is coming! The only legitimate way to fight him is to earnestly spread the good news of Jesus' love now!

# 16

## The Rise of the Antichrist

The late historian Arnold Toynbee once remarked how the world was ready for the deifying of a new Caesar who could bring peace and unity to the world.[1] Perhaps Toynbee was not aware of how significant his words really were. World leaders—even today—are perhaps at times held in too much esteem. While I do not believe nor claim that President Barack Obama is the Antichrist, the portrayal of him as a messiah figure in January 2009 further revealed humanity's capacity to embrace a counterfeit messiah. In imitation of Jesus Christ's triumphant entry into Jerusalem as recorded in Matthew 21:1–11, artist Matthew J. Clarke designed a sculpture depicting Obama riding a donkey. The sculpture was paraded down Locust Street in Des Moines, Iowa. One woman in the procession was handing out palm branches, attempting to recreate the imagery of Jesus' triumphal entry. Perhaps the world is indeed close to the "deifying of a new Caesar!" Somewhere, somehow, and at some point in the future, a dynamic world leader will arise and command the attention and worship of the world. He will be Satan's prince, the dragon's messiah.

### Throne of the "Perfect" Man

One of the most enduring aspects of the Arthurian legends is the famous Round Table where the knights sat and beheld images of the mysterious Grail. While a great number of knights are often portrayed as being able to sit at the table (up to fifteen hundred in some instances),[2] one of the more common depictions of the table has it capable of seating twenty-four. In this depiction there are actually twenty-six seats—twenty-four for the knights, one for Arthur, and an empty seat called "the Siege Perilous" (the Perilous Seat), which was reserved for the one who found the Holy Grail.[3] According to Hall, the Round Table represented the universe, while the twenty-four seats represented the twelve signs of the Zodiac in both their nocturnal (night) and diurnal (day) phases. The Siege Perilous, meanwhile, represented the throne of the *perfect man* who, as indicated by the vacant seat, had not yet arrived.

This Round Table itself has served as an inspiration behind the creation of Europe's oldest and most prestigious order of chivalry—the Most Noble Order of the Garter.[4] This order is limited to twenty-four true members (Companion Knights), plus the Sovereign (currently Queen Elizabeth II) and the Prince of Wales (currently Prince Charles), which brings the overall total number to twenty-six, matching the seats at the Arthurian table. The heraldic shield of the Order of the Garter is a red cross centered inside a circle-shaped garter. According to Laurence Gardner, the Grail itself is symbolized by a cross within a circle.[5] The red cross is also similar to the red cross of the flag of England and the red cross of the Knights Templar.

Those familiar with the fourth and fifth chapters of the Book of Revelation may notice in this twenty-six-seat arrangement a remarkable mimicry. In Revelation we read:

> Immediately I was in the Spirit; and behold, a throne was standing in heaven, and One sitting on the throne. And He who was sitting was like a jasper stone and a sardius in appearance; and there was a rainbow around the throne, like an emerald in appearance. Around the throne were twenty-four thrones; and upon the thrones I saw twenty-four elders sitting, clothed in white garments, and golden crowns on their heads. (Revelation 4:2–4)

> I saw in the right hand of Him who sat on the throne a book written inside and on the back, sealed up with seven seals. . . . And I saw between the throne (with the four living creatures) and the elders a Lamb standing, as if slain, having

> seven horns and seven eyes, which are the seven Spirits of God, sent out to all the earth. And He came and took the book out of the right hand of him who sat on the throne. (Revelation 5:1, 6–7)

These are remarkable passages of Scripture, as they give us a glimpse into the throne room of heaven. Astonishingly though, they also reveal the mimicry of God's heavenly throne by the Arthurian Table and the Order of the Garter on earth. The setting around God's throne is mimicked by the table of Arthur's earthly dwelling. The One on the throne—God the Father—is mimicked by King Arthur, while the Lamb of God—Jesus Christ, the perfect God-man—is mimicked by the perfect man of Arthur's table who is to sit at the Siege Perilous. The twenty-four elders around the throne are mimicked by the twenty-four knights of the realm. Arthur's Round Table is a close mimicry of the setting around God's throne, lacking only the twenty-sixth person, the perfect man, to take up his place.

In the Order of the Garter, God the Father is mimicked by the British sovereign, while Jesus Christ is mimicked by the Prince of Wales. The twenty-four elders meanwhile are mimicked by the twenty-four companion knights.

Regarding the Prince of Wales, in a bizarre episode just a few years ago, a bronze statue was made of the current Prince of Wales, depicting him with angel wings towering over the sea of humanity.[6] The statue was presented to Prince Charles while he was in Brazil. He was told that a larger-sized model would be erected in the Brazilian town of Palmas. The statue features the Prince wearing nothing but a garment to protect his modesty, much like what Jesus is wearing in depictions of Him on the cross, and identifies the Prince as the savior of the world. Again we see the subtle yet dangerous tendency of the human heart to seek out a savior from among ourselves rather than look to the true Savior who saves us from ourselves.

The Arthurian Round Table, the Grail, and the perfect man are all esoteric themes that speak of an ideal state, society, and humanity. These things, however, can only be found in Jesus Christ, and any attempt to establish them apart from Christ is to advance the counterfeit system of the Antichrist. The idea presented in the Arthurian legend is that there is one worthy of the Grail—a perfect man—who, upon discovering the Grail, sits upon a throne. The parallels here to the coming Antichrist should by now be obvious! The Antichrist, who upon revealing the Grail to the world (the path or key to the perfect society and existence) will sit upon a now-vacant throne, the throne of the "perfect" human being—and will usher in what will appear to be the kingdom of heaven on earth. This will be a counterfeit kingdom of heaven inaugurated by a counterfeit Christ, for there is only one perfect man, the man Christ Jesus: "He made Him who *knew no sin* to be sin on our behalf, so that we might become the righteousness of God in Him" (2 Corinthians 5:21, italics added). And "For there is one God, and one mediator also between God and men, the man Christ Jesus who gave Himself as a ransom for all" (1 Timothy 2:5–6).

### Esotericism and the Antichrist

Throughout this book we have seen the contrast between the true revelation of God that leads to Jesus Christ and the counterfeit esoteric stream of spirituality that leads to the Antichrist. We have seen how, from the very dawn of creation, this counterfeit system has run parallel to the divine revelation, at times manifesting itself quite openly. When tolerated by society, this system of worship could often be detected in the many pagan-state religions of the ancient world. When suppressed, it could be detected in various secret, esoteric organizations. We have looked in detail at several esoteric "revelations" now permeating Western civilization. These revelations have been promoted through best-selling books, blockbuster movies, academic documentaries, and apostate Christian leaders. They undermine the Christian faith and are preparing the world for the embrace of the Antichrist. Let us now take another look at these revelations in light of what we have learned concerning the Antichrist and his coming kingdom. In doing so, we shall see how each one of them is helping to further the cause of the Antichrist by preparing the world to accept this satanic prince.

***The "Bloodline of Christ" Revelation***: If the Antichrist, who according to Scripture arises to power over the Gentile world, poses as Israel's messiah, he must prove his ancestry back to the house of David, which is the royal house that the Messiah is to come from. The "bloodline of Christ" revelation provides a means by which a Gentile prince can claim Davidic ancestry. If it can be "proven" that Jesus Christ indeed did marry and sire a bloodline, then it is entirely possible that one living today could claim to be a living descendant of Jesus Christ and Mary Magdalene, and thus a descendant of Israel's King David.

The Priory of Sion, the alleged guardians of the Merovingian bloodline, supposedly had as their goal a United States of Europe, to be ruled by a descendant of Christ. Thus, under this scenario, a prince from a Gentile land would lead a reunified Europe and could also pose as Israel's messiah. The continuation of the Merovingian dynasty is not certain, and the very existence of the Priory of Sion as a historical secret society is doubtful. However, this "revelation" is extremely relevant for two main reasons. First, it tears down the person and work of Jesus Christ, making Him out to be nothing more than an ordinary man. This alone is sufficient to enable us to conclude that the bloodline of Christ "revelation" is in actuality a demonic attempt to steer people's minds away from the truth of Jesus Christ, and to prepare them to accept a counterfeit Christ.

Second, this "revelation" mirrors biblical prophecy in a very precise way concerning a coming Antichrist and a revived Roman Empire. The messianic "descendant" of Christ corresponds to the Antichrist, while the united Europe corresponds to the revived Roman Empire. The claim to the throne of Jerusalem by the messianic descendant calls to mind the possibility that the Antichrist will claim Davidic descent to deceive the Jewish people. The pact between the Merovingian Clovis and the Roman church resembles the union between the beast (political Rome) and the woman (spiritual Babylon) in Revelation 17.

The Magdalene legacy is crucial to esoteric spirituality as it also provides a means by which Christianity can be presented as an esoteric religion characterized by the ancient pagan concept of the divine male-female balance. Esoteric and pagan spirituality has always been very goddess oriented, as it was Semiramis, the supposed wife of Nimrod, who is credited with promoting many of the pagan mysteries. This Babylonian goddess has an equivalent in several cultures, including the modern West. In ancient Egypt the equivalent was Isis, widow of the Egyptian king Osiris. In Greece it was Aphrodite. The Assyrians knew her as Ishtar, while the Phoenicians knew her as Astarte. In pagan Rome she was Venus, while in Catholic Rome she is the Virgin Mary.

Meanwhile, Mary Magdalene—the "esoteric Mary Magdalene"—as the supposed wife of a "deceased" king (Jesus) serves as the goddess figure of the "Christian" West. Her prominence today in Western culture as the supposed bride of Christ represents more than just a romantic legend. She in fact represents the pagan mystery religion of the ancient world wrapped in Christian clothing, seducing men and women away from the true revelation of God and directly into pagan worship. The dual system of the kingdom of the Antichrist is depicted in Revelation 17 as a woman riding a beast. The woman, identified in Revelation 18 as a queen, is holding a chalice—a grail—and denies widowhood. This may be an allusion to the resurrection of the ancient Babylonian pagan religion, serving as the religious arm of a new Holy Roman Empire. Her "resurrected" husband is the Antichrist who, supposedly just like his prototype—Nimrod—will be deified by humanity.

Curiosity in esoteric philosophy and alternative history has been awakened within the hearts of men and women throughout Western civilization, as evidenced by the overwhelming popularity of theories concerning Magdalene and the so-called bloodline of Christ. The fact that these theories strike at the very heart of the Christian faith—while promoting ideologies and notions that resemble or relate to what is coming under the Antichrist—strongly suggests that they are preparing the world for the soon arrival of the counterfeit messiah.

***The Grail Revelation***: What is the Holy Grail? The Grail is many things to many people, but in its simplest metaphoric form it represents the *thing* that all humanity seeks, the *thing* that provides the ideal state and the ideal existence. It is the most sought-after prize! It is the philosopher's stone and the elixir of life, capable of bestowing immortality upon those who discover it. It is the crown jewel of Lucifer—the magical gem capable of resurrecting the dead, and the source of earthly kingship.

The Grail is also related to the female, who in the pagan and occult world is regarded as crucial to the success of the "male" side. King Arthur is aided by the Lady of the Lake, who brings him his magical sword. Female blood and hormones, according to some, supposedly heighten man's spiritual powers. And it is the woman, Babylon the Great, who aides the Antichrist before being turned on and annihilated by the the Antichrist and his forces.

The Grail, according to Laurence Gardner, is also the Blood Royal, the messianic bloodline of the house of David that supposedly runs through Jesus and Mary. This bloodline, according to some, has been suppressed and supplanted by the Christian establishment. Supposedly including certain European royals, this bloodline is said to represent the true line of earthly kingship reaching back to, not only to Jesus and King David, but to the pharaohs of Egypt, Cain, and (according to Nicholas de Vere) Lucifer himself.

The Grail can also be the lost knowledge of Atlantis—the ideal society and the blueprint among the secret societies for a new world order. It is also the all-seeing eye—the eye of Providence found on the US one-dollar bill that is a spin-off of the eye of Horus. Horus, as we have seen, represents the avenger, striking back at Set, who represents the true divine revelation. Horus then, represents the triumph of the kingdom of Satan over the kingdom of God. He represents the enthronement of the Antichrist and the dethronement of Christ.

The Grail in every instance is that *thing* that serves as an occult substitute for Jesus Christ, who is the true source of immortality and the only One capable of establishing a true utopian society. Men and women will look to the Antichrist to do what only Christ can do. Thus, the Grail, which will be "discovered" by the "perfect man," also points to a counterfeit messiah.

***The Tomb of Christ Revelation***: Many esoteric philosophers and some apostate Christian leaders would have us believe that the resurrection was a hoax. The Christian faith is rooted in the historical reality and spiritual significance of the resurrection. Remove the resurrection from Christianity and there is no Christianity. All that would be left would be a dead religion, revived in the eyes of the world only by giving new meaning to old concepts. The resurrection would thus become a term to describe Jesus' "heightened spiritual state."

Western civilization is the part of the globe that would be most affected by a dead-Jesus revelation. Such a revelation would also play right into the hands of the Antichrist, as apart from the grace of God and illuminating power of the Holy Spirit such a "revelation" would annihilate all confidence men and women have in the gospel. It may not be a coincidence that as we near the revelation of the Antichrist, scholars and researchers are trying to redefine the resurrection and present a Jesus whose remains are still lying in a tomb. Once again, Christ would be humiliated and the Antichrist exalted!

***The Messianic Revelation***: The Antichrist shall be aided by a religious leader known as the False Prophet. These two—the political leader and the religious leader—together institute the kingdom of the Antichrist, which is a counterfeit kingdom of heaven. How peculiar it is then, that the Rex Deus hypothesis claims that two messianic bloodlines—one from King David and the other from the priest Aaron—have been preserved in Europe and will manifest in two messiahs who shall inaugurate the "kingdom of heaven" on earth. Again, the similarities of this with what shall occur during the times of the Antichrist are too obvious to ignore. According to proponents of this view, the main ideas of Rex Deus have been preserved and disseminated through Freemasonry.

The Antichrist seeks to imitate and usurp Christ's position and authority in the earth. The messianic revelation concerning Rex Deus already does this, lacking only the visible manifestation of the two individuals at the head of each bloodline to usher in the kingdom. We do not know if the Rex Deus group is a *historical* reality or not. However, we do know from biblical prophecy that this Rex Deus *concept* of two messiah-type figures *will be realized* through the agencies of the beast from the sea (the political Antichrist) and the beast from the earth (the false religious prophet).[7] It is astounding to see a scenario so fitting and reflective of what the Bible says is to occur during the time of the Antichrist.

***The Masonic/Illuminati/Rosicrucian Revelation***: The unifying quest of esoteric societies has been the creation of a philosophic empire, re-creating the ideal conditions that are believed to have existed in ancient Atlantis. Often called the "new world order," this global setup has been linked to numerous secret societies and conspiracy theories, some more credible than others. Three of these secret societies are the Freemasons, the Illuminati, and the Rosicrucians. Supposedly all linked by a common thread, these esoteric organizations apparently have as their goal the eventual destruction of Christianity and the creation of a new global philosophic system, characterized by a world without borders (a global government) and, in the case of the Freemasons anyway, a world without religious barriers (a global religion). Such a setup reverses what occurred at the destruction of the Tower of Babel and brings all nations, religions, tongues, and ethnic groups under the umbrella of a one-world system.

As we have seen, Atlantis, upon which the new world order is supposedly modeled, is said to have been ruled by ten kings, who in turn submitted to the authority of an eleventh. Once again, we see a reflection—a specific reflection—of what the Bible says will transpire under the Antichrist's reign. His kingdom will be divided among ten kings, who will then submit to him as the eleventh king. However, in the end, it will not be a glorious democratic, philosophic empire, but the most brutal, tyrannical, and bloody dictatorship this world has ever seen. When our world leaders speak of a new world order, understand that, as well-meaning as some of them may be, they are in actual fact calling for the very kingdom of the Antichrist. The concept of a new world order, while spoken of by political and economic leaders in political and economic terms, is at its most fundamental level an esoteric concept. The world will indeed be united in one cause, even as it was during the days of the Tower of Babel. The leader of this united world will be the man of sin himself, the Antichrist!

***The New Age and the Revelation of Maitreya***: Some of the esoteric revelations being promoted today are so blatantly anti-Christian that it does not take much effort to spot demonic inspiration behind them. According to some, planet earth is in a transition phase between the "Christian" age of Pisces and the philosophical age of Aquarius. Pisces, which incorporates the symbol of the fish (supposedly linking it with Christianity), was supposedly characterized by darkness, intolerance, and conflict. With the advent of Aquarius a new society of light, tolerance, peace, and spiritual evolution is to be created. As Jesus Christ is said to have inaugurated Pisces, so Aquarius is to be inaugurated by a new "World Teacher" known as Lord Maitreya. Maitreya is to be the Christ of the Christians, the Messiah of the Jews, the Imam Mahdi of Islam, the final Buddha of the Buddhists, etc.

Maitreya is a false Christ who plays upon humanity's desire for a new world order and a new age of peace. Whether or not there is an actual Lord Maitreya somewhere in the world, we do not know. We only have the testimony of those like Benjamin Creme, a British esoteric philosopher, to go by. According to Creme, Maitreya has already met with world leaders and journalists and is awaiting what he calls the "Day of Declaration," when he will be revealed to the world. Creme also claims that a "star sign" has appeared all over the world, heralding the emergence of Maitreya, quite similar to what happened with the Star of Bethlehem when Jesus was born.[8] He claims that many have reported seeing this starlike image. Pictures of the supposed herald have been posted on the Web site of Share International,[9] which is an zation supporting Creme in his mission to make Maitreya known. Ac to Share International, the spectacular "spiral" phenomenon that appeared in the night skies over Norway on December 9, 2009, officially attributed to a failed Russian missile test, is related to this Maitreya star sign.[10]

There certainly appears to be either highly sophisticated fraud or heavy demonic power associated with Benjamin Creme and Maitreya. On July 31, 2009, while interviewing Benjamin Creme on the popular late-night radio show *Coast to Coast A.M.*, host George Noory testified of becoming intensely ill, feeling that if he continued with the interview, he would pass out. Noory made it a point of mentioning that he had conducted over five thousand interviews with various people and never felt what he felt that night interviewing Creme about Maitreya. He reportedly got notices from his listeners—hundreds of them—indicating that they felt the same thing. Noory remarked that he was not sure if, with respect to Maitreya, he was dealing with the chosen one or the Antichrist. Maitreya is also credited with performing numerous signs and wonders such as manifesting miraculous crosses of light, as well as stirring up "healing waters" in Mexico, Germany, China, and India.[11] According to Debra Lardie, Maitreya answers to no one save an entity known as Sanat Kumura, who is equated with Lucifer.[12]

Creme claims that Maitreya held a conference in London, England, in 1990 featuring 250 guests, including royalty, heads of government, and journalists. Creme released the names of two people who were at the conference, citing that these two names could be revealed since the two individuals were now deceased. These were Palestinian leader Yasser Arafat and King Hussein of Jordan. Apparently Middle East issues surrounding the Palestinians and the Israelis were discussed between Maitreya and King Hussein. Four years later, there was peace between Israel and Jordan.

Regarding the Day of Declaration, it is claimed that at some point in the future an international press conference will be held whereby Maitreya will present to the world his credentials, which will then open the door for this all-important declaration day.[13] Again, heavy-duty supernatural power is to be involved in this declaration, as all humanity will simultaneously be overshadowed by Matreiya, each hearing his words telepathically in his or her own language. It is said that hundreds of thousands of miracles will occur throughout the world on that day.

On January 14, 2010, Creme indicated that Maitreya had recently stepped forward, giving his first interview on an American television network. Millions heard him speak, Creme claims, though he was not introduced as the World Teacher but simply as "a man."[14]

It is nearly impossible to verify Creme's claims, as he supposedly receives much of his insights through telepathic means. If Maitreya really does exist, he very well may be a candidate for either the Antichrist or the False Prophet of Revelation. But regardless of whether or not he exists, it is clear that the concept of a world teacher dominates esoteric spirituality, as it is to him that esoteric philosophers and adherents of the new age movement look to and hope in.

## Pulling Everything Together: The Kingdom of the Antichrist

The "revelations" evaluated in this book and summarized above are not in and of themselves the main issue. They *do not* represent definitive scenarios as to how the Antichrist's kingdom will come together but rather are each selected manifestations of an overall *system* that is set up in opposition to the true system of worship revealed by God. These revelations, popular in today's Western society, all display esoteric tendencies, claiming "truths" or "secrets" that can be attained to through enlightenment or participation in secret societies. This affinity toward enlightenment can be witnessed very early on in humanity's existence when Satan tempted Eve by promising knowledge, to be gained only if she would disobey the *already revealed* truth of God. This right here is the great conflict: obedience to the already revealed Word of God vs. enlightenment into new and secret "truths." Each of the revelations above are linked to this latter tendency, revealing a common root—satanic paganism and disobedience to the one true God. This counterfeit system will climax in the arrival of a counterfeit messiah, the Antichrist.

What is the kingdom of the Antichrist? It is the end-time culmination of the counterfeit system of worship in one, world power structure. It is, quite literally, the government of Satan implemented on earth through the agency of a man. The roots of this kingdom reach into the distant past when Satan rebelled against the established order of God, inaugurating a rival (yet inferior) spiritual system/kingdom, and opening the door for a ferocious (humanly speaking) conflict of the ages to ensue. Satan has been striving to fully institute this rebellious kingdom upon the earth for millennia. The advent of the

Antichrist and the establishment of a new world order under the Antichrist's leadership represent this rival kingdom in a unified, visible form.

There has been continuity to this counterfeit system throughout the ages. It originated at the fall of Satan, infected humanity in the garden of Eden, reestablished itself at Babel, sprang up in the pagan empires of history, and embodied various cults and organizations throughout the ancient and medieval world. Its mysteries have been preserved through secret/esoteric societies—the Rosicrucian Order, the Freemasons, etc.,—and can be seen in the modern New Age movement. It has also influenced world leaders from all avenues of life who today have as their goal and ambition a new world order. It can also be perceived in each of the specific revelations we have looked at. Each of them casts doubt on the deity and work of Jesus Christ, who is *already revealed* in Scripture as God-made-flesh and the true redeemer of humanity. We all, like Eve, have a choice. Either we accept and believe what God has already revealed and commanded, or we bite the fruit—accepting Satan's esoteric counterfeits, thinking that they can provide immortality and societal order. Many today are choosing the latter, as evidenced by the popularity of concepts such as the bloodline of Christ, a solely human Jesus, a new utopia, Maitreya, etc. That these revelations all possess an "Antichrist bend" should convince us of the inspiration behind them. Their popularity today may also be an indication as to the nearness of the Antichrist's arrival.

In the garden of Eden, Satan tempted Eve with everlasting life apart from obedience to God. God warned that to eat of the fruit of the Tree of Knowledge of Good and Evil was to experience certain death (Genesis 2:17). Satan, meanwhile, seemingly convinced Eve that partaking of the fruit would not, contrary to God's word, bring about death (Genesis 3:4). How similar are today's "new revelations," which declare that Jesus Christ is not the only way to immortality! The Bible states: "He who believes in the Son has eternal life; but he who does not obey the Son will not see life, but the wrath of God abides on him" (John 3:36). Satan, meanwhile, seems to be arguing through the esoteric revelations: "Does the Bible say that unless you believe in Jesus Christ you will not see eternal life? Not so! God knows that if you shake off old dogma and allow your mind to be liberated, you will be enlightened—knowing the mysteries of true spirituality."

The test of a spiritual or spiritual-related concept, revelation, person, or testimony is its treatment of the Lord Jesus Christ (1 John 4:1–3). Each of the esoteric revelations evaluated in this book contradict the biblical witness concerning Jesus. Some of them, *in the place of Jesus*, offer a substitute to address the problem of human suffering. This substitute—which is in reality the counterfeit system we have referred to—can be symbolized by the Holy Grail. The Grail is that *thing* that brings about the *perfect* society, and is to be discovered by the *perfect* man, who upon doing so will take up his now-vacant throne. He is the one for whom this world waits—the "savior" who will bring about the ideal existence that humanity seeks. In a very real sense, the Holy Grail is the provision of Satan offered for human self-betterment apart from God. How similar this is indeed to what Satan offered Eve in Eden. Larkin notes:

> The inducement that Satan held out to Eve, that the *acquisition of knowledge* would put her and Adam on the same plane with God, and make them GOD-LIKE, is the same inducement that Satan offers to ambitious men today, and he is seeking through his dupes to build up a magnificent civilization on the discoveries and inventions of men, and exalt man without God, and his aim is the final "DEIFICATION OF MAN," that will find its culmination in his "SUPERMAN," "THE ANTICHRIST," . . . This accounts for all the "World Systems" of today for the social, religious, political, and commercial betterment and advancement of the race.[15]

There are only two systems—the genuine and the counterfeit, the revelation of God and the lies of Satan, the worship of Christ and the worship of the Antichrist. What are today being proclaimed as new revelations are in many cases actually ancient pagan philosophies or anti-Christian ideals wrapped up in benevolent clothes to seduce mankind into the most tyrannical system the world has ever seen. The best way for the church to counteract these heresies is to not shrink back and alter our testimony, but to reaffirm all the more the unchanging, liberating, and satisfying truth of the biblical Jesus Christ.

## The Love of God: A Way of Escape

The greatest need of the human heart is to be loved and accepted by a God who controls our very existence. Such acceptance comes by way of reconciliation to God through the cross of Jesus Christ (2 Corinthians 5:17–19). God is a personal God. He knows us and loves us intimately and desires to meet the deepest needs of our heart and existence. Our greatest fear is often the fear of death. Through Christ, God has dealt with this fear (Hebrews 2:9, 14–15). The death of Jesus Christ has satisfied God's wrath at human sin. Thus, for those who believe in Jesus, death has no sting (1 Corinthians 15:54–57). Death is a result of sin, and for those who die apart from having their sins forgiven, death is eternal (Romans 6:23; Revelation 20:11–15). By God becoming a man in the person of Jesus Christ, living a perfect, sinless life, and dying on the cross to pay humanity's sin debt, God's righteous demands—the demands of His law—have been met, freeing all those who believe in Jesus from having to try to earn God's approval.[16] All sin must be punished, and the punishment for sin is death and eternal separation for God. Either we pay this penalty, or someone pays it on our behalf. Jesus is that "someone". Though believers in Jesus still physically die, they need not fear eternal separation from God! Since God freely restores those who believe in Jesus to a relationship with Himself, we can be assured of heaven, eternal life, and be delivered from the great fear of death—if we believe this good news. Esoteric philosophy, while often promising enlightenment and peace on earth, can never deal with humanity's greatest and deepest needs and fears. We need deliverance from death, and we need to be freed from sin. This, Jesus has accomplished for us.

God is love. He did not send His Son into the world to condemn the world, but rather to save it (John 3:16–18). Belief in Jesus Christ—the Jesus of the Bible—is the only means to a relationship with God because only Jesus met the demands of God's law fully. God is holy, and as such requires holy perfection from humanity, which is to His glory. Since we, being fallen, sinful people, could never attain these standards, God became a human being in the person of Jesus Christ and took it upon Himself to attain them for us. He then freely credits all those who believe in Jesus with *the righteousness of Jesus* (Romans 3:21–31), freeing us from having to try to "earn" God's approval (Galatians 2:16), which we could never do anyway (Romans 3:20). Forgiveness of sin, then, and eternal life in heaven, are free gifts given to the one who has faith in Jesus (Romans 6:23; 10:5–13). Our God has met the deepest needs of the human heart by removing the fear of death and giving us free access to Himself through Christ Jesus, who has been raised from the dead, having accomplished the work God gave Him to do. Faith in Christ—belief in Him from the heart—is what is required of us.

So you see, God is not a distant, uninterested Being, as the deists would have us believe. He is not interested in simply enlightening us, as the esoteric and occult philosophers would have us believe. He is interested in bringing us into a deep and intimate relationship with Himself, serving as our true heavenly *Father* (Galatians 4:6). All who are willing may come to Christ to receive His free offer.

But somebody may say, "I am too great a sinner." Where sin abounded, grace did much more abound (Romans 5:20). Another may say, "God will never forgive me for what I have done." Any sin and blasphemy—except blasphemy against the Spirit—will be forgiven people (Matthew 12:31). But another might say, "I have committed the unpardonable sin." If you are willing to truly come to Christ, He will not reject you, and thus you have not committed the unpardonable sin (John 6:37; Revelation 22:17). Still, one may argue, "I was a Christian, but have sinned away my salvation, though I earnestly desire to come back." If God has granted you repentance, don't let your guilt keep you away any longer (Hebrews 6:6; Galatians 6:1–2; 1 John 1:9; 2:1–2). And yet, I think there are many who might say, "This all sounds good, but I just can't believe that it is true. Can we really trust the Bible?" Ask God to help your unbelief (Mark 9:24). The only excuse we really have for not coming to Christ is that we simply do not want to. He stands ready to receive in mercy all who come to Him in true faith.

It is true that we cannot continue to go on in sin and still enjoy fellowship with God. God's grace is not a free ticket to do as we please. We cannot love both sin and God. Repentance is a key part of the Christian experience. However, we do not do good to earn God's acceptance; rather, we do good in response to His love toward us. We walk with Him in relationship just as we would with a best friend or a loving father. This is the gospel. This is the true revelation of God. All who accept it are set free to love and worship God in truth. Those who reject it position themselves to be deceived by the counterfeit gospel and the counterfeit messiah, the Antichrist.

It is the belief of many, including this author, that God will not subject His redeemed church to the horrors of the tribulation and the times of the Antichrist—not because the church is "better" than the rest, but because it is made up of those who have already accepted Christ and stand forgiven in

God's sight. The Lord will deliver those who are now His from the days of His wrath.[17] Throughout the Bible, God has always spared the righteous while destroying the wicked. He delivered Noah from the flood, and Lot from the destruction of Sodom and Gomorrah. The means by which many feel the church will be delivered from the wrath of God during the times of the Antichrist is through a spectacular event known as the rapture of the church. Paul describes this event in 1 Thessalonians 4:14–17. Those who accept Christ now can look in hope to the coming of Jesus and need not fear the Antichrist. Christians are admonished in the Bible to eagerly look for the coming of the Lord, not to the coming of the Antichrist. Those who reject Christ now and live to see the coming of the Antichrist will be forced to either worship him or reject him. Those who worship him will lose their eternal souls (Revelation 14:9–12), while many who reject him will be executed (Revelation 20:4).

The Antichrist's reign upon the earth will be brief. God, who loves His creation, will not permit Satan and the Antichrist to bring this world to total destruction. At the right moment God will send Jesus to this earth to defeat and destroy the Antichrist and his kingdom (Revelation 19:11–21). He will then set up the genuine messianic kingdom upon the earth, with His throne being set in the city of Jerusalem. True peace will be ushered in, and planet earth will enjoy a thousand-year paradise unmatched by anything since the garden of Eden, as God will be ruling this world directly in the person of Jesus Christ (Revelation 20:1–4; Zechariah 14:9). Those who were raptured to heaven just before the Antichrist's appearance shall return with Christ to govern this world with Him (Jude 14–15; Revelation 3:21). Under the government of Jesus, righteousness and justice will flourish in the earth. God is love! He has not abandoned His creation.

The issue for us today is whom will we serve—the one true God of heaven or Satan, the prince of the counterfeit system? What "truth" will we accept—the true revelation of God in the person of Jesus Christ or the counterfeit revelations that attempt to redefine Christ and which actually prepare people for the Antichrist? The choice is ours. The God of love offers Himself to us freely through Christ. Satan offers nothing but terror and deception in the person of the Antichrist. Today we have the opportunity to choose. Tomorrow may be too late.

# Bibliography


Abane, Richard. *The Truth Behind the Da Vinci Code: A Challenging Response to the Bestelling Novel.* Eugene: Harvest House Publishers, 2004.

Anderson, Sir Robert. *The Coming Prince.* Grand Rapids: Kregel, 1957.

Andrews, Richard and Paul Schellenberger. *The Tomb of God: Unlocking the Code to a 2,000-Year-Old Mystery.* Great Britain: Time Warner Books, 1996. First published in Great Britain by Little, Brown and Company, 1996.

Baigent, Michael, Richard Leigh & Henry Lincoln. *Holy Blood, Holy Grail: Revised and updated.* United Kingdom: Arrow Books, 1996

*The Messianic Legacy.* London: Arrow Books, 1996.

Barackman, Floyd H. *Practical Christian Theology: Examining the Great Doctrines of the Faith, Fourth Edition.* Grand Rapids: Kregel, 2001.

Bush, Frederic William, David Allan Hubbard &William Sanford Lasor. *Old Testament Survey: The Message, Form, and Background of the Old Testament, Second Edition.* Grand Rapids: William B. Eerdmans Publishing Company, 1996.

Butler, Alan. *The Goddess, the Grail & the Lodge: The Real Da Vinci Code and the Origins of Religion.* Winchester, U.K., New York, U.S.A.: O Books, 2004.

Butler, Alan and Christopher Knight. *Solomon's Power Brokers: The Secrets of Freemasonry, the Church, and the Illuminati.* London: Watkins Publishing, 2007.

Carrico, David. *The Great Seal of the United States: It's Occult Meaning.* Evansville: Followers of Jesus Christ Ministries, 1997.

Church, J. R., N. W. Hutchings, Gary Stearman, Bill Uselton. *Europe is Rising.* Oklahoma City: Heathstone Publishing, 1990.

Cohen, Tim. *The Antichrist and a Cup of Tea.* Aurora: Prophecy House Inc., 1998

Cooper, William. *Behold a Pale Horse.* Flagstaff: Light Technology Publishing, 1991.

Davies, Norman. *Europe: A History.* London: Pimlico, 1997.

De Vere, Nicholas. *The Dragon Legacy: The Secret History of an Ancient Bloodline.* San Diego: The Book Tree, 2004.

Driver, Jack M. *Freemasonry: An Illustrated History.* London: Kandour Ltd., 2006.

Enns, Paul. *The Moody Handbook of Theology: Revised and Expanded.* Chicago: Moody Publishers, 1989, 2008.

Gaebelein, Arno C. *Daniel.* Grand Rapids: Kregel, 1955.

Gardiner, Philip and Gary Osborne. *The Serpent Grail: The Truth Behind the Holy Grail, The Philosopher's Stone, and the Elixir of Life.* London: Watkins Publishing, 2005.

Gardner, Laurence. *Bloodline of the Holy Grail: The Hidden Lineage of Jesus Revealed.* Gloucester: Fair Winds Press, 2002.

*Genesis of the Grail Kings: The Explosive Story of Genetic Cloning and the Ancient Bloodline of Jesus.* Gloucester; Fair Winds Press, 2002.

*The Magdalene Legacy: The Jesus and Mary Bloodline Conspiracy.* Hammersmith: Element, An imprint of HarperCollins Publishers, 2005.

*Realm of the Ring Lords: The Myth and Magic of the Grail Quest.* Gloucester: Fair Winds Press, 2002.

*The Shadow of Solomon.* London: Harper Element, 2005.

Geisler, Dr. Norman. *Christian Apologetics.* Grand Rapids: Baker Book House, 1976. *Systematic Theology: Volume 4.* Minnesota: Bethany House, 2005.

Gest, Kevin. *The Secrets of Solomon's temple: Discover the Hidden Truth that Lies at the Heart of Freemasonry.* Gloucester: Fair Winds Press, 2007.

Gilbert, Adrian. *The New Jerusalem: The Extraordinary True Story of How a Secret Society Rebuilt London.* London: Harper Element, 2005.

Gonzalez, Justo L. *The Story of Christianity: Volume 1.* New York: HarperCollins Publishers, 1984.

Hagger, Nicholas. *The Secret History of the West: The Influence of Secret Organizations on Western History from the Renaissance to the 20th Century.* United Kingdom: O Books, 2005.

Hall, Manly P. *The Lost Keys of Freemasonry.* New York: The Penguin Group, 2006. *The Secret Destiny of America.* Los Angeles: The Philosophical Research Society, 1991. *The Secret Teachings of All Ages.* New York: Penguin Group, 2003.

Harpur, Tom. *The Pagan Christ: Recovering the Lost Light.* Toronto: Thomas Allen Publishers, 2004.

Harris, Jack. *Freemasonry.* New Kensington: Whitaker House, 1983.

Hindson, Ed and Tim LaHaye. *The Popular Bible Prophecy Commentary: Understanding the Meaning of Every Prophetic Passage.* Eugene: Harvest House Publishers, 2006.

Hislop, Alexander. *The Two Babylons: Or the Papal Worship Proved to be the Worship of Nimrod and His Wife.* Neptune: Loizeaux Brothers, 1959.

Hopkins, Marilyn and Tim Wallace-Murphy. *Custodians of Truth: The Continuance of Rex Deus.* Newburyport and San Francisco: Red Wheel/Weiser LLC, 2007.

*Rosslyn: Guardians of the Secrets of the Holy Grail.* Hammersmith: HarperCollins Publishers, 1999.

Hunt, Dave. *A Woman Rides the Beast: The Roman Catholic Church and the Last Days.* Eugene: Harvest House Publishers, 1994.

Ironside, H. A. *Revelation.* Neptune, New Jersey: Loizeaux Brothers, 1996

Jeffers, H. Paul. *Freemasons: Inside the World's Oldest Secret Society.* New York: Citadel Press, 2005.

Jeffrey, Grant R. *Apocalypse: The Coming Judgement of the Nations.* New York: Bantam Books, 1994. *The New Temple and the Second Coming: The Prophecy that Points to Christ's Return in Your Generation.* Colorado Springs: Waterbrook Press, 2007. *Triumphant Return: The Coming Kingdom of God.* Toronto: Frontier Research Publications, 2001.

Kah, Gary. *On Route to Global Occupation: A High Ranking Government Liaison Exposes The Secret Agenda for World Unification.* Lafayette: Huntington House Publishers, 1992. *The New World Religion: The Spiritual Roots of Global Government.* Noblesville: Hope International Publishing, 1998.

Knight, Christopher and Robert Lomas. *The Hiram Key: Pharaohs, Freemasons, and the Discovery of the Secret Scrolls of Jesus.* London: Arrow Books, 1997. *The Second Messiah: Templars, the Turin Shroud, and The Great Secret of Freemasonry.* London: Arrow Books, 1998.

Laney, J. Carl. *Concise Bible Atlas: A Geographical Survey of Bible History,* Peabody, MA; Hendrickson Publishers, Inc., 2007.

Lardie, Debra. *Concise Dictionary of the Occult and New Age.* Grand Rapids: Kregel, 2000.

Larkin, Clarence. *The Book of Daniel.* Genside: The Rev. Clarence Larkin Estate, 1929. *The Book of Revelation: A Study of the Last Prophetic Book of Holy Scripture.* Glenside: The Rev. Clarence Larkin Estate, 1919. *Dispensational Truth of God's Plan and Purpose in the Ages,* Glenside: The Rev. Clarence Larkin Estate, 1918. *The Spirit World.* Glenside: The Rev. Clarence Larkin Estate, 1921.

Lewis, David Allen. *False Messiah: Unholy Blood, Satan's Grail.* Springfield, 1988.

Lincoln, Henry. *The Holy Place: Sauniere and the Decoding of the Mystery of Rennes-le-Chateau.* New York: Arcade Publishing, 1991.

Lunn, Martin. *Da Vinci Code Decoded: The Truth Behind the New York Times #1 Bestseller.* New York: The Disinformation Company, 2004.

Marrs, Jim. *Rule By Secrecy: The Hidden History that Connects the Trilateral Commission, the Freemasons, and the Great Pyramids.* New York: Perennial, 2000.

Marrs, Texe. *Circle of Intrigue: The Hidden Inner Circle of the Global Illuminati Conspiracy.* Austin: Living Truth Publications, 1995.

Martin, Malachi. *The Keys of This Blood: Pope John Paul II versus Russia and the West for Control of the New World Order.* New York: Touchstone, 1990.

Matthews, John. *King Arthur: Dark Age Warrior and Mythic King.* London: Carlton Books, 2004.

McDowell, Josh. *The New Evidence that Demands a Verdict: Evidence I & II Fully Updated In One Volume to Answer Questions Challenging Christians in the 21st Century.* Nashville: Thomas Nelson Publishers, 1999.

Ovason, David. *The Secret Symbols of the Dollar Bill: A Closer Look at the Hidden Magic And Meaning of the Money You Use Every Day.* New York: Perennial Currents, 2005.

Pentecost, J. Dwight. *Things to Come: A Study in biblical Eschatology.* Grand Rapids: Zondervan Publishing House, 1964.

Picknett, Lynne and Clive Prince. *The Sion Revelation: Inside the Shadowy World of Europe's Secret Masters.* Great Britain: Time Warner Books. In the United States: New York, Touchstone, a division of Simon & Schuster), 2006.

Prophet, Elizabeth Clare (With Annice Booth). *Mary Magdalene and the Divine Feminine: Jesus' Lost Teaching on Women.* Gardiner: Summit Publications Inc., 2005.

Quantum Books. *The Encyclopaedia of Ancient Myths and Cultures.* London: Quantum Books, 2003.

Schiffman, Lawrence. *Society of Biblical Literature Monograph Series: The Eschatological Community of the Dead Sea Scrolls.* Atlanta: Scholars Press, 1989.

Sinclair, Andrew. *The Sword and the Grail: The Story of the Grail, the Templars, and the True Discovery of America.* United Kingdom: Birlinn Ltd., 2005.

Southwell, David and Sean Twist. *Conspiracy Files: Paranoia Secrecy Intrigue.* London: Sevenoaks, 2004.

Starbird, Margaret. *Mary Magdalene, Bride in Exile.* Rochester: Bear & Company, 2005.

Still, William. *New World Order: The Ancient Plan of Secret Societies.* Lafayette: Huntington House Publishers, 1990.

Strong, James. *The New Strong's Exhaustive Concordance of the Bible.* Nashville: Thomas Nelson Publishers, 1995, 1996.

Stubbs, Richard and Geoffrey R.D. Underhill. *Political Economy and the Changing Global Order.* Toronto: McClelland & Stewart Inc., 1994.

Telushkin, Rabbi Joseph. *Jewish Literacy: The Most Important Things to Know About the Jewish Religion, Its People, and its History.* New York: HarperCollins Publishers, 2001.

Time Life Books. *Mysteries of the Unknown: Mystic Places.* Alexandria: Time Life Books.

Time Magazine. *Visions of Europe.* Winter 1998–1999.

Twyman, Tracy R. *The Merovingian Mythos: And the Mystery of Rennes-le-Chateau.* Portland: Dragon Key Press, 2004. *Solomon's Treasure: The Magic and Mystery of America's Money.* Portland: Dragon Key Press, 2005.

Vanity Fair Magazine. *20th Anniversary Issue, Special Collector's Edition.* September 2003.

Wallace-Murphy, Tim. *The Enigma of the Freemasons: Their History and Mystical Connections.* New York: The Disinformation Company Ltd., 2006.

Walvoord, John F. *The Blessed Hope and the Tribulation: A Historical and Biblical Study of Posttribulationism.* Grand Rapids: Zondervan Publishing House, 1976.

Yeago, David. *The Apostolic Faith: A Catholic and Evangelical Introduction to Christian Theology, Part One: The Gift of the Life of the Triune God in Jesus Christ* 2005.

# Notes and References

## CHAPTER 1


1. Debra Lardie (Dan Lioy and Paul Ingram Contributing Editors), *Concise Dictionary of the Occult and New Age*, Kregel Publications, Grand Rapids, 2000, 98.
2. H. A. Ironside, *Revelation*, Loizeaux Brothers Inc. New Jersey, 1996, 158.
3. Ibid., 108. (Parenthesis added).
4. Laurence Gardner, *Bloodline of the Holy Grail: The Hidden Lineage of Jesus Revealed*, Fair Winds Press, Gloucester, MA, 2002, 1.
5. Laurence Gardner, *Realm of the Ring Lords: The Myth and Magic of the Grail Quest*, Fair Winds Press, Gloucester, MA, 2002, 14.
6. Christopher Knight and Robert Lomas, *The Second Messiah: Templars, the Turin Shroud, and the Great Secret of Freemasonry*, Arrow Books Limited, London, 1998, 103–104.
7. Christopher Knight and Alan Butler, *Solomon's Power Brokers: The Secrets of Freemasonry, the Church, and the Illuminati*, Watkins Publishing, London, 2007, 255.
8. Ibid., 284–285.
9. William Still, *New World Order: The Ancient Plan of Secret Societies*, Huntington House Publishers; Lafayette, Louisiana, 1990, 41.
10. Manly P. Hall, *The Secret Destiny of America*, The Philosophical Research Society, Inc., Los Angeles, 1991, 59.
11. Martin Lunn, *Da Vinci Code Decoded: The Truth Behind the New York Times #1 Bestseller*, The Disinformation Company, New York, NY, 2004, 3–4.
12. Tim Wallace-Murphy and Marilyn Hopkins, *Rosslyn: Guardians of the Secrets of the Holy Grail*, Element Books Ltd, 2000; 210.
13. Ibid., 210–211, ©1999, Tim Wallace-Murphy and Marilyn Hopkins. Copyright in the customized version vests in Adrian Isaacs.
14. Tom Harpur, *The Pagan Christ: Recovering the Lost Light*, Thomas Allen Publishers, Toronto, 2004, 183–184.
15. Hopkins and Wallace-Murphy, *Rosslyn*, 211. ©1999, Tim Wallace-Murphy and Marilyn Hopkins. Copyright in the customized version vests in Adrian Isaacs.
16. Excerpted from *Custodians of Truth: The Continuance of Rex Deus* ©2007 *By Tim Wallace-Murphy and Marilyn Hopkins* with permission from Red Wheel/Weiser LLC Newburyport, MA and San Francisco, CA. www.redwheelweiser.com, 268.
17. Lardie, *Concise Dictionary of the Occult and New Age*, 164.
18. Taken from *Concise Dictionary of the Occult and New Age*, © Copyright 2000 by Debra Lardie. Published by Kregel Publications, Grand Rapids, MI. Used by permission of the publisher. All rights reserved, 164.
19. Share International, 'Highlights from the Text', *Maitreya's Mission: Volume 1, A New Age and the Appearance of the World Teacher* (April 1999), http://www.share-international.org/background/printed/mission_1.htm.
20. Lardie, *Concise Dictionary of the Occult and New Age*, 164.

**CHAPTER 2**

1. Wikipedia: The Free Encyclopedia, *George H.W. Bush* (20 August 2009), *http://en.wikipedia.org/wiki/George_H._W._Bush.*
2. Darris McNeely, Managing Editor, *World News and Prophecy Online: Biblical Perspectives on Current Events* (28 September 2006), http://www.wnponline.org/newsletter/2006/wnp09282006.htm.
3. William Sanford Lasor, David Allan Hubbard, Frederick William Bush, *Old Testament Survey: The Message, Form, and Background of the Old Testament, Second Edition*, William B. Eerdmans Publishing Company, Grand Rapids, Michigan, 1996; 689.
4. Ibid., 691
5. Rabbi Joseph Telushkin, *Jewish Literacy: The Most Important things to Know About the Jewish Religion, Its People, and its History*, HarperCollins Publishers, New York, 2001, 601.
6. See Exodus 3, 4.
7. See Exodus 28:1, 29: 7–9.
8. Zechariah 6:12–13.
9. See Luke 19:28–40.
10. Josh McDowell, *The New Evidence that Demands a Verdict: Evidence I and II Fully Updated in One Volume to Answer Questions Challenging Christians in the 21st Century*, Thomas Nelson Publishers, Nashville, 1999, 164.
11. James Strong, *The New Strong's Exhaustive Concordance of the Bible*, Thomas Nelson Publishers, Nashville, 1995, 1996, 67.
12. See Acts 2:22–24, 3:13–15, 17–19.
13. See Isaiah 53:10, 1 John 1:7, Romans 5:9.
14. Tim Wallace-Murphy and Marilyn Hopkins, *Rosslyn: Guardian of the Secrets of the Holy Grail*, HarperCollins Publishers Ltd, Hammersmith, London, ©1999, Tim Wallace-Murphy and Marilyn Hopkins. Copyright in customized version vests in Adrian Isaacs, 210.
15. Michael Baigent, Richard Leigh and Henry Lincoln, *The Messianic Legacy*, Arrow Books, London, 1996, 451.

**CHAPTER 3**

1. J. Dwight Pentecost, *Things to Come: A Study in Biblical Eschatology*, Zondervan Publishing House, Grand Rapids, 1964, 337.
2. Pentecost, *Things to Come*, 322.
3. Arno C. Gaebelein, *Daniel*, Kregel Publications, Grand Rapids, 1955, 82.
4. Pentecost, *Things to Come*, 321.
5. See Matthew 11:12–14; 17:10–13; Luke 1:8–17.

**CHAPTER 4**

1. The seven hills of Rome are: Aventine, Caelian, Capitoline, Esquiline, Palatine, Quirinal, and Viminal.
2. Dave Hunt, *A Woman Rides the Beast: The Roman Catholic Church and the Last Days*, Harvest House Publishers; Eugene, Oregon, 1994; 69.

3. See Ephesians 5:22–32; Revelation 20:8–14.
4. Grant R. Jeffrey, *Apocalypse: The Coming Judgment of the Nations*, Bantam Books, New York, NY, 1994, 202.
5. J. Carl Laney, *Concise Bible Atlas: A Geographical Survey of Bible History*, Hendrickson Publishers Inc., Peabody, MA, 2007, 30–31.
6. See Genesis 11:5–9.
7. Ephesians 2:8–10.
8. Revelation 5:9–10.
9. See Revelation 5:9.
10. Clarence Larkin, *The Book of Revelation: A study of the Last Prophetic Book of Holy Scripture*, Rev. Clarence Larkin Estate; Glenside, PA, 1919, 152.
11. Ibid.
12. Alexander Hislop, *The Two Babylons: Or the Papal Worship Proved to be the Worship of Nimrod and His Wife*, Loizeaux Brothers, Neptune, NJ, 1959, 32.
13. Ibid., 66.
14. Ibid.
15. Ibid., 66–67.
16. Ibid.
17. H. A. Ironside, Ironside Commentaries, *Revelation*, Loizeaux Brothers, Inc., New Jersey, 1996, 188.
18. Ibid.
19. Alan Butler, *The Goddess, the Grail and the Lodge*, O Books, United Kingdom, 2004, 49.
20. Hislop, *The Two Babylons*, 74–75.
21. Ibid., 75.
22. J. Dwight Pentecost, *Things to Come*, Zondervan Publishing House, Grand Rapids, Michigan; 1958, 366.
23. Ironside, *Revelation*, 188.
24. *Tim Lahaye Prophecy Study Bible*, AMG Publishers, United States, 2000, 704–705.
25. Clarence Larkin, *The Spirit World*, The Rev. Clarence Larkin Estate, Glenside, PA., 1921, 8.
26. Ezekiel 28: 14–15.

**CHAPTER 5**

1. Tim Wallace-Murphy, *The Enigma of The Freemasons: Their History and Mystical Connections*, The Disinformation Company Ltd., New York, NY 2006, 40.
2. Laurence Gardner, *Realm of the Rings Lords: The Myth and Magic of the Grail Quest*, Fair Winds Press, Gloucester, MA; 2003, 3.
3. Wikipedia, The Free Encyclopedia, Camelot (16 August 2009), http://en.wikipedia.org/wiki/Camelot
4. Laurence Gardner, *Bloodline of the Holy Grail: The Hidden Lineage of Jesus Revealed*, Fair Winds Press, Gloucester, MA; 2002, 171.
5. Manly P. Hall, *The Secret Teachings of All Ages, Reader's Edition*, Penguin Group, New York, 2003, 309.

6. Tracy R. Twyman, *The Merovingian Mythos: And the Mystery of Rennes-le-Chateau*, Dragon Key Press, Portland, 2004, 9.
7. Ibid.
8. Ibid.
9. Gardner, *Realm of the Rings Lords*, 2.
10. Ibid., 3.
11. Ibid.
12. John Matthews, *King Arthur: Dark Age Warrior and Mythic King*, Carlton Books, London, England 2004, 69.
13. Nicholas de Vere, *The Dragon Legacy: The Secret History of an Ancient Bloodline*, The Book Tree, San Diego, 2004, 242.
14. J. R. Church, N. W. Hutchings, Gary Stearman, Bill Uselton; *Europe is Rising*, Heathstone Publishing Ltd., Oklahoma City, 1990, 48.
15. David Ovason, *The Secret Symbols of the Dollar Bill: A Closer Look at the Hidden Magic and Meaning of the Money You Use Every Day*, Perennial Currents, New York, NY 2005, 99.
16. Ibid., 52, 54.
17. David Carrico, *The Great Seal of the United States: It's Occult Meaning*, Followers of Jesus Christ Ministries, Evansville, IN, 1997, 30.
18. Taken from *Concise Dictionary of the Occult and New Age*, © Copyright, 2000, by Debra Lardie. Published by Kregel Publications, Grand Rapids, MI. Used by permission of the publisher. All rights reserved, 101.
19. Lardie, *Concise Dictionary of the Occult and New Age*, 101.
20. Ibid.
21. Revelation 17:8.
22. Lardie, *Concise Dictionary of the Occult and New Age*, 101.
23. Twyman, *The Merovingian Mythos*, 132.
24. Taken from *Concise Dictionary of the Occult and New Age*, © Copyright 2000, by Debra Lardie. Published by Kregel Publications, Grand Rapids, MI. Used by permission of the publisher. All rights reserved, 189.
25. Gardner, *Bloodline of the Holy Grail*, 297.
26. Manly P. Hall, *The Secret Destiny of America*, The Philosophical Research Society, INC.; Los Angeles, 1991, 179.
27. Ibid.
28. William Still, *New World Order: The Ancient Plan of Secret Societies*, Huntington House Publishers, Lafayette, Louisiana, 1990, 41.
29. Genesis 6:4.
30. Philip Gardiner, Gary Osborne, *The Serpent Grail: The Truth Behind the Holy Grail, the Philosopher's Stone, and the Elixir of Life*, Watkins Publishing, London, 2005, 39–40.
31. Gardner, *Realm of the Rings Lords*, p. 3.
32. Genesis 3: 2–7.
33. De Vere, *The Dragon Legacy*, 318.
34. Ibid., 318–319.

**CHAPTER 6**

1. Genesis 3:5.
2. Laurence Gardner, *Genesis of the Grail Kings: The Explosive Story of Genetic Cloning and the Ancient Bloodline of Jesus*, Fair Winds Press, Gloucester, MA; 2002, 120.
3. Henry Lincoln, *The Holy Place: Sauniere and the Decoding of the Mystery of Rennes-le-Chateau*, Arcade Publishing, New York, NY 1991, 69.
4. Gary Kay, *The New World Religion: The Spiritual Roots of Global Government*, Hope International Publishing, Inc., 1998, Hope for the World, P.O. Box 899, Noblesville, IN., 46061-0899, U.S.A., www.garykah.com, used by permission, 246–247.
5. *Tim LaHaye Prophecy Study Bible*, AMG Publishers, United States, 2000, 6.
6. H. A. Ironside, Ironside Commentaries, *Revelation*, Loizeaux Brothers Inc. Neptune, NJ, 1996, 188.
7. Ibid.
8. Matthew 1:16.
9. Luke 3:23–38.
10. Gardner, *Genesis of the Grail Kings*, 157.
11. Nicholas de Vere, *The Dragon Legacy: The Secret History of an Ancient Bloodline*, The Book Tree, San Diego, CA; 2004, 391.
12. De Vere, *The Dragon Legacy*, 376 (Parentheses added).
13. Gardner, *Genesis of the Grail Kings*, 131.
14. Ibid.
15. Genesis 12:1–3; 15:1–21.
16. David S. Yeago, *The Apostolic Faith: A Catholic and Evangelical Introduction to Christian Theology, Part One: The Gift of the Life of the Triune God in Jesus Christ*, 98.
17. See Amos 5:25–26 for an example of this.
18. Gary Kah, *The New World Religion: The Spiritual Roots of Global Government*, Hope International Publishing, Inc, 1998, Hope for the World, P.O. Box 899, Noblesville, IN., 46061-0899, USA, www.garykah.com, used by permission, 249.
19. Taken from *Practical Christian Theology: Examining the Great Doctrines of the Faith, Fourth Edition*, © 2001, by Floyd H. Barackman. Published by Kregel Publications, Grand Rapids, MI. Used by permission of the publisher. All rights reserved, 237.
20. Taken from *Concise Dictionary of the Occult and New Age*, © 2000, by Debra Lardie. Published by Kregel Publications, Grand Rapids, MI. Used by permission of the publisher. All rights reserved, 114.
21. Gary Kah, *En Route to Global Occupation: A High Ranking Government Liaison Exposes the Secret Agenda for World Unification*, Huntington House Publishers, Lafayette, LA, 1992, 99–100.
22. Tim Cohen, *The Antichrist and a Cup of Tea*, Prophecy House Inc., Aurora, CO, 1998, 235.
23. Kah, *En Route to Global Occupation*, 100–101.

24. Jim Marrs, *Rule By Secrecy: The Hidden History That Connects the Trilateral Commission, the Freemasons, and the Great Pyramids*, Perennial, New York, NY 2000, 277–278.
25. Ibid., 298.
26. Michael Baigent, Richard Leigh, and Henry Lincoln, *Holy Blood, Holy Grail, Revised and Illustrated Edition*, Century, UK, 2005, 315.
27. Ibid., 316.
28. Excerpted from *Custodians of Truth: The Continuance of Rex Deus*, ©2007 *By Tim Wallace-Murphy and Marilyn Hopkins* with permission from Red Wheel/ Weiser LLC Newburyport, MA and San Francisco, CA. www.redwheelweiser.com, 131, 134, 137.

**CHAPTER 7**

1. Elizabeth Clare Prophet (with Annice Booth), *Mary Magdalene and the Divine Feminine: Jesus' Lost Teaching on Women*, Summit Publications Inc., Gardiner MT, 2005, 167.
2. *Mary Magdalene, Bride in Exile* by Margaret Starbird, Bear & Company, Copyright © 2005, Inner Traditions www.BearandCompanybooks.com, 6.
3. Jim Marrs, *Rule by Secrecy: The Hidden History that Connects the Trilateral Commission, the Freemasons, and the Great Pyramids*, HarperCollins Publishers, New York, NY, 2000, 328.
4. Ibid., 329.
5. Michael Baigent, Richard Leigh, and Henry Lincoln, *Holy Blood, Holy Grail, Revised and Updated Edition*, Arrow Books, U.K., 1996, 207.
6. Ibid., 435.
7. Ibid.
8. Michael Baigent, Richard Leigh, and Henry Lincoln, *The Messianic Legacy*, Arrow Books, UK, 1996, fig. 28–29.
9. Baigent, Leigh, and Lincoln, *Holy Blood, Holy Grail*, 438.
10. David Allen Lewis, *False Messiah: Unholy Blood, Satan's Grail*, Menorah Press, Springfield, MO, 1988, 5.
11. Marrs, *Rule by Secrecy*, 337.
12. Ibid., 316.
13. Martin Lunn, *Da Vinci Code Decoded: The Truth Behind the New York Times #1 Bestseller*, The Disinformation Company Ltd., New York, NY, 2004, 75.
14. Texe Marrs, *Circle of Intrigue: The Hidden Inner Circle of the Global Illuminati Conspiracy*, Living Truth Publishers, Austin, Texas, 1995, 62.
15. Baigent, Leigh, and Lincoln, *Holy Blood, Holy Grail*, 93.
16. Marrs, *Rule by Secrecy*, 319.
17. Baigent, Leigh, and Lincoln, *Holy Blood, Holy Grail*, 107.
18. Ibid., 235–236.
19. Ibid., 299.
20. Ibid., 305.
21. Ibid., 313.

22. Ibid., 329.
23. Lunn, *Da Vinci Code Decoded*, 24.
24. Ibid.
25. Laurence Gardner, *The Magdalene Legacy: The Jesus and Mary Bloodline Conspiracy*, *Element*, an Imprint of HarperCollins Publishers, Hammersmith, London, 2005, 287.
26. Ibid., 289.
27. Richard Abanes, *The Truth Behind the Da Vinci Code: A Challenging response to the Best-selling Novel*, Harvest House Publishers, Eugene, OR, 2004, 49.
28. Lynne Picknett and Clive Prince, *The Sion Revelation*, Time Warner Books, Great Britain, 2006, 467. In the United States: The Sion Revelation by Lynn Picknett and Clive Prince. (N.Y.: Touchstone, a division of Simon & Schuster, 2006), 429.
29. Ibid., 369.
30. Ibid., 370.
31. Jim Marrs, *Rule by Secrecy*, 318.
32. Picknett and Prince, *The Sion Revelation*, 89–90.

**CHAPTER 8**

1. Christopher Knight and Alan Butler, *Solomon's Power Brokers: The Secrets of Freemasonry, the Church, and the Illuminati*, Watkins Publishing, London, UK, 2007, 285.
2. Ibid., 255.
3. Ibid.
4. Ibid.
5. Richard Andrews and Paul Schellenberger, *The Tomb of God: Unlocking the Code to a 2,000-Year-Old Mystery*, Time Warner Books, Great Britain, 1996, 431–432. First Published in Great Britain by Little, Brown And Company, 1996.
6. Ibid., 433.
7. William Cooper, *Behold a Pale Horse*, Light Technology Publishing, Flagstaff, AZ, 1991, 76.
8. Ibid., 79.
9. See Romans 10:4–10, 1 Thessalonians 4:14–18.
10. Christopher Knight and Robert Lomas, *The Second Messiah: Templars, the Turin Shroud, and the Great Secret of Freemasonry*, Arrow Books, London; 1998, 6.
11. Christopher Knight and Robert Lomas, *The Hiram Key: Pharaohs, Freemasons, and the Discovery of the Secret Scrolls of Jesus*, Arrow Books, United Kingdom, 1997, 50.
12. Ibid.
13. Manly P. Hall, *The Secret Teachings of All Ages*, Penguin Group, New York, NY; 2003, 91.
14. Ibid.
15. Tim Wallace-Murphy, *The Enigma of the Freemasons: Their History and Mystical Connections*, The Disinformation Company Ltd., New York, NY, 2006, 16.
16. Lawrence Schiffman, Society of Biblical Literature Monograph Series, *The Eschatological Community of the Dead Sea Scrolls*, Scholars Press, Atlanta, 1989, 6.

17. Ibid., 7.
18. Knight and Lomas, *The Hiram Key*, 278.
19. Ibid., 282.
20. Wallace-Murphy, *The Enigma of the Freemasons*, 16.
21. Ibid.
22. Tim Wallace-Murphy and Marilyn Hopkins, *Custodians of Truth: The Continuance of Rex Deus*, Weiser Books, York Beach, ME, 2005, 73.
23. Knight and Lomas, *The Hiram Key*, 271.
24. Jack M. Driver, *Freemasonry: An Illustrated History*, Kandour Ltd., London, 2006, 174.
25. Knight and Lomas, The Second Messiah, 102.
26. Ibid., 104.
27. Ibid., 105.
28. Ibid., 104.
29. Knight and Butler, *Solomon's Power Brokers*, 285.

**CHAPTER 9**

1. Taken from *Concise Dictionary of the Occult and New Age*, © 2000, by Debra Lardie. Published by Kregel Publications, Grand Rapids, MI. Used by permission of the publisher. All rights reserved, 98.
2. Taken from *Concise Dictionary of the Occult and New Age*, © 2000, by Debra Lardie. Published by Kregel Publications, Grand Rapids, MI. Used by permission of the publisher. All rights reserved, 201.
3. Tony Blair Faith Foundation, Faith and Globalisation, *Seeking to Understand Faith and Globalisation*, http://tonyblairfaithfoundation.org/projects/faith-and-globalisation/.
4. Katie Hunt, BBC News, *Will The US Dollar Remain King?* (26 March 2009), http://news.bbc.co.uk/1/hi/business/7965518.stm.
5. Manly P. Hall, *The Secret Destiny of America*, The Philosophic Research Society, Inc., Los Angeles, 1991, 73.
6. Ibid., 72.
7. Ibid., 77.
8. Ibid.
9. Some who see Merovingian/Rex Deus/Grail bloodline involvement in European history and politics maintain that it was only against the "illegitimate nobility"—the "church nobility"—that the esoteric fraternities set themselves against. The fraternities, in actual fact, supported monarchy, but only those royal houses which governed purely by dynastic inheritance, not through the sanction of the church. The Merovingian dynasty, believed by some to be of the bloodline of David and Jesus, would be such a "legitimate" royal house.
10. Manly P. Hall, *The Secret Teachings of All*, Penguin Group, New York, 2003, 240 (parentheses added).
11. Hall, *The Secret Destiny of America*, 23.
12. Ibid., 24.
13. William T. Still, *New World Order: The Ancient Plan of Secret Societies*, Huntington

House Publishers, Lafayette, LA, 1990, 41.
14. Hall, *The Secret Destiny of America*, 15.
15. Still, *New World Order*, 44.
16. Hall, *The Secret Destiny of America*, 63.
17. Still, *New World Order*, 44.
18. Hall, *The Secret Destiny of America*, 79.
19. Ibid., 78.
20. Ibid., 79.
21. Clarence Larkin, *The Book of Daniel*, The Rev. Clarence Larkin Estate, Glenside, Pa., 1929, 49.
22. Arno C. Gaebelein, *Daniel*, Kregel Publications, Grand Rapids, 1955, 82.
23. J. Dwight Pentecost, *Things to Come: A Study in Biblical Eschatology*, Zondervan Publishing House, Grand Rapids, 1964, 319.
24. See Daniel 2:41–43.
25. Gary Kah, *The New World Religion: The Spiritual Roots of Global Government*, Hope International Publishing Inc., Noblesville, IN., 1998, 39.
26. Prince Michael of Greece, Vanity Fair, 20th Anniversary Issue, Special Collector's Edition, *The Case for Kings* September 2003, 402.
27. Tracy R. Twyman, *The Merovingian Mythos and the Mystery of Rennes-le-Chateau*, Dragon Key Press, Portland OR, 2004, 90.
28. Ibid., 91.
29. Still, *New World Order*, 41.
30. Time Life Books, Mysteries of the Unknown, *Mystic Places*, Time Life Books, Alexandria, Virginia, 12.
31. Clarence Larkin, *The Spirit World*, Rev. Clarence Larkin Estate, Glenside, PA, 1921, 36.
32. Twyman, *The Merovingian Mythos*, 97.
33. Hall, *The Secret Teachings of All Ages*, 85.
34. Ibid.

**CHAPTER 10**

1. Laurence Gardner, *The Shadow of Solomon: The Lost Secret of the Freemasons Revealed*, Harper Element, London, 2005, 3–4.
2. Adrian Gilbert, *The New Jerusalem: The Extraordinary True Story of How a Secret Society Rebuilt London*, Corgi Books, London, UK, 2002, 108.
3. Gary Kah, *En Route to Global Occupation: A High Ranking Government Liaison Exposes the Secret Agenda for World Unification*, Huntington House Publishers, Lafayette, LA, 1992, 105.
4. Manly P. Hall, *The Secret Teachings of All Ages*, Penguin Group, New York, 2003, 579.
5. Christopher Knight and Robert Lomas, *The Second Messiah: Templars, the Turin Shroud, and the Great Secret of Freemasonry*, Arrow Books, United Kingdom, 1998, 153.
6. Gardner, *The Shadow of Solomon*, 111.

7. Ibid.
8. Jim Marrs, *Rule By Secrecy*, 338.
9. Gardner, *The Shadow of Solomon*, 112.
10. Debra Lardie (Dan Lioy and Paul Ingram), *Concise Dictionary of the Occult and New Age*, Kregel Publications, Grand Rapids, 2000, 223.
11. Ibid., 224.
12. Laurence Gardner, *Bloodline of the Holy Grail: The Hidden Lineage of Jesus Revealed*, Fair Winds Press, Gloucester MA, 2002, 261, 263.
13. Ibid.
14. Laurence Gardner, *Realm of the Ring Lords: The Myth and Magic of the Grail Quest*, Fair Winds Press, Gloucester MA, 2000, 2.
15. Ibid., 3.
16. Marrs, *Rule by Secrecy*, 265.
17. Ibid., 266.
18. Manly P. Hall, *The Secret Teachings of All Ages*, 463.
19. Marrs, *Rule by Secrecy*, 266.
20. Hall, *The Secret Teachings of All Ages*, 463.
21. Marrs, *Rule by Secrecy*, 266.
22. Hall, *The Secret Teachings of All Ages*, 464.
23. Ibid.
24. Gilbert, *The New Jerusalem*, 317.
25. Ibid.
26. Knight and Butler, *Solomon's Power Brokers*, 196.
27. Gilbert, *The New Jerusalem*, 348.
28. The Architect of the Capitol, http://www.aoc.gov/cc/plaques/cornerstone_masonic.cfm.
29. Marrs, *Rule by Secrecy*, 228.
30. Ibid., 230.
31. Gardner, *The Shadow of Solomon*, 112.
32. Marrs, *Rule by Secrecy*, 228.
33. William T. Still, *New World Order: The Ancient Plan of Secret Societies*, Huntington House Publishers, Lafayette, LA, 1990, 50.


**CHAPTER 11**


1. Kevin Gest, *The Secrets of Solomon's temple: Discover the Hidden Truth that Lies at the Heart of Freemasonry*, Fair Winds Press, Gloucester MA, 2007, 344.
2. Tim Wallace-Murphy and Marilyn Hopkins, *Rosslyn: Guardians of the Secrets of the Holy Grail*, HarperCollins Publishers Ltd, Hammersmith, London, 1999, 13.
3. For a detailed illustration of how Rosslyn architecturally coincides with the Jerusalem temple, see Christopher Knight and Robert Lomas's *The Second Messiah*.
4. Andrew Sinclair, *The Sword and the Grail: The Story of the Grail, the Templars, and the True Discovery of America*, Birlinn Limited, United Kingdom, 2005, 96.
5. Christopher Knight and Alan Butler, *Solomon's Power Brokers: The Secrets of Freemasonry, the Church, and the Illunminati*, Watkins Publishing, London, 2007, 149.

6. Wallace-Murphy and Hopkins, *Rosslyn*, 107.
7. Ibid., ©1999, Tim Wallace-Murphy and Marilyn Hopkins. Copyright in the customized version vests in Adrian Isaacs.
8. Christopher Knight and Robert Lomas, *The Hiram Key: Pharaohs, Freemasons and the Discovery of the Secret Scrolls of Jesus*, Arrow Books, 1997, London, UK, 407.
9. Jack M. Driver, *Freemasonry: An Illustrated History*, Kandour Ltd., London, 2006, 9.
10. Debra Lardie (Dan Lioy and Paul Ingram Contributing Editors), *Concise Dictionary of the Occult and New Age*, Kregel Publications, Grand Rapids, 2000, 98.
11. Tim Cohen, *The Antichrist and a Cup of Tea*, Prophecy House, Inc., Aurora CO, 1998, 235.
12. Lardie, *Concise Dictionary of the Occult and New Age*, 108.
13. Jack Harris, *Freemasonry*, Whitaker House, New Kensington, PA, 1983, 13.
14. Lardie, *Concise Dictionary of the Occult and New Age*, 108.
15. H. Paul Jeffers, *Freemasons: Inside the World's Oldest Secret Society*, Citadel Press, New York NY, 2005, 128.
16. Driver, *Freemasonry*, 175.
17. Ibid., 174.
18. Ibid.
19. Manly P. Hall, *The Lost Keys of Freemasonry*, The Penguin Group, New York NY, 2006, 153.
20. Ibid.
21. Ibid., 152.
22. William T. Still, *New World Order: The Ancient Plan of Secret Societies*, Huntington House Publishers, Lafayette, LA, 1990, 98.
23. Ibid.
24. Ibid.
25. Ibid.
26. Harris, *Freemasonry*, 25.
27. Ibid., 25–26.
28. Ibid., 27.
29. Tim Wallace-Murphy, *The Enigma of the Freemasons: Their History and Mystical Connections*, The Disinformation Company Ltd., New York, NY, 2006, 36.
30. Ibid., 51.
31. Knight and Butler, *Solomon's Power Brokers*,173.
32. Jack M. Driver, *Freemasonry: An Illustrated History*, Kandour Ltd., London, 2006, 19.
33. Ibid., 20.
34. Christopher Knight and Robert Lomas, *The Second Messiah: Templars, the Turin Shroud and the Great Secret of Freemasonry*, Arrow Books Limited, London, 1998, 262.
35. See 2 Samuel 20:25; 1 Kings 2:27.
36. Knight and Lomas, *The Second Messiah*, 274.
37. Ibid., 279.

38. Ibid., 281.
39. Ibid., 90.
40. Ibid., 285.
41. Ibid.
42. Lardie, *Concise Dictionary of the Occult and New Age*, 108.
43. William Cooper, *Behold a Pale Horse*, Light Technology Publishing, Flagstaff, AZ, 1991, 71.
44. Knight and Lomas, *The Second Messiah*, 281.

**CHAPTER 12**

1. William T. Still, *New World Order: the Ancient Plan of Secret Societies*, Huntington House Publishers, Lafayette LA, 1990, 71.
2. Ibid., 46.
3. Jim Marrs, *Rule by Secrecy: The Hidden History that Connects the Trilateral Commission, the Freemasons, and the Great Pyramids*, HarperCollins Publishers, New York, NY, 2000, 230.
4. Still, *New World Order*, 46.
5. Ibid., 50.
6. Manly P. Hall, *The Secret Destiny of America*, The Philosophic Research Society, Inc., Los Angeles, 1991, 128, 129.
7. Ibid., 129.
8. Ibid., 191.
9. David Ovason, *The Secret Symbols of the Dollar Bill: A Closer Look at the Hidden Magic and Meaning of the Money You Use Every Day*, Perennial Currents, New York NY, 2004,viii.
10. Nicholas Hagger, *The Secret History of the West: The Influence of Secret Organizations on Western History from the Renaissance to the 20th Century*, O Books, United Kingdom, 2005, 224.
11. Hall, *The Secret Destiny of America*, 191.
12. Gary Kah, *En Route to Global Occupation: A High Ranking Government Liaison Exposes the Secret Agenda for World Unification*, Huntington House Publishers, Lafayette, LA, 1992, 62.
13. Drew Zahn, WorldNetDaily, *Kissinger: Obama primed to create 'New World Order'—Policy Guru Says Global Upheaval Presents 'Great Opportunity'* (6 January 2009), http://www.worldnetdaily.com/index.php?fa=PAGE.view&pageId=85442.
14. Marrs, *Rule By Secrecy*, 232.
15. Still, *New World Order*, 61.
16. Ibid.
17. Ibid.
18. *The Encyclopaedia of Ancient Myths and Cultures*, Quantum Books, London, U.K., 2003, 591.
19. The Supreme Council: Ancient and Accepted Scottish Rite, Southern Jurisdiction, USA, http://www.scottishrite.org/who/faqs.html.
20. Ovason, *The Secret Symbols of the Dollar Bill*, 5.

21. Ibid., 93.
22. Ibid., 86.
23. CNN.com International, Politics, *Bush: 'No Justice Without Freedom,'* Thursday, January 20, 2005; http://edition.cnn.com/2005/ALLPOLITICS/01/20/bush.transcript/index.html.
24. Ovason, *The Secret Symbols of the Dollar Bill*, 86.
25. The State of Israel, The Judicial Authority, http://elyon1.court.gov.il/eng/siyur/index.html.
26. Ovason, *The Secret Symbols of the Dollar Bill*, p. 85.
27. David L. Carrico, *The Great Seal of the United States: It's Occult Meaning, Followers of Jesus Christ Ministries*, Evansville, IN, 1997, 41.
28. Tracy R. Twyman, *Solomon's Treasure: The Magic and Mystery of America's Money*, Dragon Key Press, Portland OR, 2005, 188.
29. Carrico, *The Great Seal of the United States*, 30.
30. Ibid., 31.
31. Ibid., 44
32. Ovason, *The Secret Symbols of the Dollar Bill*, 125,126.
33. Ibid., 129.
34. Hagger, *The Secret History of the West*, 257.
35. Twyman, *Solomon's Treasure*, 3.
36. Ibid.
37. Ibid.

**CHAPTER 13**

1. Pentecost, *Things to Come*, 325–326.
2. Norman Davies, *Europe: A History*, Reprinted with Corrections, Pimlico, London, 1997, 1066.
3. Grant R. Jeffrey, *Triumphant Return: The Coming Kingdom of God*, Frontier Re search Publications, Inc., Toronto, ON, 2001, 242.
4. Barroso: European Union is 'empire' (long version), http://www.youtube.com/watch?v=-I8M1T-GgRU.
5. Clarence Larkin, *The Book of Revelation: A Study of the Last Prophetic Book of Holy Scripture*, The Rev. Clarence Larkin Estate, Glenside, PA, 1919, 122.
6. Pentecost, *Things to Come*, 324.
7. Sir Robert Anderson, *The Coming Prince*, Kregel Publications, Grand Rapids, MI, 1957, 271.
8. Bruno Waterfield, Telegraph.co.uk, *Gaddafi Attacks Sarkozy Plan for Union of the Med* (10 July 2008), http://www.telegraph.co.uk/news/worldnews/europe/2277517/Gaddafi-attacks-Sarkozy-plan-for-Union-of-the-Med.html.
9. Tim Lahaye and Ed Hindson, *The Popular Bible Prophecy Commentary: Understanding the Meaning of Every Prophetic Passage*, Harvest House Publishers, Eugene, OR, 2006, 532.
10. Ibid.

11. Ibid., 534.
12. Lahaye and Hindson, *The Popular Bible Prophecy Commentary*, 534.
13. Pentecost, *Things to Come*, 326.
14. The brand of Christianity that came out of this council was Nicene Christianity, which maintained belief in the Trinity, the deity of Christ, and the oneness between the Son and the Father.
15. Dave Hunt, *A Woman Rides the Beast: The Catholic Church and the Last Days*, Harvest House Publishers, Eugene, OR, 1994, 54.
16. Ibid., 46.
17. Ibid.
18. The Rev. Alexander Hislop, *The Two Babylons: Or Papal Worship Proved to be the Worship of Nimrod and His Wife*, Loizeaux Brothers, Neptune, NJ, First Edition, 1916, First American Edition, 1943, Second American Edition, 1959, 167–168.
19. Ibid., 157.
20. Ibid., 197.
21. Paul Enns, *The Moody Handbook of Theology: Revised and Expanded*, Moody Publishers, Chicago; 1989, 2008; 372
22. Alan Butler, *The Goddess, the Grail and the Lodge*, O books; Winchester, U.K.; New York, U.S.A.; 2004, 123.
23. David Southwell and Sean Twist, *Conspiracy Files: Paranoia Secrecy Intrigue*, Sevenoaks, London, UK, 2004, 112–113.
24. Ibid., 112.
25. Economist.com, Charlemagne, *The European Commission and Religious Values* (28 October 2004), The Economist Print Edition, http://www.economist.com/agenda/displaystory.cfm?story_id=3332056.
26. Southwell and Twist, *Conspiracy Files*, 113.
27. Laurence Gardner, *The Magdalene Legacy: The Jesus and Mary Bloodline Conspiracy, Element*, An Imprint of HarperCollins Publishers, Hammersmith, London, 2005, 25.
28. http://www.economist.com/agenda/displaystory.cfm?story_id=3332056.
29. Time Magazine, *Visions of Europe*, Winter 1998–1999, 30–31.
30. Norman Davies, *Europe: A History*, Pimlico; London, UK, 1997, xx.
31. Europa, The European Anthem, http://europa.eu/abc/symbols/anthem/index_en.htm.
32. Ibid.
33. Tim Cohen, *The Antichrist and a Cup of Tea*, Prophecy House Inc., Aurora, CO, 1998, 27.
34. Sir Robert Anderson, *The Coming Prince*, Kregel Classics, Grand Rapids, MI, Reprinted from the Tenth Edition, 1957, 190.

**CHAPTER 14**

1. Sir Robert Anderson, *The Coming Prince*, Kregel Classics, Grand Rapids, MI, Reprinted from the Tenth Edition, 1957, 271.

2. For a detailed explanation as to why—from a biblical, exegetic standpoint—Syria has been identified as a possible place of Antichrist origin, see *The Book of Daniel* by Clarence Larkin.
3. William T. Still, *New World Order: The Ancient Plan of Secret Societies*, Huntington House Publishers, Lafayette, LA, 1990, 41.
4. Anderson, *The Coming Prince*, 191.
5. Ibid.
6. Time Life Books, Mysteries of the Unknown, *Mystic Places*, Time Life Books, Alexandria, Virginia, 16.
7. Clarence Larkin, *The Book of Revelation: A Study of the Last Prophetic Book of Holy Scripture*, The Rev. Clarence Larkin Estate, Glenside, PA, 1919, 122.
8. Ibid.
9. Norman Davies, *Europe: A History, Reprinted with Corrections*, Pimlico, London, 1997, 151.
10. J. R. Church, N.W. Hutchings, Gary Stearman, Bill Uselton, *Europe is Rising*, Heathstone Publishing Ltd., Oklahoma City, 1990, 73.
11. Ibid., 44.
12. Ibid., 73.
13. Ibid., 46.
14. Jim Marrs, *Rule By Secrecy: The Hidden History that Connects the Trilateral Commission*, the Freemasons, and the Great Pyramid, Perennial, New York, NY, 2001, 337.
15. Laurence Gardner, *Bloodline of the Holy Grail: The Hidden Lineage of Jesus Revealed*, Fair Winds Press, Gloucester, MA; 2002, 1.
16. Gardner, *Bloodline of the Holy Grail*, xvii.
17. Laurence Gardner, *Genesis of the Grail Kings: The Explosive Story of Genetic Cloning and the Ancient Bloodline of Jesus*, Fair Winds Press, Gloucester, MA; 2002, 131.
18. Nicholas de Vere, *The Dragon Legacy: The Secret History of an Ancient Bloodline*, The Book Tree, San Diego, 2004, 340.

**CHAPTER 15**

1. Tim Lahaye and Ed Hindson, *The Popular Bible Prophecy Commentary: Understanding the Meaning of Every Prophetic Passage*, Harvest House Publishers, Eugene, OR, 2006, 537.
2. *Tim LaHaye Prophecy Study Bible* (King James Version): Red Letter Edition, AMG Publishers, 2000, 1130.
3. See 1 John 2:22; 4:1–3; 2 John 7.
4. By referring to the death of God, we are referring to His ceasing to exist as a Being, not the earthly, human death of Jesus Christ, which is a separate matter all together. It is beyond the focus and scope of this book to delve into the mysteries of the death of the God-man Jesus Christ.
5. Norman L. Geisler, *Christian Apologetics*, Baker Book House, Grand Rapids, MI, 1976, 314.
6. Ibid., 350–351.
7. Ibid., 351.

8. Josh McDowell, *The New Evidence that Demands a Verdict: Evidence II and II, Fully Updated in One Volume to Answer Questions Challenging Christians in the 21st Century*, Thomas Nelson Publishers, Nashville, TN, 1999, 215–216.
9. Tom Harpur, *The Pagan Christ: Recovering the Lost Light*, Thomas Allen Publishers, Toronto, 2004, 84.
10. Ibid.
11. McDowell, *The New Evidence that Demands a Verdict*, 21.
12. Ibid.
13. Ibid., 22.
14. Richard Banes, *The Truth Behind the Da Vinci Code: A Challenging Response to the Best-selling Novel*, Harvest House Publishers, Eugene, OR, 2004, 26.
15. Ibid., 27.

**CHAPTER 16**

1. Dr. Ken Culver, The Christian Arsenal, *The Time is Near to Recognize the Beast, The Time is Near: Part 6*, http://www.christianarsenal.com/study/Misc/The TimeIsNear6.pdf.
2. Manly P. Hall, *The Secret Teachings of All Ages*, Penguin Group, New York, NY, 2003, 590.
3. Ibid.
4. Adrian Gilbert, *The New Jerusalem: The Extraordinary True Story of How a Secret Society Rebuilt London*, Corgi Books, London, UK, 2002, 161.
5. Laurence Gardner, *Realm of the Ring Lords: The Myth and Magic of the Grail Quest*, Fair Winds Press, Gloucester MA, 2000, 2.
6. For a detailed report on the statue, see:http://news.bbc.co.uk/2/hi/americas/ 1857482.stm and http://www.two-olive-trees.org/antichrist/charles_statue.jpg.
7. See Revelation 13.
8. *Benjamin Creme Talks About the 'Star'* http://www.youtube.com/watch?v=9 JihYJhfAs4.
9. Share International, *Star Sign* http://www.share-international.org/maitreya/Ma_ starsign.htm#Anchor-Share-49575
10. Ibid., http://www.share-international.org/maitreya/Ma_starsign.htm.
11. Share International, *Healing Wells*, http://www.share-international.org/back ground/miracles/MI_water.htm.
12. Lardie, *Concise Dictionary of the Occult and New Age*, 164.
13. Share International, *Maitreya's Mission: Volume 1*, http://www.share-international. org/background/printed/ mission_1.htm.
14. Benjamin Creme, Share International, *Maitreya Steps Forward*, January 14, 2010: http://www.share-international.org/.
15. Clarence Larkin, *Dispensational Truth or God's Plan and Purpose in the Ages*, Rev. Clarence Larkin Est., Glenside, PA, 1918; 33.
16. See Matthew 5:17; Romans 4; 6:14.
17. See Revelation 3:10; 1 Thessalonians 1:10.